"Filling a huge gap in pastoral care, Dr. Mason has provided a remarkable manual and guide for understanding the causes of suicide and how to care for the family and friends who have been shattered in its wake. Mason's work is both practical, as in her dispelling of common myths about suicide, as well as theological, providing a much-needed integration between theology and clinical theory. This is the manual the church has been waiting for! I heartily recommend it!"

Timothy C. Tennent, president, Asbury Theological Seminary

"This book probes the stigma-filled tragedy of suicide and closes a yawning gap in the literature of practical pastoral care. Every church has members who live with mental illness, and every church may at some point have members at risk of suicide. No pastor can afford to wait until a mental health care crisis arises or suicide strikes the parish to learn what this book can teach. This is a must-read for all Christian clergy, regardless of denomination."

Kathryn Greene-McCreight, author of *Darkness Is My Only Companion: A Christian Response to Mental Illness*

"Unequivocally the best book on suicide prevention I've ever read. This reaches far beyond a typical textbook. It is extremely practical in addressing, with insight and compassion, what I've witnessed as a pastoral practitioner for thirty years. I wish I had this powerful resource my first year as a chaplain. Every Christian chaplain needs a copy."

Alan T. "Blues" Baker, rear admiral and chaplain of the Marine Corps, retired

"Losing a loved one to suicide is one of the most devastating experiences a family or community can experience. But suicide is preventable, and pastors and caregivers can intervene to help those at risk. This book is a comprehensive, useful and hopeful resource, and readers will become better equipped to save lives because of it."

Albert Y. Hsu, author, *Grieving a Suicide*

"Without reservation I highly recommend Dr. Karen Mason's book, *Preventing Suicide*, as a must-read for every pastor, missionary, chaplain and pastoral counselor. Plus, I suggest adding to that must-read list every psychologist, social worker, school counselor, family member of a suicide victim and seminary student. All of these will benefit from this book's wisdom and practicality. I believe Dr. Mason's book will become one of the classics in its field."

Jim Stout, pastor, counselor and author of *Bipolar Disorder: Rebuilding Your Life*

"*Preventing Suicide* is a comprehensive resource for clergy across denominational lines and in various settings. Dr. Mason has done her homework, and her book integrates diverse theological understandings and biblical perspectives with practical pastoral advice and solid psychological research. As a pastor who has served local congregations for over thirty years, I recommend it highly."

Talitha Arnold, senior minister, coleader of the Faith Communities Task Force with the National Action Alliance for Suicide Prevention

"Most pastors, chaplains and pastoral counselors already know someone they could help choose living instead of dying, if only they knew how. If you're in that role, this book is for you. And if you're preparing for ministry, this book is also for you, because there is little doubt that you are going to find yourself in this dark trysting place where death meets life more often than any of us would wish."

David B. Biebel, coauthor of *Finding Your Way After the Suicide of Someone You Love*

"Mental illness exists inside and outside of the church community. Christians struggle with depression and even suicidal thoughts. It does not make you less of a Christian. Just like heart disease or cancer does not dilute our Christianity, neither does mental illness.

Nevertheless, we must stand committed to 'creating space' and providing ministry to those who struggle with depression and other mental illnesses. In partnership with medical professionals, the church of Jesus Christ can bring attention to this silent illness with grace, compassion and love. Karen Mason's book provides such space. For at the end of day, suffering from mental illness is not a sin. Yet not addressing it may very well be."

Samuel Rodriguez, president, Hispanic Evangelical Association

"Karen Mason has with this book made a monumental contribution to helping us better understand suicide and our ministry responsibilities to those impacted by it. I wish it was available when I, as a young pastor, had to deal pastorally with all the complicated realities of several heart-breaking suicides within six years in my small Florida congregation. This book is a must-read for anyone dealing with persons in deep depression that could be life threatening."

John Huffman Jr., author, pastor, Christianity Today board chairman

"The book, written by an expert in the field of suicide prevention, intervention and post-vention, is thoughtful, even gentle, but grapples head-on with theological issues in offering practical and biblical insights into the world of those contemplating suicide and provides a plethora of practical help for survivors, caregivers and the church. It is an engagingly readable book that is high on my recommendation list for students and caregivers."

Kenneth L. Swetland, senior professor of ministry, Gordon-Conwell Theological Seminary

"In *Preventing Suicide: A Handbook for Pastors, Chaplains, and Pastoral Counselors,* Dr. Karen Mason applies psychology and theology to this complex and heart-breaking issue. She incorporates a spiritual perspective into a biopsychosocial model to understanding suicide—a perspective that has long been missing from discussions about prevention and intervention."

Pamela Caudill Ovwigho, executive director, Center for Bible Engagement

"Karen Mason's *Preventing Suicide* is a valuable, well-documented resource for pastors, chaplains and pastoral counselors. Mason's work dealing with these issues . . . has provided her with extensive in-the-trenches experience and academic expertise, which manifest themselves throughout the book. Perhaps her most important point is one she emphasizes frequently—the need to be open about the fact of suicide, both among family and among friends, but more particularly among the clergy and those who serve with them."

G. Lloyd Carr, professor emeritus of biblical and theological studies, Gordon College

"Most pastors and almost every chaplain will encounter suicide at some point in their ministry. The complexities involved in seeking to prevent, intervene and follow up can seem overwhelming, but Karen Mason's clear, but not simplistic, exploration offers a helpful guide. She raises questions often asked and provides suggestions of what to say—and what not to say—to provide faithful pastoral care, helping to reflect Christ's light even in this darkest of situations."

David A. Currie, associate professor of pastoral theology and director of the doctor of ministry program, Gordon-Conwell Theological Seminary

"Dr. Karen Mason's new book, *Preventing Suicide: A Handbook for Pastors, Chaplains and Pastoral Counselors,* provides us with an invaluable resource to deal with one of the most difficult challenges anyone can face. If you live in the same complicated and painful world I do, you need all the help you can get. Dr. Mason's wisdom, experience and insight helps avoid the delusion that Christians don't have the same problems as other humans, while at the same time offering practical hope for addressing this most painful reality."

Frank A. James, president, Biblical Theological Seminary

KAREN MASON

PREVENTING SUICIDE

A HANDBOOK FOR PASTORS, CHAPLAINS AND PASTORAL COUNSELORS

IVP Books

An imprint of InterVarsity Press
Downers Grove, Illinois

InterVarsity Press
P.O. Box 1400, Downers Grove, IL 60515-1426
World Wide Web: www.ivpress.com
Email: email@ivpress.com

InterVarsity Press® is the book-publishing division of InterVarsity Christian Fellowship/USA®, a movement of students and faculty active on campus at hundreds of universities, colleges and schools of nursing in the United States of America, and a member movement of the International Fellowship of Evangelical Students. For information about local and regional activities, write Public Relations Dept., InterVarsity Christian Fellowship/USA, 6400 Schroeder Rd., P.O. Box 7895, Madison, WI 53707-7895, or visit the IVCF website at www.intervarsity.org.

Scripture quotations, unless otherwise noted, are from the New Revised Standard Version of the Bible, copyright 1989 by the Division of Christian Education of the National Council of the Churches of Christ in the USA. Used by permission. All rights reserved.

While any stories in this book are true, some names and identifying information may have been changed to protect the privacy of individuals.

Cover design: David Fassett
Interior design: Beth McGill
Images: feeling blue watercolor: © stereohype/iStockphoto
blank lined paper: © GrabillCreative/iStockphoto

ISBN 978-0-8308-4117-2 (print)
ISBN 978-0-8308-9647-9 (digital)

Printed in the United States of America ∞

As a member of the Green Press Initiative, InterVarsity Press is committed to protecting the environment and to the responsible use of natural resources. To learn more, visit greenpressinitiative.org.

Library of Congress Cataloging-in-Publication Data
Mason, Karen, 1955-
  Preventing suicide : a handbook for pastors, chaplains, and pastoral counselors / Karen
Mason.
      pages cm
  Includes bibliographical references and index.
  ISBN 978-0-8308-4117-2 (pbk. : alk. paper)
  1. Suicide--Religious aspects—Christianity. 2. Pastoral counseling. I. Title.
  BV4012.2.M297 2014
  259'.428—dc23
                                                                2014013853

P	22	21	20	19	18	17	16	15	14	13	12	11	10	9	8	7	6	5	4	3	2	1
Y	32	31	30	29	28	27	26	25	24	23	22	21	20	19	18	17	16	15	14			

This book is dedicated to my parents, Randall and Alice Mathews,

who modeled for me how to build lives worth living.

CONTENTS

ACKNOWLEDGMENTS

My clients have taught me the most about suicide prevention. The courage with which they live challenging lives has been inspiring. The many clergy who generously shared their experiences have been no less inspiring. I gratefully acknowledge the Lilly Theological Research Grants Program, administered by the Association of Theological Schools, which made possible two of my research studies of clergy and their engagement with suicide. I am appreciative of those who have collaborated with me on these projects: Dr. James D. Wines Jr., Dr. Monica Geist, Dr. Raymond Pendleton and Dr. Pablo Polischuk. My student assistants have provided invaluable help. I couldn't have completed this work without them. Thanks to Elizabeth Bousa, Rebekah Doreau, Heather Thornburg, Day Marshall and Richard Kuo. The thoughtful feedback on previous drafts from my parents and my editor, David Congdon, has been invaluable. I claim all mistakes as mine.

INTRODUCTION

Most suicides, although by no means all, can be prevented.

KAY REDFIELD JAMISON

I am not sure when it finally hit me that suicide can be prevented. I think it was somewhere in a therapy session several years ago with Jane,[1] a woman who suffered from multiple personalities who had been suicidal all her life. I realized one day that she hadn't yet killed herself and she wanted me to help her not do so. I was somewhat afraid to wade into a life-and-death issue and not very optimistic, but I was willing to try for her sake. As a psychologist I also had a professional commitment to prevent suicide.[2] Typically suicide prevention involves hospitalizing suicidal clients and Jane wanted to stay out of the hospital. I wasn't sure this was doable or how to do it.

All this occurred for me within a complicated set of attitudes toward suicide picked up throughout my life. As I had read Sophocles and Shakespeare, as I had watched films and news reports on suicide, I had begun to develop the expectation that certain clients in certain situations might claim a right to suicide.[3] I was intrigued by the fact that Jane did not. I realize now that, in these depictions of suicide, I was absorbing diverse attitudes about suicide that I needed to examine, because attitudes can affect behaviors.[4] Some depictions of suicide were affecting my attitudes and muddling my thinking about how to help Jane.

DIVERSE DEPICTIONS OF SUICIDE

Here are some typical depictions of suicide that may affect attitudes about suicide and suicide prevention:

Suicide as duty. An example of a duty suicide is a Hindu widow who immolates herself on her deceased husband's funeral pyre. This type of suicide, though considered a duty, also had a voluntary aspect, as is evidenced by the fact that although the British declared this type of suicide illegal in 1829, they found it difficult to stop the practice.[5] Central African and Melanesian wives were buried alive with their deceased husbands, and among the Natchez of North America and the Maoris the wife was strangled.[6] I remember seeing a television program on old gypsies who were too feeble to migrate across the great rivers of Europe who stayed behind to die for the good of the family group. A captain going down with his sinking ship is a modern version of a duty or honor suicide.[7]

Suicide when honor is at stake. A second depiction is that suicide is honorable in certain situations. The Japanese custom of hara-kiri, a type of honor suicide reserved for nobility and members of the military caste,[8] is described by Fedden as follows:

> In 1868 twenty Japanese knights involved in the murder of a French officer were condemned to execute hari-kari before the French ambassador. The latter, however, found it impossible to appreciate to the full this token of Nipponese friendship. When eleven of the victims had done their duty he could bear the sight no longer and the remainder were reprieved and banished.[9]

The high honor of this type of suicide led Seneca to describe Cato's suicide like this: "Surely the gods looked with pleasure upon their pupil as he made his escape by so glorious and memorable an end!"[10] A more modern example of honor suicide would be Japanese kamikaze pilots in World War II.

Suicide as political protest. As in the case of suicide bombers in the Middle East, suicide has been used as political protest. In A.D. 73, 960 Jews died together by suicide at Masada.[11] Gandhi's several fasts were threats of suicide for political purposes.[12] Jan Palach immolated himself in Prague in 1969 to protest the demoralization of the Czech people after the Soviet invasion of Czechoslovakia.[13] Thích Quảng Đức, a Vietnamese Mahayana Buddhist monk, burned himself to death at a Saigon intersection on June 11, 1963, to protest the persecution of Buddhists by South Vietnam's government. On November 18, 1978, 914 adherents to Jim Jones's People's Temple killed themselves.[14] Jim Jones is reported to have said, "We are not committing suicide; we are committing a revolutionary act."[15]

Suicide as a rational choice. Another perspective is that suicide is a rational and philosophical choice. The Babylonian Dialogue of Pessimism, written around 2500 B.C., concludes that the meaninglessness of life must logically result in suicide:

> Now then what is good?
> To break my neck and thy neck,
> To fall into the river is good.[16]

Greek Cynic, Stoic and Epicurean philosophies upheld the right to rational suicide. For example, the Stoic Seneca wrote, "As I choose the ship in which I will sail, and the house I will inhabit, so I will choose the death by which I will leave life. . . . The lot of man is happy because no one continues wretched but by his own fault."[17] He suggested that suicide may be not only rational but also wise: "The wise man will live as long as he ought, not as long as he can."[18] An unhappy Athenian was given permission to kill himself if he could convince the Senate of the rationality of his choice, as stated in Athenian law:

> Whoever no longer wishes to live shall state his reasons to the Senate, and after having received permission shall abandon life. If your existence is hateful to you, die; if you are overwhelmed by fate, drink the hemlock. If you are bowed with grief, abandon life. Let the unhappy man recount his misfortune, let the magistrate supply him with the remedy, and his wretchedness will come to an end.[19]

The Greeks who founded Marseilles perpetuated this practice by keeping poison on hand for those who were able to convince the Senate they had adequate reason and were given permission to kill themselves.[20] The Roman Pliny wrote, "Wherefore hath our mother the earth brought out poisons in so great a quantity, but that men in distress might make away themselves?"[21] In fairness, not all Greeks believed in rational suicide. For example, Pythagoreans argued against suicide from a rational moral perspective: "We must wait to be set free in God's appointed time."[22] Suicide was illegal if deemed irrational, and this type of suicide resulted in mutilation. The hand that had implemented death was cut off.[23]

Fedden has argued that Renaissance philosophers revived Greek and Roman philosophy and its focus on rational suicide within a context of growing melancholy or depression at that time.[24] He also points out that later in the seventeenth century, poverty was despised as morally inferior and therefore became a reason for suicide.[25] Some Renaissance philosophers upheld the rational right to suicide either on the basis of the insignificance of human life or human liberty.[26] For example, Montaigne wrote, "The most voluntary death is the finest. Life depends upon the pleasure of others; death upon our own."[27]

Other philosophers since the Renaissance have also argued the rational suicide perspective. In the nineteenth century Schopenhauer wrote, "It is perfectly clear that no one has such indisputable right over anything in the world as over his own person and life."[28] Existentialism at times considered suicide as the ultimate act that defined a person. The poet William Carlos Williams writes, "The perfect type of the man of action is the suicide."[29] Reybaud's character Jérôme Paturot conveys this thought: "A suicide establishes a man. One is nothing standing; dead one becomes a hero. . . . All suicides have success. . . . I must decidedly make my preparations."[30] Though Jean-Paul Sartre and Albert Camus were against suicide personally, they contributed to this philosophical debate.[31] Albert Camus wrote, "There is but one truly serious philosophical problem, and that is suicide. Judging whether life is or is not worth living amounts to answering the fundamental question of philosophy."[32]

Another version of rational suicide is suicide to avoid the humiliations or pain associated with old age, disability or illness, as advocated by Jack Kevorkian and Derek Humphry.[33] Arthur Koestler, vice president of the Voluntary Euthanasia Society, died by suicide with his wife Cynthia in 1983.[34] Dr. and Mrs. Henry Pitt Van Dusen, members of the Euthanasia Society, overdosed in January 1975 after a period of physical decline. He had been past president of Union Theological Seminary.[35] Freud died September 23, 1939, asking his physician for a lethal dose of morphine.[36] As far back as 1250 B.C., Rameses the Great of Egypt killed himself after the loss of his sight.[37]

A last type of rational suicide is the perspective that suicide is the appropriate response to economic disaster or dire circumstances. Gambling debts were linked with suicide in eighteenth-century England.[38] The British press inaccurately portrayed the 1929 Great Crash in New York as teeming with suicides: "In the week or so following Black Thursday, the London penny press told delightedly of the scenes in downtown New York. Speculators were hurling themselves from windows; pedestrians picked their way delicately between the bodies of fallen financiers."[39]

Suicide as destiny for artists. One perspective suggests that artists are prone to kill themselves because suicide is "one of the many prices to be paid for genius."[40] Novelist David Foster Wallace argued that suicide is shooting "the terrible master" of one's mind.[41] Alvarez argues that artists are doomed to suicide "not as an end of everything, but as the supreme, dramatic gesture of contempt toward a dull bourgeois world."[42] In addition, suicide can also be considered theatrical: "Killing yourself is considered dramatic; there is a certain cachet to knocking on death's door instead of waiting for it to sneak up on you when you are not looking."[43]

Suicide as joining "star-cross'd lovers." We see another perspective in thwarted lovers uniting in suicide, like Romeo and Juliet or Mark Antony and Cleopatra. John Dryden in 1678 ends his play *All for Love* about Antony and Cleopatra with this line: "No lovers lived so great, or died so well."[44] Winslow gives the example of a boatman on the Seine who found

> two bodies, a young woman about twenty, tastefully dressed, and a young man in the uniform of the eighth hussars. . . . A bit of paper . . . told their names and motives:—
>
> "O you, whoever you may be, compassionate souls, who shall find

these two bodies united, know that we loved each other with the most ardent affection, and that we have perished together, that we may be eternally united. Know, compassionate souls that our last desire is, that you should place us, united as we are, in the same grave. Man should not separate those whom death has joined." (Signed) Florine Goyon.[45]

The "Lovers of Lyons" were well-known in the eighteenth century as examples of this type of suicide. They had not been allowed to marry and shot each other simultaneously.[46] Related is suicide resulting from unrequited love, an example of which is Goethe's Werther.[47] Suicide, for some, may also be a way of reuniting in the afterlife. Plato wrote, "Many a man has been willing to go to the world below animated by the hope of seeing there an earthly love, or wife, or son, and conversing with them."[48]

In addition to depicting some situations that seem to justify suicide, many have just as clearly explored the brutal consequences of suicide, further complicating my attitudes about the subject.

The consequence of suicide is damnation to hell. This perspective states that people who die by suicide languish in eternal punishment. In the fourteenth century, Dante wrote about people who killed themselves as being tortured in circle seven of hell with Satan in the ninth circle.[49] Dante based his *Inferno* on Virgil's *Aeneid*, in which Aeneas visits the underworld and there finds those who killed themselves:

> Then the next place
> is held by those gloomy spirits who, innocent of crime,
> died by their own hand, and, hating the light, threw away
> their lives. How willingly now they'd endure
> poverty and harsh suffering, in the air above![50]

Hamlet contemplates suicide—"To be, or not to be, that is the question"—but decides against it because of "the dread of something after death."[51] Adam in Milton's *Paradise Lost* argues against suicide because of God's "vengeful ire."[52]

The consequence of suicide is haunting. Another fearsome consequence to suicide is that the suicide ghost terrorizes the living. It is assumed that a person who dies by suicide is so gravely wronged or disturbed that the ghost is especially vengeful.[53] Winslow gives the example of a servant girl who tells another servant, "I will have a swim, and afterwards I will haunt you." She was later found drowned.[54] For this reason, people who died by suicide in the fifteenth century in Metz, France, were put in a barrel and floated down the Moselle River; the idea was to keep them far from the region and the people they would want to haunt.[55] The fear of haunting explains why suicides in England were buried with a stake in the heart at a crossroads—so that the ghost could not find its way home.[56]

What Does the Church Have to Do with Suicide Prevention?

With all these depictions and attitudes toward suicide swirling about, it's no wonder I approached my client Jane with confusion. Because I'm a Christian, I wondered if the church would be a resource for her. William James, who suffered from depression with suicidal thoughts, "regarded religious faith as the most powerful safeguard against suicide."[57]

However, Jane explained that her church had held an exorcism for her and she said she would never set foot in a church again. The church is not always the resource it could be. Angie died when she picked up a handgun and it went off. Though no one will ever know Angie's intentions, Angie's mother received a letter from her brother, a Protestant minister, that said, "I can't absolve her; you'll have to accept that she's probably in hell."[58] This type of pronouncement can have long-term negative consequences. Biebel and Foster note, "Within two years of a suicide, at least 80 percent of survivors will either leave the church they were attending and join another or stop attending church altogether. The two most common reasons for this are (1) disappointment due to unmet expectations and (2) criticism or judgmental attitudes and treatment."[59]

Despite these complications, I am convinced of the importance of pastors, chaplains and pastoral counselors in suicide prevention for two reasons: Science and my own experience tell me that faith is important in suicide prevention. Studies have found that religiosity protects against suicide.[60] In my own life, I recognize how important my faith is to me in difficult times, and I know I would never want to live life without it. In addition, more than any other professionals, pastors, chaplains and pastoral counselors minister at the intersection of theology and moral practice. They teach people to choose life. They provide guidance in how to build lives worth living. They teach how to manage suffering. They monitor and intervene when suicidal people come to them for help. They guide faith communities in how to support suicide survivors. They partner with others in their communities. In fact, the US government recognizes the key role of faith-based leaders and communities in its *2012 National Strategy for Suicide Prevention: Goals and Objectives for Action* report.[61] Pastoral caregivers have a vital and unique role to play in suicide prevention.

But if you're a pastor, chaplain or pastoral counselor, you may not always know what to do. You may feel the same confusion I did with my suicidal client. This book is designed to help you recognize and use your ministry preparation to come alongside those who intend to take their lives and provide comfort to those who have lost someone to suicide. As a pastor, chaplain and pastoral counselor, you can help prevent suicide by:

1. Teaching a theology of life and death, including moral objections to suicide.

2. Teaching theodicy, or how to understand and manage suffering.

3. Directly engaging the issue of suicide—stigma-free—when people become suicidal, attempt suicide or die by suicide.

4. Teaching how to build a life worth living with meaningful purpose and belongingness.

5. Offering community where relationship skills are learned and practiced and where those who need support can get it.

6. Partnering with others in preventing suicide.

Though these tasks are huge, I hope to convince you by the end of this book that they are achievable.

DEFINITIONS

Before proceeding further, I must define suicide so that we know what pastoral caregivers are preventing. In order to determine that a suicide has occurred, the event must (1) involve a self-inflicted act, (2) result in death and (3) include intent to die.[62] "Intent to die" is a crucial aspect of this definition because a person may die accidentally or may not be sure he or she wanted to die.[63] The following examples show how intent to die is sometimes present, sometimes absent and sometimes unclear:[64]

Self-harm with no suicidal intent. Sandy comes to a therapy session on a hot summer day wearing a long-sleeved shirt and long pants. In response to her therapist's questions, she shows the therapist cuts across her arms. She says she also cuts her thighs the same way. She says she cuts herself when conflict with her mom escalates into a screaming match. She says that when she cuts she has no intent to kill herself and afterward she feels better.

Suicide attempt with clear suicidal intent. Stuart sustained traumatic brain injury during military combat. After hospitalization, and since his return home, he and his wife have been experiencing intense marital conflict. During one of his wife's business trips, Stuart feels hopeless about their fighting and experiences intense thoughts of suicide he feels he can't resist. He leaves a goodbye note for his grown daughter, locks his bedroom door and takes all of his pain medication ("a handful") and plans to die. Unexpectedly his daughter drops by. She sees the note and, when she can't get into his room, she calls the police, who break down his door and bring him to the local emergency department. He tells the doctor who questions him that he is sorry he didn't die.

Suicide-related behavior with undetermined intent. Jenny had a neglectful mother who drank, and Jenny started drinking while still a preschooler. Jenny's alcohol use has rocketed into the abuse of other drugs, her preferred being cocaine. As an adult she is diagnosed with bipolar disorder based on her experience of phases of depression followed by phases of mania in which her activity is frenzied and she becomes irritable. During these manic phases, she often stops taking her medication because she feels she doesn't need it.

One day while Jenny is in a manic phase, she and her boyfriend have a "big fight." After he leaves their home, she jumps into a bathtub with a plugged-in toaster. Her son is home and calls 911. After a brief hospitalization, she tells her therapist that she isn't sure she wanted to die because when she's manic she doesn't always think clearly. But she also muses that her boyfriend has just left her, and she knows that plugged-in appliances and water create the possibility of electrocution and death. She doesn't remember any suicidal thinking. Nor does she remember making a decision to kill herself. She isn't sure whether or not she intended to die.

Of these examples, only Stuart reported clear intent. Determining intent is complicated. It depends on the person's accurate self-report, which depends on how ambivalent they feel about dying and on their memory.[65] Intent is important and hard to determine.

My working definition of *suicide* is death caused by self-inflicted injuries with some intent to die. A *suicide attempt* is a self-inflicted, nonfatal injury with some evidence of intent to die.[66] Just as intent is important to the definition, so is injury. When one of my adolescent clients scraped her wrist with a key, her mom was worried about this being a suicide attempt. However, the scrape didn't cause injury.

The pathway to suicide attempt and suicide is *suicidal ideation*, which includes any thoughts or mental images of suicide or of intent to take one's life.[67] A *suicidal crisis* is "a discrete, intense episode of suicide ideation accompanied by suicidal desire, a suicide attempt, or other suicide-relevant behavior."[68] *Suicidality* is a broad term that captures the spectrum of suicidal thinking and behaviors.

A last note about language: There is nothing "successful" about a suicide and nothing "failed" about surviving an attempt, so I will avoid this language except in quotations. Also, I will say "die by suicide" and avoid the expression "commit suicide" out of respect for suicide survivors who have reminded me that suicide is no longer a crime.

THE CRIMINALITY OF SUICIDE

Suicide was a criminal act in England as early as the tenth century.[69] After suicide, the two possible legal verdicts were *felo de se* (felon of self) or *non compos mentis* (not of sound mind), depending on intentionality. Children and the insane were exempt from guilt because they were deemed unable to understand the consequences of their behavior; the jury would bring a *non compos mentis* verdict in these cases.[70]

Following a *felo de se* verdict, the corpse was desecrated—dragged through the streets by a horse in France, buried at a crossroads with a stake through the heart in England, buried with a load of rocks piled on the grave in the American colonies—with the victim's goods forfeited to the crown.[71] Montesquieu wrote in 1715, "The laws in Europe are furious against suicides, who are made to die a second time; they are dragged shamefully through the streets; they are marked by infamy and their goods are confiscated."[72] In April 1707 an American judge gave an order "to Cause the Body of the said Abraham Harris [who hanged himself] to be buried upon Boston Neck near the High-way, leading to Roxbury over against the Gallows and to Cause a Cart-Load of Stones to be laid upon the Grave of the said Harris as a Brand of Infamy."[73] John Wesley called for the bodies of suicide victims to be gibbeted, a practice typical of his times.[74] Donne explains that these customs were engaged in "for the reason common to almost all nations, to deter men from doing it and not to punish its being done."[75] Winslow adds that in the fifteenth century the body of Louis de Beaumont was to be dragged "the most cruelly possible to show others."[76]

With the publication of several pioneering works—including those of Burton and Winslow,[77] which will be discussed in chapter four—the criminalization of suicide as a prevention method began to fade to the background and mental illness as a cause of suicide moved to the foreground. Kushner writes:

> William Bond, a thirty-one-year-old unemployed master mariner, "came to his Death by discharging the contents of a large pistol into his head" on 27 March 1828. Nevertheless, the jury did not find suicide because it accepted testimony that Bond had been "quite down-hearted" prior to this death. A sailor, Jacob Wilson, who hanged himself in 1828 with "his suspenders round his neck," was determined to have done so "in a fit of insanity."[78]

By the late eighteenth century, juries typically adjudicated *non compos mentis*.[79]

Changing jury verdicts led to changes in the laws. George III's parliament in England abolished the practice of burial with a stake through the heart, and the last man to be thus buried was named Griffiths in 1823.[80] In 1870, the confiscation of goods of a victim of suicide was abolished. In 1879 and 1882, the maximum sentence for attempted suicide was reduced to two years and suicides were granted the right of burial at normal hours; the question of religious rites was left to the minister.[81]

Some US states changed suicide laws after the American Revolution, as did France after the French Revolution of 1789.[82] Though most US juries rendered *non compos mentis* verdicts, some state laws did not officially reflect this position until the twentieth century. For example, as recently as 1974, attempted suicide was still a crime in nine states.[83] Suicide remained a crime in England and Wales until 1961, when the Suicide Act of 1961 abolished the criminalization of suicide and attempted suicide, and in Ireland until 1993.[84] Alvarez recounts meeting with police after his suicide attempt: "At some point the police came, since in those days suicide was still a criminal offense. They sat heavily but rather sympathetically by my bed and asked me questions they clearly didn't want me to answer. When I tried to explain, they shushed me politely. 'It was an accident, wasn't it, sir?' Dimly, I agreed. They went away."[85]

THIS BOOK'S FOCUS

This book will focus primarily on suicidal acts that include at least some intent to die, as was the case with my client who spent her life wanting to die and also wanting to find a way to live. While the current suicide classification system is broad enough to include intentional self-harm with no intent to die, such as cutting oneself (which can be called self-harm, self-mutilation, nonsuicidal self-injurious behavior or parasuicide), I will not cover nonsuicidal self-harm because the behavior is so complex that this book would not be able to deal justly with it.[86] I will also not cover what Karl Menninger, the "grandfather of modern suicidology," calls "chronic suicides," people who are slowly dying from poor choices—for example, people who "drink themselves to death" or "starve themselves to death."[87] Though these types of behavior are extremely serious and pose moral dilemmas, this book will focus on acts with at least some clear intent to die.[88] I will also not cover some specific types of suicide with intent to die: physician-assisted suicide, suicide bombing, suicide by cop (provoking a law enforcement officer to take lethal action), murder-suicide, or bullycide. These deserve books of their own.

INTEGRATION OF THEOLOGY AND PSYCHOLOGY

Because this book will include both theology and psychology, it's important that I clarify how I integrate them. For me, psychology is the science of systematic observation of mental processes and behavior, whereas theology is reasoned discourse about God. Some have pitted theology and psychology against each other as "mortal enemies."[89] But I see theology and psychology as different disciplines that both contribute to the practice of suicide prevention and that require integration. The domain of theology is God and his revelation through Christ and the Bible. The domain of psychology is empirical observation. Psychology as an empirical science can provide pastoral caregivers a great deal of information about suicide but cannot make pronouncements about what's morally objectionable about suicide, whereas theology can.

The Bible determines my theological beliefs about God and the world, but it presupposes that I have a certain knowledge of the world gained from various sources, such as personal experience, science and general human reason. For example, many biblical concepts rest on the assumption that readers know the world they live in. Understanding how the law of the Lord is more to be desired than gold (Ps 19:10) requires that the reader observe people enough to appreciate how basic monetary units are desired. Understanding how the law of the Lord is sweeter than honey requires that the reader pay attention to how uniquely delectable honey can be. Science is a source of knowledge.[90] Psychology as a science has truths worthy of consideration because while the Bible is all true, it does not contain all truth. Arthur Holmes puts it like this:

> To say that all truth is God's truth does not mean that all truth is either contained in the Bible or deducible from what we find there. Historic Christianity has believed in the truthfulness of Scripture, yet not as an exhaustive revelation of everything men can know or want to know as true, but rather as a sufficient rule for faith and conduct.[91]

For example, in Matthew 28:19, we are told to "go . . . and make disciples of all nations," but the Bible doesn't tell us how to build an internal combustion engine. The Bible tells us to avoid alcoholism (Prov 23:29-35) but not that cues in the environment can activate expectations of positive outcomes of drinking for problem drinkers.[92] The Bible describes several suicides, but psychology fleshes out more completely the many factors that contribute to suicide. The Bible is God's gift of inspired revelation for how to be in a relationship with him, not a 1-2-3 manual on how to do suicide prevention.[93]

Some readers might be concerned that discovery of truth outside the Bible is a criticism of the Bible. It is not. The Bible is not diminished one bit when we supplement its observer phenomenological perspective with the science of astronomy, which informs us that the earth turns and the sun doesn't rise. The Bible is not diminished because as God's inspired revelation it provides us the meaning of what we observe in science.[94] Science has its limitations. The revelation of God is required in order to make sense of what we observe empirically. Elizabeth Barrett Browning writes,

> Earth's crammed with heaven,
> And every common bush afire with God;
> But only he who sees, takes off his shoes,
> The rest sit round it and pluck blackberries.[95]

Some psychologists pluck blackberries without seeing God. They apprehend the complexity of the human being but do not see the relational, personality-full Creator whose image we all bear. During my training I asked one of my supervisors why people should value themselves. His answer was that people should value themselves because they occupied space in the universe. The science is flawless: people do indeed occupy space. But he missed the meaning found in Psalm 8: "You have made [people] a little lower than God, and crowned them with glory and honor" (Ps 8:5). When apprehending what's there, people engage in science. When apprehending the meaning of what they see as determined by God, people engage in theology. These are separate disciplines, and science, in fact, does not do theology well.

For example, Freud was an avowed materialist who believed that religion was an illusion based in the helplessness people felt as children.[96] And while Christians disagree with the meaning he drew because it's in conflict with a Christian perspective, we do adopt his concepts of the unconscious, defensiveness and the Freudian slip. We value psychology for what it can do. To blame psychology that it doesn't do theology is like being disappointed that a hammer can't bake bread. And to throw that hammer away is a waste of a good tool.[97]

SUMMARY

Pastors, chaplains and pastoral counselors have a unique and vital role to play in suicide prevention but they may face the same quandary I did, which is how to work with someone who is suicidal. Many different perspectives on suicide contributed to some of my confusion early in my career and, like me, pastoral caregivers need help knowing how to minister to the Janes in their faith communities. They need tools, the first of which is a framework for suicide prevention, including appropriate definitions and an approach to the integration of psychology with theology.

However, perspectives on suicide are not the only contributions to confusion about suicide. Myths about suicide are pervasive. One of the most prominent is that teen girls are at the highest risk for suicide. How can we know who is most at risk? We'll focus on this question in chapter one.

DISCUSSION QUESTIONS

1. A book about suicide with stories about real people is hard to read. How will you take care of yourself as you read this book?

2. Suicide is mentioned in the Bible: Abimelech (Judg 9:52-54), Samson (Judg 16:30), Saul (1 Sam 31:4), Ahithophel (2 Sam 17:23), Zimri (1 Kings 16:18) and Judas (Mt 27:5; Acts 1:18). How do these biblical accounts of suicide fit with the perspectives in this chapter?

3. What is your perspective on suicide?

4. What, if anything, do you think pastors, chaplains and pastoral counselors should do to prevent suicide?

RESOURCES

National Suicide Prevention Lifeline, 1-800-273-TALK, a free, 24-hour confidential hotline available to anyone in suicidal crisis or emotional distress, including veterans and Spanish speakers. Also visit the Lifeline's profile on MySpace: www.myspace.com/800273talk.

Canadian Association for Suicide Prevention (CASP/ACPS), www.suicideprevention.ca.

T. D. Doty and S. Spencer-Thomas, *The Role of Faith Communities in Suicide Prevention: A Guidebook for Faith Leaders* (Westminster, CO: Carson J. Spencer Foundation, 2009).

K. J. Kaplan and M. B. Schwartz, *A Psychology of Hope: A Biblical Response to Tragedy and Suicide* (Grand Rapids: Eerdmans, 2008).

Suicide Prevention Resource Center, *The Role of Faith Communities in Preventing Suicide: A Report of an Interfaith Suicide Prevention Dialogue* (Newton, MA: Education Development Center Inc., 2009).

U.S. Department of Health and Human Services Office of the Surgeon General and National Action Alliance for Suicide Prevention, *2012 National Strategy for Suicide Prevention: Goals and Objectives for Action* (Washington, DC: HHS, 2012).

1

WHO DIES BY SUICIDE?

The phone rings at your home at 10:30 p.m. Jim is sobbing. Bit by bit he tells you that he plans to kill himself tonight because his wife has discovered his ongoing affair. He says he has disappointed God, his family and himself in an unforgivable way.

Jim is the last person in your congregation you would have expected to experience suicidal thinking. He's an involved member of your church, a committed Christian. He has never discussed any concerns about his marriage. And even if he had, he is upbeat and positive, and people describe him as "dependable" with "a winning personality." You wonder: If Jim is suicidal, are there others in your faith community who might be as well? Suicidal thinking and suicide are a lot more common than we often believe.

IS SUICIDE THAT WIDESPREAD?

The World Health Organization has found that for every death due to war in the world, there are three deaths due to homicide and five due to suicide.[1] Closer to home in the United States, suicide was the tenth leading cause of death across all ages in 2010 (affecting 38,364 people), ahead of homicide (16,259 people) and HIV (8,352 people).[2] Even as you read this chapter, there will be one US suicide every sixteen minutes.[3] Suicide is a serious threat and must be taken seriously, especially because these numbers are underreported. Take this example from 1899 cited by Kushner: A 34-year-old woman inhaled gas but revived. She then swallowed morphine and lost consciousness, but again she recovered and showed improvement. She died five days later of pneumonia, which is listed as the cause of death on both the coroner's report and her death certificate in 1899.[4]

Those who actually die by suicide are just the tip of the iceberg. Based on large national surveys, it is estimated that for every fourteen suicides per hundred thousand people each year, approximately five hundred people attempt suicide and three thousand think about it.[5] Therefore, there's a significant chance suicidal thinking occurs in your faith community. Individuals in your pews, those who request counseling and even members of your governing board may at some point have thought about suicide or even attempted it. And you may experience a suicide death in your faith community.

Jim's story ended well. He called his pastor who talked about God's forgiveness (Rom 5:20-21) and prevented his suicide. But what happens when the Jim in your church doesn't call you? Is there a way to identify him and help him anyway?

We can try to answer that question using the same approach that helps doctors understand what causes high blood pressure. A public health approach involves (1) surveillance, or tracking who gets high blood pressure—which ages, sex and races are affected?—and (2) research on what factors tend to co-occur with high blood pressure— being overweight, eating a high-salt diet, smoking. Let's apply these same methods to suicide to see if we can identify the Jim in your faith community.

WHICH GROUPS DIE BY SUICIDE?

Let's start with surveillance to discover which groups experience more suicide and attempts.

Age. On the evening news we hear about teens like Phoebe Prince, who was bullied and took her own life, and we know that suicide is a serious problem for teens.[6] In 2010 in the United States, suicide was the third-leading cause of death among 10- to 14-year-olds, the third-leading cause of death among 15- to 24-year-olds, and the second-leading cause of death among 25- to 34-year-olds.[7] Suicide is a problem for teens because psychiatric illnesses and suicidal behavior start to emerge as a serious concern in the 10- to 14-year-old age group, and suicide attempts are highest in adolescence and young adulthood.[8]

But when we look at the number of people who actually die, people in the middle years of life are at higher risk. In 2010, 4,600 young people in the 15- to 24-year-old age group died by suicide, while 6,571 35- to 44-year-olds, 8,799 45- to 54-year-olds, and 6,384 55- to 64-year olds took their own lives.[9]

Even young children think about suicide and, though rare, die by suicide. In 2010, seven US children in the five- to nine-year-old age range died by suicide.[10] Researchers have found that preschool children aged two-and-a-half to five years old think about and attempt suicide.[11] Jane told me that her earliest memory of a suicidal thought was of holding a knife to her stomach around age three.

We can talk about these numbers in a different way if we look at the rates for these different groups. The suicide rate is simply the number of people in a group who die by suicide divided by the larger number of people in that group, and standardized by multiplying by 100,000 to permit meaningful comparisons between groups. When we look at suicide rates, we discover that 45- to 54-year-olds had the highest rate of suicide in 2010: There were 19.55 suicide deaths per 100,000 compared to 12.43 suicide deaths per 100,000 Americans of all ages.[12] The second-highest rate occurred in the 85-plus age range (17.62 per 100,000), with the 55- to 64-year-old age range a close third (17.50 per 100,000).[13] The rate for the oldest Americans is especially unexpected because older adults made up 13 percent of the 2010 population but represented 15.6 percent of suicide deaths.[14]

So how does this information help us identify Jim or Joan in our faith community? By reminding us not to exclude anyone. Every age group thinks about and dies by suicide. If we pay particular attention to middle-aged congregants and do not remain alert to warning signs among other age groups, we might miss people who need our help.

Sex. Almost four times more men than women die by suicide each year. In 2010 in the United States, 30,277 males died by suicide compared to 8,087 females; the suicide rate for males was 19.95 per 100,000 compared to 5.15 per 100,000 for females.[15] But more women than men attempt suicide. Women made up 57 percent of all people treated for nonfatal self-harm in a US hospital emergency department in 2010. Of the 464,995 people with nonfatal self-harm injuries treated, 199,204 were men with a rate of 131.67 per 100,000, and 265,727 were women with a rate of 180.59 per 100,000.[16]

Males. Many theories exist about why more men die by suicide than women. One is that men use firearms. In 2010, 56 percent of men who died by suicide used firearms as opposed to 30 percent of women.[17] In that same year, 88 percent of suicide deaths involving firearms were men,[18] perhaps related to the fact that three times more men than women own a gun.[19] A striking characteristic of most people contemplating suicide is their ambivalence: a part of them wants to die and often another part wants to find reasons to live. William Cowper, a Christian hymnodist, planned to overdose on the narcotic laudanum but experienced this ambivalence when he brought a vial of laudanum to his mouth twenty times and each time set it back down, "distracted between the desire for death, and the dread of it."[20] Kevin Hines, who suffers from bipolar disorder and who started hearing voices in high school, jumped from the Golden Gate Bridge in 2000. As soon as he jumped he realized he did not want to die. Miraculously, he survived.[21] Another example of someone who survived is Ken Baldwin, who jumped from the Golden Gate and then realized his ambivalence: "I instantly realized that everything in my life that I'd thought was unfixable was totally fixable—except for having just jumped."[22] A woman may swallow pills and then suddenly realize she wants to live. She can pick up the phone and dial 911 for help. But a man using a firearm has little opportunity for a second thought. I am not suggesting that women are more ambivalent, but I am highlighting a gender difference in method. If a woman uses a method that allows the desire to live to emerge, she may be more likely to survive an attempt than a man who uses a firearm.

Other theories attempting to explain why more men die by suicide include the cultural script theory, which suggests that masculinity is associated with killing oneself and femininity with nonfatal attempts.[23] Another theory is that men have higher substance abuse rates, which are related to greater impulsivity and impaired judgment as well as problems in relationships.[24] Men fall in love earlier in a relationship, they cling longer to a "dying love," and three times as many men as women die by suicide after a failed intimate relationship.[25] Shneidman cites this suicide note written by a 31-year-old separated male:

> Forgive me, for today I die. I just cannot live without you. I might as well be dead. Maybe there will be peace. I have this empty feeling inside me that is killing me. I just can't take it anymore. When you left me I died inside. I have to say, nothing left but the broken heart that is leading me into this. I cry to God to help me but he doesn't listen. There is nothing else for me to do.[26]

Another circumstance that may help explain why men may have higher suicide rates is incarceration.[27] In 2010, men made up about 88 percent of jail inmates.[28] Suicide is the leading cause of jail deaths and the second-leading cause of prison deaths following illnesses.[29] (A jail holds people awaiting a trial or those sentenced for a short duration. A prison holds people convicted of crimes serving longer terms.) Most jail suicides occur during the inmate's first week after admission, either on the date of admission or the next.[30] Plus, a recent release from prison increases suicide risk,[31] and an association may exist between committing crimes and suicide: "Murderers have a suicide rate several hundred times greater than people of the same age and sex who have not committed murder, and . . . people found guilty of violent and impulsive crimes, such as arsonists, have . . . a very high incidence of violent suicide attempts."[32] Aggression and suicide are related.[33]

Another theory is that men are more apt to be fearless or acquire the fearlessness required to go against the self-preservation instinct.[34] Voltaire wrote, "None but a strong man can surmount the most powerful instinct of nature."[35] Thomas Joiner has theorized that suicidal people develop the ability to harm themselves through practice, with an "escalating trajectory" toward more and more serious and potentially lethal attempts.[36] This theory is consistent with the finding that people who have previously attempted suicide are up to forty times more likely to die by suicide.[37] Joiner believes that men have more opportunity to acquire the ability to enact lethal self-injury through "more exposure to guns, to physical fights, to violent sports like boxing and football, and to self-injecting drug use."[38] Acquired fearlessness may also help explain suicides among service men and women and veterans.[39] As a former Special Forces officer who served multiple combat tours in Iraq and Afghanistan explained, "We know what death looks like and we're comfortable with it."[40]

Females. Though men die at greater rates than women, we cannot worry less about women. McKeon writes, "It is critical to remember that even if a group has a lower suicide rate than the national average this does not mean that hundreds, if not thousands, from that demographic group may not die by suicide every year."[41] Not only do women die, but one study found that women attempted suicide five times more often than men.[42] In 2010 in the United States women had a higher attempt rate (180.59 per 100,000) than men (131.67 per 100,000).[43] And it is likely that these numbers are underestimates, because not everyone who attempts suicide actually goes to a hospital emergency department. Robins provides an example of a 34-year-old woman who attempted suicide with an overdose of sleeping pills but whose children kept her awake with coffee and walking.[44] The woman was never seen by medical professionals. When she was later hospitalized, she denied any previous attempts. As another example, one of my clients took pills intending to harm herself. She woke up later and never went to an emergency room, so her attempt was never reported.

Pastoral caregivers need to be concerned about women because women tend to experience higher rates of anxiety and mood disorders such as depression than men (though men have higher rates of attention-deficit/hyperactivity disorder, conduct disorder and substance disorders).[45] In the next section of this chapter we'll see that mental disorders increase the risk of suicide. Women also report more suicidal ideation.[46] They tend to experience more sexual abuse and intimate partner violence, which are associated with higher rates of suicide attempts.[47] But women may be more protected because they seek mental health care more than men[48] and have higher involvement in religion and in social networks.[49] Their greater help-seeking suggests that pastors may encounter more suicidal women than men in their ministry.

Does this information help identify the Jim or Joan in your congregation? It prompts us to realize that, as a man, Jim is part of a group with high suicide rates, but women also die by suicide, and they think about and attempt suicide more than men.

Race. The 2010 US suicide rate for whites is 14.13 per 100,000 people. For blacks it's 5.1 people per 100,000, for American Indian/Alaska natives it's 11 per 100,000, and for Asian/Pacific Islanders it's 6.24 per 100,000 people who die by suicide. Of the 30,277 men who died of suicide in 2010 in the United States, 27,422 were white, 1,755 were black, 344 were American Indian/Alaska Native, and 756 were Asian/Pacific Islanders.[50] White individuals also made up the majority of suicide attempts.[51] People from all races die by suicide, though white individuals have higher rates.

Suicide surveillance, or tracking who dies by suicide, has given us some helpful information about the higher risk of white middle-aged males for death and young white females for attempts. But it also shows us that people across all age groups and races and in both sexes die by suicide or attempt suicide. Another question we can ask to help identify the Jim or Joan in our faith community is, what factors are related to suicidal thinking? Just as weight, diet, stress, genetics and smoking may be related to high blood pressure, what factors might be related to Jim's suicidal thinking? And will these factors help identify Joan?

Risk and Protective Factors: Researching Suicide

You may wonder how we answer this question about factors when "the chief source of information is no longer available."[52] One method employed is psychological autopsy, which comprises in-depth interviews with family, friends and colleagues of the person who died by suicide, as well as professionals who worked with him or her, in order to clarify intent to die.[53]

Another method is epidemiology, which involves the study of patterns related to suicide deaths in order to identify risk factors (factors that increase the likelihood of suicide) and protective factors (factors that decrease the likelihood). Durkheim calls these factors the "coefficient of aggravation" and the "coefficient of preservation."[54] Epidemiology can also help quantify the amount of risk a factor adds—for example, researchers have found that almost six times as many people who have a diagnosis of alcohol abuse or dependence die by suicide compared to the general population.[55] Based on these methodologies, researchers have identified the following risk and protective factors, which may be factors in Jim's and Joan's suicidal thinking.

Mental health factors. A prominent factor associated with suicide is the presence of a mental health problem. In a large national survey, a mental health disorder was present in 82 percent of people with suicidal thoughts, 94.5 percent of those who made a suicide plan, and 88.2 percent of those who had attempted suicide in the previous twelve months.[56] Major depression was the most common disorder. The "big five" mental health disorders are of particular concern for suicide risk: borderline personality disorder (400 times higher suicide rate than that of the general population), anorexia nervosa (which increases suicide risk 23 times), major depressive disorder (20 times more risk), bipolar disorder (15 times greater risk), and schizophrenia (8.5 times greater risk).[57] Joiner assumes that everyone who dies by suicide experiences at least some symptoms of a mental health problem.[58] Mental health factors are important to know about because one in five Americans has a mental health problem and this may confer some suicide risk.[59] For example, John, an unemployed contractor in his fifties, lived with depression and thoughts of suicide since his college days, experiencing a lifelong struggle with not meeting his father's expectations. One in five members of your congregation may be at some risk of suicide because of a mental health disorder.

Having more than one mental health problem increases the risk of suicide attempt five times.[60] Fifty-one percent of people who attempt suicide have both a mental health problem and a substance abuse problem.[61] Use of drugs or alcohol can be particularly dangerous in young people, where alcohol intoxication has been found in approximately half of suicides, but it is a risk factor in all age groups.[62] Substance use tends to disinhibit and impair judgment such that McKeon concludes, "For both death by suicide and suicide attempts, acute alcohol use played a role in over one third of the cases, a finding of great clinical significance."[63] Substance abuse can also create other risk factors, such as relationship problems and social disconnection.[64] Other mental health symptoms add risk as well. For example, anxiety or agitation can facilitate the change from thinking about suicide to acting on those thoughts.[65] Sleep problems have been found to confer risk even after controlling for depression.[66] People with suicidal thinking often report nightmares.[67]

Other biological factors. Having a mental health problem is not the whole story of suicide because only one to three percent of people who have a mental health problem die by suicide. Joiner points out that mental illness as an explanation for suicide is dissatisfying because mental illness is much more common than suicide.[68]

To explain how people come to take their own lives, we also have to consider the possibility of a genetic component. For example, one twin study found that identical twins have significantly greater risk for suicide and suicide attempt than fraternal twins.[69] In a study of the Amish, suicides clustered in just a few families.[70] Agerbo, Nordentoft and Mortensen found youth suicide to be nearly five times more likely in the offspring of mothers who had died by suicide and twice as common in the offspring of fathers who had died by suicide, even after adjusting for parental mental disorders.[71] The Institute of Medicine reports that having a first-degree relative die by suicide increases the risk of suicide six times.[72] However, it's also important to put these statistics in context. As Joiner notes, the risk of suicide for any given person is one out of 10,000; having a family member die by suicide increases this risk to no more than five out of 10,000.[73] Genetic predisposition to suicide does not in any way, shape or form make suicide inevitable.[74] In addition to genetics, the associations between lower levels of scrotonin, a neurotransmitter in the brain, and impulsivity and violence point to the part biology plays in suicide.[75]

Circumstances. It's a myth that people in difficult circumstances kill themselves as a matter of course. People survive great horror and do not kill themselves. Kushner contrasts Meriwether Lewis and Abraham Lincoln, who both suffered from depression and faced great challenges, but it was Meriwether Lewis who killed himself.[76] In fact, suicide is never a normal response to difficult events. Circumstances are just one part of the story. Jim struggled with a circumstance—his wife's discovery of his affair—but it was not the circumstance alone that affected his thinking. The circumstance occurred in the context of his theology that God could not forgive him. As a Centers for Disease Control report states, "Suicide is never the result of a single factor or event, but rather results from a complex interaction of many factors and usually involves a history of psychosocial problems."[77]

Some of the circumstances that confer risk for suicide include:

- Childhood sexual abuse, which is more common among females[78]

- Intimate partner conflict[79]

- Intimate partner violence, which is more frequently perpetrated on females[80]

- Social isolation in many forms, such as being single, divorced or widowed, or having lost a parent in childhood[81]

- Firearm ownership, which tends to be higher in rural areas and among men[82]

- Low socioeconomic status[83]

- Economic recession for working-age people (ages 25 to 64)[84]

- Chronic pain[85]

- Homelessness[86]

- Being a veteran[87]

- Immigration[88]

- Sexual orientation[89]

Among adolescents, problems with parents play an important role in suicidal behavior, especially in younger adolescents.[90] And as

Miller and colleagues note, "Romantic difficulties are more common precipitants among older adolescents, while parent-child conflicts are more common among younger adolescents."[91] Other factors that confer suicide risk for adolescents include conflict with friends, disciplinary events and legal problems.[92] In fact, in adolescents these stressful life events may contribute as much risk for suicide as a mental health problem.[93]

But even as we point to these general risk factors based on population statistics, we must recognize that every suicide is unique and involves many factors. Styron wrote, "The greatest fallacy about suicide lies in the belief that there is a single immediate answer—or perhaps combined answers—as to why the deed was done."[94] Durkheim adds, "Each victim of suicide gives his act a personal stamp which expresses his temperament, the special conditions in which he is involved, and which, consequently, cannot be explained by the social and general causes of the phenomenon."[95]

For example, Sally died by suicide. She had struggled with depression and suicidal thoughts every day of her life. Her first suicidal thought was around three years old. Her father had fluctuated between neglecting her and abusing her and her siblings both sexually and physically. Though Sally begged her mother for help, she not only did not protect Sally but locked her in her room for days at a time. Sally was sexually assaulted and experienced domestic violence as a young woman. Before she died, she was living alone with little positive contact with family. She prepared for her death by taking out an insurance policy, then waiting the necessary years. She got used to pain by cutting herself. Sally is an example of the complexity of factors that contribute to suicide. Jim experienced several risk factors but he also had an important protective factor. He felt comfortable pouring out his heart to his pastor, who shared with him a theology of forgiveness.

Protective factors. Even if a person has several risk factors, protective factors can buffer the effects.[96] These are "the mirror image of the risk factors," meaning that they are the reverse of risk factors.[97] A desire to live, fear of pain and suffering, and not having access to a firearm are protective factors. Among adults, protective factors include:

- Support by family, friends and significant others[98]

- The presence of an intimate partner[99]

- Church attendance[100]

- Religious coping, including prayer, worshiping God, meditation, reading scriptures and meeting with a spiritual leader[101]

- Moral objection to suicide (believing suicide is unacceptable)[102]

- Reasons for living,[103] including survival and coping beliefs (such as believing one will be able to find solutions to problems), a feeling of responsibility to family, child-related concerns, fear of suicide or death, and fear of social disapproval[104]

- Coping strategies focused on solving and managing a problem and regulating one's emotional responses[105]

- Having a child less than 18 years old (this is especially true for women)[106]

- The strengths of the suicidal person. I have a client with great persistence who loses hope but then problem-solves and generates solutions. I have another suicidal client who is very likeable and people offer him social support.

Among adolescents, family cohesion (a feeling of togetherness in the family) and parental support, ethnic identity, and self-esteem have been found to be protective against suicidal thinking and behaviors as well as social support and connection to school.[107]

CONCLUSIONS

How can pastors, chaplains and pastoral counselors use this information? One way is to realize that suicidal thinking, attempts and deaths are more common than you think. People in your faith community are struggling today. Another way is to realize that it's difficult to predict who the Jim or Joan in your congregation is or will be. While it's possible to identify a person who may be at higher risk—

such as a white middle-aged divorced male who just lost his job and is abusing alcohol—it is also possible that someone you least expect may attempt suicide. Surveillance and risk and protective factors are based on general population statistics and each suicide is a unique interaction among many factors and therefore in many ways unique and unpredictable.[108] Despite all the information we have on suicide, human beings are not clairvoyant. We can in hindsight notice risk factors that were there, but to expect to predict suicide is unreasonable. McKeon writes, "Prediction of death by suicide was probably never a feasible goal."[109]

But prediction and prevention are different. While we struggle to predict suicide, we can help to prevent it. Pastoral caregivers can monitor a person's risk factors and are especially able to build protective factors that buffer vulnerabilities to suicide. In addition to encouraging involvement in religious activities, clergy also help strengthen people's reasons for living, giving them a place to belong and serve, teaching them how to build enduring marriages, strong cohesive families and identities and esteem founded on God's everlasting love.

SUMMARY

One of the top ten causes of death in the United States is suicide. It can show up unexpectedly in people like Jim. Even though white middle-aged men have high vulnerability, people from every group die by suicide. People at higher risk are those with mental health problems such as depression who have developed the ability to harm themselves. Irving Selikoff is quoted as saying, "Statistics are people with the tears wiped away."[110] What is sad about these statistics is that they describe real people who have died. What is positive is that suicide is often preventable, as we saw with Jim when his pastor intervened.[111]

As we have looked at the factors associated with people wanting to harm themselves, you may have found yourself wondering how a Christian gets to that point. For example, Jack was teaching at a Christian college and directing the choir at his evangelical church. Why did he kill himself? Myths about suicide abound—myths such as

"Christians don't kill themselves," and "Talking about suicide will give the person the idea," and "If someone really wants to kill himself, there's nothing I can do." Is there any truth to these? We'll look at these questions next.

DISCUSSION QUESTIONS

1. What is the difference between Judas and Peter (Mt 26:75) after their betrayal of Jesus? Why did one kill himself and the other did not?

2. Of all the factors related to suicide discussed in this chapter, which were the most surprising to you? Which ones had you already expected?

3. How do you imagine these factors might be the same or different for Christians?

4. How would you apply knowledge of risk and protective factors to preventing suicide?

RESOURCES

K. Hawton, ed., *Prevention and Treatment of Suicidal Behaviour: From Science to Practice* (Oxford: Oxford University Press, 2005).

K. R. Jamison, *Night Falls Fast: Understanding Suicide* (New York: Vintage, 1999).

T. Joiner, *Why People Die by Suicide* (Cambridge, MA: Harvard University Press, 2005).

National Suicide Prevention Lifeline, 1-800-273-TALK, a free, 24-hour confidential hotline available to anyone in suicidal crisis or emotional distress. You can call for yourself or someone you care about.

National Institute of Mental Health, www.nimh.nih.gov/health/topics/suicide-prevention.

2

SHATTERING MYTHS ABOUT SUICIDE

Even Christians can, and do, take their own lives.

LLOYD AND GWEN CARR

Whenever I give a talk on suicide prevention invariably someone will say that anyone who kills himself wasn't really a Christian or that people who kill themselves are selfish or that most suicides happen over the holidays. Myths about suicide abound and can keep us from taking steps to prevent it. In this chapter we will examine ten myths about suicide in the light of the Bible and science.

MYTH 1: REAL CHRISTIANS DO NOT EXPERIENCE SUICIDAL THOUGHTS

Emily is a Christian seminarian. One night she seriously contemplated suicide, but a friend intervened the next morning, getting her the help she needed. Joe, a pastor, experienced thoughts of suicide a few times a week for an entire year. He had a typical childhood, but he became depressed as a young adult. Dr. Kathryn Greene-McCreight, an Episcopal priest and theologian, and Rev. Dr. James T. Stout, a Presbyterian minister, have struggled with bipolar illness and suicidal thinking.[1] Francis Schaeffer, theologian, pastor and founder of L'Abri Fellowship, also struggled with suicidal thoughts. His son writes, "Dad did contemplate suicide. He sometimes spoke in detail about hanging himself. I went through childhood knowing that there were two things we children were never to tell anyone. The first was that Dad got insanely angry with my mother; the second was that from time to time he threatened suicide."[2]

Are you surprised that such committed Christians would consider suicide? Most of us think that God's blessing of the righteous (Ps 5:12) would prevent a person from becoming suicidal. What's more, from a scientific perspective we know that religion provides some protection against suicide.[3] Religious involvement is linked with longevity.[4] Religious people are less likely to drink, smoke and experience depression, and they are more likely to wear their seatbelts and see their dentists than less religious people.[5] However, Christians do become depressed—contrary to a sign I saw in front of a church that declared, "We are too blessed to be depressed"—and some Christians do long for death and think about suicide.

Christians become depressed. C. H. Spurgeon, the nineteenth-century revivalist, in 1866 told his congregation, "I am the subject of depressions of spirit so fearful that I hope none of you ever gets to such extremes of wretchedness as I go to."[6] Martin Luther also experienced recurrent depression and anxiety.[7] According to J. R. Watt, he believed that "an element of despair was a necessary part of spiritual life and conceded that such fears might lead some to take their lives."[8] Edward John Carnell, a leading theologian in the evangelical movement and past president of Fuller Seminary, struggled with depression and insomnia for which he took medication.[9] Psalm 102 depicts someone struggling with symptoms consistent with depression. Elsewhere in Scripture we read about the despondency of Rebekah (Gen 27:46), Rachel (Gen 30:1), Job (Job 3:24) and Jeremiah (Jer 20:18).

Christians contemplate death and suicide. The Old Testament records people with close relationships to God who wished for death: Job (Job 3:20-22; 7:15-16), Moses (Num 11:15), Elijah (1 Kings 19:4) and Jonah (Jon 4:8). Should it surprise us, then, that Christians such as Emily, Joe, Kathryn Greene-McCreight, Jim Stout and Francis Schaeffer actively thought about suicide and that some even die by suicide?[10] Puritan Increase Mather was tempted to suicide and in a sermon referred to Luther's temptations to "self-murder."[11] John Donne, seventeenth-century poet, Anglican priest and dean of St. Paul's Cathedral, wrote, "I often have such a sickly inclination [to suicide]."[12] Edward J. Carnell, a Christian apologist, describes an event when "one Friday afternoon . . . I emotionally exploded. . . . Even suicide took on a certain attractiveness."[13] Carnell died in 1967 from a drug overdose; the coroner was unable to determine whether the death was accidental or intentional.[14] Young Martin Luther King Jr. is said to have attempted suicide.[15]

Christians might become suicidal for four reasons. First, we are both fallen and redeemed, which means that we are both new creations in Christ (2 Cor 5:17) and we also live with sin (1 Jn 1:8).[16] As we move on to maturity in Christ, living more and more for God and dying more and more to sin, we still continue to struggle with the sin in us (Rom 7:21-23). Sin affects us in three ways. We suffer the effects of living in a sin-broken world, we sin, and we are sinned against. Mark McMinn describes these three types of sin as sinfulness (our general state of brokenness, which might manifest as a genetic vulnerability to suicide), sin or sinful acts (for example, committing murder), and the consequences of sin (such as vulnerability to suicide because of a parent's abuse).[17] What this means is that Christians will live in a broken world with broken bodies and broken selves touched by sin, and some will become suicidal.

A second reason Christians might become suicidal lies in Satan's determination to destroy those created in God's image. The early church believed the devil instigated Christians to suicide, a view consistent with the Bible (1 Pet 5:8).[18] However, another age-old biblical perspective is that Christians are to resist the devil (Eph 6:11). The Puritans believed that suicide was not only the work of the devil but also a personal decision.[19] Those who believe that suicide is a result of Satan's influence need to recognize this as well. Albert Hsu writes, "What I must grapple with is not that God wanted my dad to die [by suicide], or that Satan wanted my dad to die, but that my dad wanted to die. I can't know for sure what spiritual forces were at work to influence my father's decision. All I know for certain is that whatever the reasons, my dad decided that death was better than life."[20]

A third reason Christians may become suicidal is that real Christians experience real suffering. That God blesses the righteous and

allows suffering in life even when we are virtuous is empirically veri-
fiable by reading the book of Job and opening our eyes to the suffering
of the Christians around us. The Carrs ask:

> Why do we want to hush up the [suicide], bury the scandal, deny the
> reality, and torture ourselves for years? Is it because we believe we are
> the only (or at least the very rare) Christian family that has had a
> suicide? . . . Are we still caught up in the false theology that if we have
> enough faith we will never have the problems that our less believing
> brothers and sisters have? Do we actually believe, deep down, that bad
> things really don't happen to good (truly spirit-filled) people?[21]

Christians also struggle through their suffering both in Christian
ways and in broken ways. Carnell describes his Christian approach to
his suffering in a letter to a former student:

> I still have periodic visits with my psychiatrist, and now and then I have
> an electric shock treatment (when I suffer from a build-up of anxieties
> and my brain feels like it is going to split; and when I feel like going to
> the top of Mt. Wilson and screaming with all my might). I sincerely am
> resting in the Lord and his providence, trusting that this terrible expe-
> rience will make me a more compassionate and humble teacher; for I
> now know a bit more about the complexity of human nature, for I
> know a bit more about the complexity of Carnell.[22]

In contrast, William Cowper, a poet, hymnodist, Christian and
friend of John Newton, often struggled with suffering in a broken
way. He experienced at least three episodes of "derangement" and
attempted suicide several times, believing after these attempts that
he was beyond God's forgiveness.[23] Suicidal Christians who struggle
with suffering in broken ways are unable to grab onto some of God's
love, forgiveness or hope, perhaps because their Christian beliefs are
not fully internalized or apprehended. Psychological science tells us
that Christians internalize their religious beliefs to different de-
grees.[24] Science also tells us that having wrong Christian beliefs increases our risk for mortality from medical illnesses.[25] In one study,
Christians feeling unloved or abandoned by God, or believing their
medical illness to be caused by the devil, increased their risk of dying

from the illness by 19 to 28 percent.[26] Christians with wrong beliefs are at higher risk.

But does this mean the person isn't a Christian? Consider that all Christians are blind to some of God's truths (1 Cor 13:12). We have all experienced immaturity as Christians and have become more mature as our understanding of God's truths has grown (1 Cor 3:1-2). To argue that a suicidal Christian is an unworthy Christian or non-Christian because he or she does not apprehend some of God's truths is to argue that we are all unworthy Christians or non-Christians because we all know God imperfectly. Not apprehending all the truths about God does not necessarily disqualify a person from being a Christian.

A fourth reason Christians might become suicidal comes from how we view our soul and body connection. Christian views on biblical anthropology are myriad, ranging from reductive materialism to radical dualism.[27] I hold a dualist perspective, which maintains that a person consists of the material and the immaterial, body and soul. Both body and soul are good, though affected by sin, and they function as an integrated living whole, though on some level body and soul are different aspects.[28] By observation, we know that the soul does not trump the body. The body can be diseased (with cancer) but the soul can be healthy (with a beneficial dependence of God), and though a healthy soul may promote healing, a Christian with a healthy soul may die of cancer. We are regenerated at conversion (Tit 3:5) but we groan while we wait for the redemption of our bodies (Rom 8:23).

This integrated whole can also be construed as having such capacities as intellect, will, emotion, mood, thought, spirit and relationality.[29] Mood can be sick (such as experiencing depression) but the spirit can be healthy (such as holding on to Christian hope). Bess was sexually abused by her father as a child. This abuse affects her whole self. When her body is touched in certain ways, she can be flooded with anxiety. And her emotion, which has been shaped by her parents as her earthly caretakers, can affect the way she relates to God as her heavenly father. In the same way, an understanding of God's presence can buttress Bess's courage as she confronts these memories and proceeds through a process of healing her vulnerability to suicide and the hatred she feels for herself. Though a Christian, she still experiences the violence done to her. And each of these aspects of her whole self needs healing. If Bess kills herself, it may not be an entirely spiritual decision. Suicide is sometimes related to a biologically based depression with spiritual effects: a depressed brain, a despondent soul and a hopeless spirit. These human aspects and capacities are different and yet interrelated within an integrated whole person. Plantinga writes, "In tragedy, sin is surely one of the forces at work, but it is by no means the only force and sometimes not even the most obvious one."[30]

In summary, Christians do become depressed, long for death and contemplate suicide because Christians are both fallen and redeemed. Satan is determined to destroy Christians, though they should resist him. Christians suffer in Christian ways and in broken ways because some Christian beliefs aren't understood or internalized, a state common to all Christians. And the soul and body connection results in connected but separate aspects that don't trump one another.

Myth 2: Prayer Is All a Christian Needs—Just Pray Harder

Healing is a process. Dallas Willard cites Francis de Sales, who "wisely counsels us not to expect transformation in a moment, though it is possible for God to give it."[31] Healing requires prayer, but prayer is sometimes not all that goes into healing. Stauffacher writes, "[Suicidality] is not something that can be resolved with a quick-fix prayer."[32] I have talked with many Christians who are distraught because they believe prayer should be enough. There are two reasons it sometimes is not: (1) God is not in the business of eliminating our suffering, and (2) while our soul needs healing through prayer, our body might also need healing through medical or psychological interventions, which take time. First let's look at God and suffering.

Prayer is not a magic wand that eliminates our suffering. Dr. Gay Hubbard writes:

Contrary to [the thinking that "he'll fix it so I won't have to live through it"], God refuses to play the magician's role, nor is God in the business of providing free placebos or heavenly strength aspirin. The idea that if we can only get our burdens to God He will make us instantly feel better is bitterly unfair misdirection to people in pain. . . . This "fix-it" approach makes pain a measure of our distance from God. Indirectly, this idea encourages us to think, "If I hurt, I'm a long way from God. If I were close to Him, He would make the hurt go away." The God of all comfort . . . is an identity quite different . . . from the idea of God as the "Great Pain Reliever."[33]

Greene-McCreight adds, "Suffering is not eliminated by the resurrection but transformed by it."[34]

There are no guarantees that we'll be spared from suffering. Regarding the healing "promised" in James 5:13-15, the Spencers write, "Forgiveness of sins has no doubt of fulfillment (v. 15). Healing does have some doubt of fulfillment: 'You may be healed' (5:16). James uses the aorist passive subjunctive. . . . The subjunctive is a mood of doubt."[35] In other words, by using this subjunctive tense, James is telling us that healing is possible but not guaranteed.

Despite the absence of guarantees, Christians should still pray and ask God for healing (Jas 5:13) because whatever God uses (therapy, medications and/or prayer), he is the ultimate healer (Ps 103:3). Greene-McCreight writes about healing from her depression: "I feel that God is the ultimate source of that healing, even though medications and therapy are part of it."[36] At the same time it's important to remember that a Christian who asks for healing may not be healed. If healing does not happen, a Christian is in good company. The apostle Paul himself lived with a thorn in the flesh (2 Cor 12:7-9).

Guarantees aside, some Christians may get the idea from James 5 that if they are righteous enough, God will answer their prayer for healing, and that if God does not answer their prayer, they must not be righteous enough. But that is an error in logic. While we are assured in James 5:16 that the prayer of a righteous person is "powerful and effective," it is not logical to conclude that not being healed suggests that the person who prays is not righteous. Jesus was righteous and he asked God, "May this cup be taken from me" (Mt 26:39), and God did not do it. Jesus also said, "Yet not my will, but yours be done" (Lk 22:42). Ask God, but do not make the outcome proof of your righteousness or influence with God.

A second reason that prayer alone may not result in healing is that Christians take advantage of medicine and the science of the day. The apostle James recommended the use of oil, used as medicine by the good Samaritan (Lk 10:34), and the apostle Paul recommended wine for Timothy's stomach, not prayer alone (1 Tim 5:23). Christians can do more than pray.

In summary, we pray for healing but healing is not guaranteed because God is not in the business of eliminating suffering. Also, we may require a process of healing using the medicine and science of the day.

MYTH 3: PEOPLE WHO ARE SUICIDAL ARE JUST TRYING TO GET ATTENTION

Some people assume that a common reason people kill themselves is to get attention, but the most common reason people attempt to kill themselves is that they want to escape intense psychological pain. This suicide note captures this pain: "Dear God forgive me for what I'm about to do. I can't stand it any longer."[37] Iris Bolton's 20-year-old son told his mother before his suicide, "Mom, I don't want to die, but I can't stand the pain of living."[38] In the 1950s, a 47-year-old woman who was still depressed after twenty electroshock treatments and five insulin shock treatments and who was scheduled for a lobotomy left this suicide note:

> The past six months of torture and agony for me and all my loved ones who have been so good to me, don't hate me for this. The past two months [sic] a living Hell on earth, no more, no more, and this operation would just not bring me out of my misery, to go on and on to the end and no one knows, no one.[39]

Supportive evidence that most suicidal people aren't seeking attention is that they ask those left behind to forgive them or try to protect the person who will discover their body. For example: "Everyone has been so good to me—has tried so hard. I truly wish that I could be different, for the sake of my family. Hurting my family is the worst of it, and that guilt has been wrestling with the part of me that wanted only to disappear."[40] Another example is the Christian college professor and choir director who posted a note on his apartment door warning the person to call the building superintendent instead of entering the apartment. Dr. Thomas Joiner shatters the attention-seeking myth by comparing suicide talk to heart-attack talk:

> A key point is that, in the case of severe chest pain, it is relatively rare for the reaction to be "He's faking!" or "She's just trying to get attention!" Indeed, most people would find these reactions cruel, rightly. And this despite the fact that a sizable proportion of chest-pain scenarios actually are false alarms. . . . It would be ridiculous to say something like, "If the guy were going to die from heart disease, he would have done it already; he's been having heart problems for years."[41]

The myth about attention seeking is an important one to challenge because not taking suicidal talk or a suicide attempt seriously is a life-and-death gamble that you might lose. Shneidman figures that, prospectively, about two or three percent of people who threaten suicide will die by suicide. Retrospectively, about 90 percent of people who die by suicide have talked about suicide. Therefore, Shneidman cautions that it is wisest to take a conservative, retrospective view and take any suicide talk seriously.[42] In summary, people die by suicide to escape pain, not to get attention.

MYTH 4: PEOPLE WHO KILL THEMSELVES ARE JUST BEING SELFISH

Foster writes about her anger toward her daughter who killed herself: "This was a senseless act of pure rejection of everyone who has ever loved you."[43] Suicide might look like a selfish rejection, but one of the factors in Foster's daughter's suicide was depression and hopelessness.[44] Similarly, Albert Hsu writes, "Suicide feels like a total dismissal, the cruelest possible way a person could tell us that they are leaving us behind."[45] Hsu also notes that his father was depressed.[46] He goes on, "What has been helpful to me is the realization that my father did not kill himself to abandon me. He did what he did to end his pain, not to cause pain for me."[47] A young chemist before taking his life put it like this: "The question of suicide and selfishness to close friends and relatives is one that I can't answer or even give an opinion on. It is obvious, however, that I have pondered it and decided I would hurt them less dead than alive."[48] Though suicide might look like selfishness to those left behind, those who die by suicide "believe their deaths will be a blessing to others."[49]

Myth 5: People Who Kill Themselves Are Angry and Vengeful

Anger and vengeance are at times motives for suicide. Kushner tells the story of Max White, who left this suicide note: "Ah, you false friends, who with your mouth claimed your friendship and with your hands withheld it! My curse upon you. May you ever feel misfortune blighting your whole career. My hatred is indescribable against you."[50] When revenge motivates suicide, this might represent more about a person's personality than about suicide in general. Joiner suggests, "People who had anger problems throughout their lives may, when planning their deaths by suicide, express anger in their deaths. This does not mean that suicide is about anger; it only means that people with anger issues may express anger in many things they do, including death by suicide."[51] Though some suicide deaths are motivated by anger and vengeance, many are not.[52]

However, some suicide attempts may be efforts at communicating something important—and sometimes this is anger. Where suicide deaths are motivated by intent to die, Stengel believes every suicide attempt is a "cry for help," which functions as an appeal or alarm system to the people around because it elicits an upsurge of activity directed to the attempter.[53] Susan Rose Blauner writes of why she attempted suicide three times:

> Whenever I had suicidal thoughts, I was in one or more of these feeling states: I felt painfully alone; I felt volcanic anger and wanted to punish someone; I felt free-floating anger and had no healthy outlet for it; I felt afraid of being abandoned (so I thought I'd abandon first); I felt afraid that my needs would never be met (so I'd create a crisis to get them met); I felt

overwhelmed by responsibility or financial stress; or I felt completely hopeless that my life would ever improve. At times it hurt to live.[54]

In one study, Linehan and her colleagues found that suicide attempts were more often motivated by a desire to make others better off whereas self-harm behavior without intent to die (i.e., self-injury) more often was intended to express anger, punish oneself, regain normal feelings and distract oneself.[55] I once talked to a client who said that he wanted to kill himself because he was angry with his sister, who had said some things that hurt him. When I questioned him further, he said that what he really wanted was for the hurt to end. It's best not to make assumptions about another person's motives. While suicide deaths are not usually motivated by anger, a suicide attempt may be an effort to communicate.

MYTH 6: DEPRESSED PEOPLE SHOULD JUST "BUCK UP"

A mental health problem is a common risk factor for suicide, and depression is the most common disorder associated with suicide.[56] One day my client's daughter called me and asked why her father couldn't just snap out of depression. Most people don't know how debilitating depression is. William Styron, who experienced depression, wrote, "The pain of severe depression is quite unimaginable to those who have not suffered it."[57] Most of us don't understand depression because it's hard to explain. Styron continues, "The horror of depression is so overwhelming as to be quite beyond expression."[58] One thing is clear: depression is an illness that a person no longer knows how to fix on his or her own. If my client could have fixed it, he would have. Styron goes on:

> In depression this faith in deliverance, in ultimate restoration, is absent. The pain is unrelenting, and what makes the condition intolerable is the foreknowledge that no remedy will come—not in a day, an hour, a month, or a minute. If there is mild relief, one knows that it is only temporary; more pain will follow. It is hopelessness even more than pain that crushes the soul.[59]

People who are depressed cannot snap out of it. If they could, they would.

Myth 7: People Who Are Suicidal Don't Tell Anyone

Dr. Eli Robins studied 134 suicides deaths during a one-year period (1956–1957) in the city of St. Louis and in St. Louis County. He found that 69 percent (ninety-three people) communicated their intent to kill themselves an average of three times, the maximum number of communications by one individual being twelve.[60] Sixty percent of the subjects communicated intentions of suicide to their spouses, one-half communicated to relatives, including in-laws, one-third communicated to friends, and less than one-fifth communicated to physicians, job associates, ministers, police and landladies. For example, Robins writes about a 67-year-old widower who gave his daughter-in-law his insurance policies, told his neighbors they would "find a dead man on the street," and told his companions in a tavern that he was going to die by suicide. They did not believe him and the next day he killed himself.[61] Based on Robins's study, not all but many people give us a chance to do something. Many of them visit a doctor in the year before they die and some talk to clergy.[62] Robins describes a 38-year-old press operator and welder who four weeks before his suicide told his pastor and family he was going to kill himself. On the day of the suicide he called his pastor, who was not able to come over to talk. He shot himself.[63]

Sometimes these warnings can be indirect. Suicidal people might drop hints like "I'm going away" or "You won't have to worry about me anymore," or they offer an explicit "I'm going to kill myself." It's important to take those comments seriously. One of my acquaintances bought a gun and told her friends she was worried about safety in her neighborhood; no one knew she actually was planning her death. One of my clients announced to me one day that she had gotten her life insurance policy in order. These are examples of indirect warnings.

Some also can threaten so often that it's difficult to know whether to take the threats seriously. For example, Robins describes the suicide of a 61-year-old retired pharmacist who threatened suicide so often that his wife and primary care physician stopped paying attention to these threats, which included "I am going to kill myself," "I'd be better off dead," "I'm going to blow my head off" and "I'm going to jump off the bridge." His wife and physician did not notice any increase in the frequency of these suicidal threats in the year preceding his death.[64] Despite frequent threats, it's important to take each threat seriously.

If you have lost someone to suicide, remember that some people don't communicate intent. Robins gives us an example of a 63-year-old woman who was devoutly religious and a regular churchgoer whose minister visited her four days before she killed herself. Though she was depressed, in constant pain, and said she wasn't sure how much longer she could stand it, she never spoke directly about suicide. Her husband told the minister after her death that they had sometimes talked about the suicide of others but she never mentioned thinking of suicide herself.[65] And some communication is so cryptic that only in hindsight do you realize what the person was intending. Robins gives an example of a cryptic statement from a 62-year-old woman who told her husband when he left for work, "That's your last kiss."[66] Remember that while most people in Robins's study communicated their intent, 31 percent did not. For the ones who do, we can do something.

MYTH 8: TALKING ABOUT SUICIDE MAY GIVE THE PERSON THE IDEA TO COMPLETE SUICIDE

One of the most important things we can do for someone who is suicidal is to ask her directly if she is thinking about suicide. Science has shown that it is a myth that talking openly about suicide might put the idea in a person's mind.[67] Another fear that stops some from asking about suicide directly is fear of embarrassing the person. Robins describes the suicide of a 58-year-old printer who attempted suicide and was rescued by his son. The printer's wife had never discussed the suicide attempt with her husband because she felt "it would have embarrassed him." Two years later he killed himself.[68] In fact, talking openly may be the most caring thing to do.

Suicidal thoughts are terrifying and isolating. Shneidman describes Beatrice's experience:

> At age 15 . . . I remember trying to explain it to my friends, who shook their heads in disbelief at my descriptions of falling in a black hole and my declarations that life was meaningless, but they simply could

not relate to my morbid thoughts. Once I realized I was alone in my thoughts, I stopped talking about them. I was terrified that I was insane and didn't want anyone to find out, so I continued to mimic the behaviors of my "normal" friends and put on a smile everywhere I went.[69]

Imagine having suicidal thoughts. You never expected to have them. Your parents didn't teach you what to do if you had them. They are frightening, disturbing, alarming, perplexing. Many people keep these thoughts to themselves because suicide is stigmatized and taboo. The best gift you can give someone suicidal is to start that conversation for her. Shneidman describes one suicidal woman's disappointment when others didn't ask her directly about her suicidal thoughts and plans for immolation:

> When her friends do nothing when she visits them, sobbing (ostensibly to return a toaster), it tells her that her ties with others have been broken and that she is hopelessly alone in the world. And she even has the fantasy that the gasoline station attendant will magically read her mind and ask her why she is purchasing a gallon of gasoline.[70]

When should you ask someone outright if they're having thoughts of suicide? Usually when some of the common warning signs appear, such as depression, worsening performance at work or school, giving away prized possessions, an increase in reckless behavior like using substances, worsening hygiene, sleep problems, talking about death or seeming to be preoccupied with death. Later we'll discuss in greater detail how to ask someone directly about suicidal thoughts. Contrary to what many people believe, it's important to start the conversation: ask about suicidal thinking.

Myth 9: If Someone Wants to Kill Himself, There's Nothing I Can Do

Remember Kevin Hines from chapter one, who jumped from the Golden Gate Bridge, realized he did not want to die and, miraculously, survived?[71] Many suicidal people are ambivalent—a part of them wants to die and a part of them wants to stay alive. Shneidman writes, "I have never known anyone who was 100 percent for wanting to commit suicide without any fantasies of possible rescue. Individuals would be happy not to do it, if they didn't 'have to.' It is this omnipresent ambivalence that gives us the moral imperative for clinical intervention."[72] Because there's typically a part of a suicidal person that wants to live, we can do something to help. As McKeon says, "Suicide is never inevitable."[73]

Myth 10: Most Suicides Occur over the Holidays

Most suicides occur in the spring and early summer, not over the winter holidays when people get together.[74] Joiner and colleagues write, "Suicide rates go down during times of celebration (when people pull together to celebrate . . .) and during times of hardship or tragedy (when people pull together to commiserate)."[75] For some suicidal people, the extreme contrast between the beautiful weather outdoors and their own inner darkness becomes unbearable.[76] Most suicides also occur during the day and at the beginning of the week.[77] One exception to this general rule is that suicides sometimes can occur on anniversary dates. Robins describes the suicide of a 47-year-old man who killed himself on the first anniversary of his father's death.[78] But most suicides don't occur over the holidays.

Summary

Strong Christians become depressed and consider suicide, and myths can get in the way of pastoral caregivers offering these individuals help. Myths can make us assume the worst about someone who is truly suffering—that she's just trying to get attention, that she's selfish to consider suicide or just too lazy to snap out of her depression. It's important to challenge these myths because they can keep us from taking steps to prevent suicide.

But if a Christian can get to the point of being suicidal, what happens if they die? Will a person who dies by suicide go to hell? What do Christians believe about the sinfulness of suicide and the question of eternal security? These questions are the focus of the next chapter.

Discussion Questions

1. How do you explain Christians who get to the point of being suicidal?

2. Discuss how prayer heals.

3. If suicidal people tend to warn others and it's sometimes easy to miss the warnings, what can you do to help prevent suicide?

4. Describe a time when you were ambivalent: a part of you wanted one thing and another part of you wanted the opposite. How is ambivalence important in working with a suicidal person?

Resources

K. Greene-McCreight, *Darkness Is My Only Companion: A Christian Response to Mental Illness* (Grand Rapids: Brazos, 2006).

T. Joiner, *Myths About Suicide* (Cambridge, MA: Harvard University Press, 2010).

W. Styron, *Darkness Visible: A Memoir of Madness* (New York: Random House, 1990).

SUICIDE AND CHRISTIAN THEOLOGY

*If there be a hell upon earth, it is to be found
in a melancholy man's heart.*

ROBERT BURTON, SEVENTEENTH-
CENTURY ENGLISH PARSON

Some suicidal people in crisis say fear of hell has kept them from killing themselves.[1] However, telling these people that suicide condemns them to hell may not keep them from the act, because the hell they are experiencing inside may be worse than any eternal hell they fear. As one chemist wrote in his suicide note, "If there is any eternal torment worse than mine I'll have to be shown."[2] Suffering, not theology, is the dominant focus.[3]

In addition, some people who die by suicide anticipate going to heaven. One man who killed himself said, "It's hell here on earth; it'll be Heaven after I'm dead."[4] Heaven may be yearned for as a place of reunion with those who have died. For those who are unsure, the future may be unknown enough to justify a gamble.[5]

If theology does not deter some people from suicide, does it have a place in suicide prevention? Yes. For some, theological beliefs are a detriment. And for you, as a practical theologian, it's important to reflect on your own theology of suicide. Here's why: (1) your theology affects what you do, (2) Christians hold a spectrum of nuanced beliefs and (3) few denominations have a stated position on suicide.

Shneidman tells the story of a woman who attempted suicide and was berated by a hospital nun for her actions.[6] This encounter was driven by the nun's theology. Theological convictions drive our approach to this work, because suicide suggests theological questions such as "If a Christian kills herself, will she go to hell?" While the answer may seem straightforward to you personally, Christians differ on their views, resulting in highly nuanced and complex theologies of suicide, which can be confusing. For example, in interviews with pastors, my research team has noticed that pastors struggle with the paradox of telling suicidal individuals that suicide is a sin—as a deterrent—and talking about God's mercy to loved ones who have lost someone to suicide—as a comfort.[7] Clemons writes, "It is precisely this complexity, and the resulting confusion, uncertainty, and discouragement, along with a lack of understanding of what the Bible says and does not say, that have kept most religious communities from addressing suicide with the urgency and careful attention it deserves in the midst of today's crisis."[8] The goal of this chapter is to offer you the opportunity to clarify your theology of suicide. Following is a spectrum of views and reasons used to support these views: four views that suicide is not a sin, four views that suicide is sin, four views that suicide is a forgivable sin and one view that suicide is an unforgivable sin.

VIEWS THAT SUICIDE IS NOT A SIN

Christians who do not believe that suicide is a sin may base their view on one or more of the following arguments.

Some Christians hold that suicide is not a sin, citing diminished responsibility. Some Christians believe that suicide is not a sin because a person who kills himself is a victim of insanity or demonic possession, unable to make rational decisions.[9] For example, Luther said, "I don't share the opinion that suicides are certainly to be damned. My reason is that they do not wish to kill themselves but are overcome by the power of the devil."[10] In other words, the person who attempts or dies by suicide has diminished responsibility and is therefore not guilty of sin. For these Christians, suicide within the context of depression would not be sin any more than getting the flu would be. Within this position, the theological question of eternal security is immaterial because suicide is not a sin.

Some Christians hold that suicide is not a sin, citing the Bible's silence. The Bible mentions suicide seven times, but none of these narratives condemns it. What stands out in reading the accounts of Abimelech (Judg 9:52-54), Samson (Judg 16:30), Saul (1 Sam 31:4), Saul's armor-bearer (1 Sam 31:5), Ahithophel (2 Sam 17:23), Zimri (1 Kings 16:18) and Judas (Mt 27:5; Acts 1:18) is that the manner of death is not associated with dishonor. Samson is listed among the heroes of faith (Heb 11:32). Both Samson and Ahithophel are buried in the family tomb. Saul and his sons were honored by a proper burial by the Israelite men of Jabesh-gilead. David's lament for Saul and Jonathan (2 Sam 1:19-27) passes no condemnation on Saul's manner of death. In addition, not all Christians view the sixth commandment as prohibiting suicide.[11] If a Christian adheres to this position, the question of eternal security again is immaterial because suicide is not a sin.

Some Christians hold that suicide is not a sin, citing the early church's silence. Fedden suggests that, historically, "the Church offers no opposition to suicide before the third century" because the apostolic fathers (except for Clement of Alexandria) merged the concepts of suicide and martyrdom: "St. Jerome and the Venerable Bede reverently place even Christ among the suicides."[12] Because of Christ's example, zeal for death in this era was notorious.[13] Tertullian wrote in 197, "Nothing matters to us in this age but to escape from it with all speed."[14] All types of voluntary death were believed to bring with them assurance of salvation.[15] Some of these voluntary deaths look like suicide. Droge and Tabor write, "One person's martyr was another person's suicide, and vice versa."[16]

For example, early in the fourth century St. Ambrose praised Pelagia, who leaped from a building to avoid rape.[17] Germanicus "drew the beast to himself and forced it to tear his body," and a woman from Edessa "dragged her son through the streets . . . saying 'I do it lest, when you have slain all the other Christians, I and my son should come too late to partake of that benefit.'"[18] Fedden describes a horde of Christians demanding martyrdom of a proconsul, who shouted, "Goe [*sic*] hang and drown your selves and ease the Magistrates."[19] The early church fathers grouped all voluntary death together and did not condemn suicide.

Some Christians hold that suicide is not a sin, citing John Donne.
A perhaps unexpected late Christian voice for suicide was John Donne
(1572–1631), an Anglican priest and dean of St. Paul's Cathedral. As
noted previously, suicide in seventeenth-century England was a felony
crime.[20] In this context, Donne writes that there are some situations
where suicide is justifiable, such as (1) "when I am weather-beaten and
in danger of betraying the precious soul that God has embarked on
me," (2) when God can be glorified in no other way, as in an act that
builds the faith of a weaker Christian, (3) when God tells you to kill
yourself, as Donne believed was true for Samson, and (4) because
some biblical passages tell Christians to follow the Good Shepherd in
giving up their lives, to have "a just contempt of this life."[21] It is important to note that Donne himself was suicidal. He wrote a long
treatise on the moral theology of suicide, but he himself did not
choose suicide in the end.[22]

VIEW THAT SUICIDE IS A SIN

Christians who believe that suicide is a sin may base their view on one
or more of these arguments.

*Some Christians hold that suicide is a sin, stating that the Bi-
ble's silence does not imply approval.* Winslow in the nineteenth
century assumed that the Bible didn't need to speak out against
suicide because suicide is so obviously "atrocious."[23] Bonhoeffer
argued that the silence of the Bible on suicide is not a basis for con-
doning suicide.[24] And the Bible does not always comment on the sinfulness of acts. For example, though the Bible is silent on Samson's
visit to a prostitute (Judg 16:1), he committed the sin of adultery. Hsu
makes the point that the biblical narratives of suicide do not end well
and therefore do not suggest approval or indifference to suicide.[25]

*Some Christians hold that suicide is a sin, citing the sixth com-
mandment.* The sixth commandment states, "You shall not murder"
(Ex 20:13; Deut 5:17) and Genesis 9:6 reads, "Whoever sheds the blood
of a human, by a human shall that person's blood be shed; for in his
own image God made humankind."[26] Augustine's position in the
fourth century was: "The law, rightly interpreted, prohibits suicide,

where it says, 'You shall not kill,'" and "No man ought to inflict on himself voluntary death . . . for those who die by their own hand have no better life after death," and "It is therefore wicked to kill oneself."[27] He argues, "Since the sixth commandment does not have the qualification 'your neighbor,' as do the ninth and tenth commandments, . . . the commandment applies both to other people and to oneself."[28]

In addition to the sixth commandment, Augustine marshaled four other arguments against suicide: Christ never recommended it, Christians should live lives of faith and trust in God even in the midst of suffering, death cuts off the possibility of repentance, suicide (a certain sin according to Augustine) should not be chosen instead of an uncertain sin, a sin which may not happen (like the rape of Pelagia, which is not certain to have occurred), and instead of a sin which is not one's own (because the rapist, not Pelagia, would own the guilt). According to Augustine, the only time a person may take his or her own life is if God commands it. He distinguished between suicide and martyrdom, viewing voluntary martyrdom as a possible Christian response, but only if prompted by God and when one is very sure that "the divine command" has been made, as in the case of Samson.[29] Augustine believed that suicide was not to be considered an option for a Christian except in these very unusual circumstances.

The distinction between suicide and martyrdom is relevant today.[30] Martyrs die at another's hand or in specific circumstances as a witness to their beliefs, and in suicide, death is instigated by one's own hand.[31] Bonhoeffer maintains the distinction: "As surely as one should offer one's life as a sacrifice for others, so surely one should not turn one's hand against oneself."[32] Chesterton agrees: "A suicide is the opposite of a martyr."[33]

Following Augustine, church councils explicated the church's anti-suicide position over time.[34] The Council of Arles (A.D. 452) declared suicide "to be an act inspired by diabolical possession" and condemned the suicide of servants.[35] The Council of Orleans (A.D. 533) denied funeral rites to suicides accused of crime, though it allowed funerals to ordinary criminals.[36] The Council of Braga (A.D. 563) condemned suicide more generally, forbidding burial with "great ceremony" and burial inside the church for all suicides.[37] Aquinas (1225–1274) argued against suicide because:

> It is altogether unlawful to kill oneself, for three reasons. First, because everything naturally loves itself. . . . Secondly, because every part, as such, belongs to the whole. Now every man is part of the community, and so, as such, he belongs to the community. . . . Thirdly, because life is God's gift to man, and is subject to His power, Who kills and makes to live. Hence whoever takes his own life, sins against God, even as he who kills another's slave, sins against that slave's master, and as he who usurps to himself judgment of a matter not entrusted to him.[38]

Some Christians hold that suicide is a sin, citing the sanctity of life. These Christians emphasize that life is sacred and inviolable (Deut 32:39; Job 1:21; 1 Cor 6:19-20; Eph 5:29; Phil 1:20-26). Calvin believed that suicide was sin on three counts: only God can take life away, suicide goes against self-preservation, and one can resist diabolical possession. Calvin said, "Let us wait for the highest commander, who sent us into this world, to call us out of it."[39]

Chesterton had a slightly different perspective: Suicide is sin because it denies life. He writes:

> Not only is suicide a sin, it is the sin. It is the ultimate and absolute evil, the refusal to take an interest in existence; the refusal to take the oath of life. The man who kills a man, kills a man. The man who kills himself, kills all men; as far as he is concerned he wipes out the world. . . . The suicide insults everything on earth. . . . He defiles every flower by refusing to live for its sake.[40]

Chesterton wrote this during a period when suicide had become a poetic vocation.[41]

Some Christians hold that suicide is a sin, citing the person's lack of faith. Bonhoeffer writes, "Because there is a living God, therefore self-murder is reprehensible: the sin of unbelief. . . . Unbelief does not reckon, in good things or bad, with the living God. That is its sin."[42] During his early days in prison, Bonhoeffer wrote on a scrap of paper, "Suicide, not out of a sense of guilt, but because I am practically dead already, the closing of the book, sum total."[43] Despite his own despair, Bonhoeffer did not take his life.

VIEW THAT SUICIDE IS A FORGIVABLE SIN

Among Christians who believe that suicide is a sin, many believe that the sin of suicide or self-murder is forgivable.

The current Roman Catholic view. Historically, Roman Catholics held that suicide was an unforgivable mortal sin that condemned a person to hell without forgiveness or absolution.[44] It was viewed as unabsolvable because the sin occurred concurrently with death. In the current Roman Catholic view, suicide is considered "gravely contrary to the just love of self. It likewise offends love of neighbor because it unjustly breaks the ties of solidarity with family, nation, and other human societies to which we continue to have obligations. Suicide is contrary to love for the living God."[45] On the other hand, the Roman Catholic Church has included in its current catechism that "grave psychological disturbances, anguish, or grave fear of hardship, suffering, or torture can diminish the responsibility of the one committing suicide" and that "we should not despair of the eternal salvation of persons who have taken their own lives. By ways known to him alone, God can provide the opportunity for salutary repentance. The Church prays for persons who have taken their own lives."[46] The current Roman Catholic position raises the question of whether or not suicide is an unforgivable sin.

Suicide is like any sin. Some Christians believe suicide is forgivable because the sin of suicide is no different from any other. In Revelation 22:15, murder is listed as one sin in a list of sins. Biblically, the only unpardonable sin is blasphemy against the Holy Spirit (Mt 12:31), or the sin unto death (1 Jn 5:16). This view emphasizes that all Christians are miserable sinners, equally in need of God's grace and forgiveness. Even our righteousness is as filthy rags (Is 64:6) and any one sin damns to hell. If any one of these sins (including murder) precludes a Christian from God's forgiveness, then all humanity would despair of God's forgiveness. For all Christians, the focus is on Christ's righteousness and grace and on his intercessional ministry

(Rom 8:34; Heb 7:24-25) with the Holy Spirit (Rom 8:26-27).[47] Nothing can separate us from God's love (Rom 8:38-39). Lewis Smedes, theologian and ethicist, writes, "Will Jesus welcome home a believer who died at her own hands? I believe he will, tenderly and lovingly. My biblical basis? It is the hope-giving promise of Romans 8:32 that neither life nor death can separate the believer from the love of God in Christ Jesus. . . . I believe that Jesus died not only for the sins of us all but for all of our sins."[48]

Suicide doesn't preclude repentance. Some Christians believe that suicide should be considered forgivable because it is presumptuous to assume a person did not repent: "To presume an inability to repent because you were not nearby to hear it is a usurpation," writes Donne.[49] For example, the Carrs' daughter-in-law, who died by suicide, repented before the act, as written in her suicide note: "All I can ask is Christ's forgiveness and understanding. . . . I feel sick, sick at heart and tired of living."[50]

All of us will die with unrepented-of sins. Many argue against a concern with unrepentance based on our covenant relationship with God.[51] God's covenant is one of steadfast love of his children, whom he knows to be sinners, rather than a transactional and mechanistic demand for repentance of every misdeed. Bonhoeffer writes, "The widespread argument in the Christian church that self-murder makes repentance, and therefore forgiveness, impossible, is also insufficient. Through sudden death, many Christians have died with unrepented sins. This argument overvalues the final moment of life."[52] Smedes adds, "But all of us commit sins that we are too spiritually cloddish to recognize for the sins they are. And we all die with sins not named and repented of."[53] While God clearly condemns sin, the paradox is that he is also merciful (Ex 34:6-7), he deals with our sin not as we deserve (Ps 103:10), and he can be trusted to be a fair judge (Is 61:8) because he is a friend of sinners (Lk 7:34).[54]

The theological issue of eternal security. Within this position that suicide is a forgivable sin, a classical Calvinist would argue that a Christian who dies by suicide remains secure in salvation. For example, Greene-McCreight writes:

Mental illness can potentially damage the soul, since it preys on the brain and the mind, but it cannot destroy the soul, for God holds the soul in his hands. . . . The Christian's relation with the triune God may not stop with suicide. Even though suicide is clearly an ultimate separation from fellow creatures, it is not more so than natural death. And natural death does not stop God from loving the soul, or the soul from loving God.[55]

The View That Suicide Is an Unforgivable Sin

Some Christians believe that damnation to hell follows the unconfessed sin of self-murder.[56] For others, suicide is the unpardonable sin of blasphemy against the Holy Spirit in that it may represent a complete loss of faith in God.[57] A possible Wesleyan Arminian approach would argue that a Christian in the act of suicide commits either a sin that remains unconfessed or the sin of apostasy, either of which might result in damnation.[58] It's interesting that Wesley himself could "hardly believe the possibility that grace would ever be eclipsed by human choice."[59] Because the Apostles, Nicene and Athanasian creeds are silent on the issue of eternal security, a range of beliefs based on biblical texts proliferates (Rom 8:29-30; Heb 6:4-6).

Three Important Theological Perspectives to Consider

A theology of suicide will include beliefs about sin and hell. The following three theological perspectives ought also to be considered as you develop your theology of suicide.

Suicide's impact. Some sin has greater impact than other sin.[60] Some Christians might argue that though the sin of suicide does not damn a person to hell any more than lying or coveting, it certainly has a deep impact. These Christians are distinguishing two ways to think about sin: (1) vertically, how sin affects our relationship with God, and (2) horizontally, how sin affects our relationship with others and ourselves. While Christ's atonement can cover suicide as equally as any other sin, suicide is an act that leaves a large wake of destruction behind it. It destroys a person and leaves many others to make sense of their own loss, shock, guilt and anger.[61] For example, Plantinga writes, "All sin is equally wrong, but not all sin is equally bad."[62] He points out that a neighbor would rather us covet her house than steal it. He concludes, "The badness or seriousness of sin depends to some degree on the amount and kind of damage it inflicts."[63] And this damage argues for the fact that suicide cannot be condoned.

Choose life. Regardless of whether you call suicide "sin" or something else, many people feel that suicide is a violation of something deep in the human psyche, something that is morally objectionable.[64] Durkheim, a secular Jew, writes, "Common morality reproves [suicide]."[65] One clergy person I spoke with said, "We're all here for a reason, and I don't think that choosing your own end . . . counts as fulfilling your purpose."[66] Her point is that suicide is not an appropriate choice. Even secular mental health professionals who value tolerance of diversity will do what they can to prevent suicide.[67] For example, Joiner and colleagues write, "We do not believe that people who die by suicide are making informed, rational decisions to do so. We also strongly believe in the value in preventing something that causes so much suffering for those directly affected by suicidal thoughts as well as their loved ones."[68] Whether suicide is called "sin" or "a violation of God's will" or "wrong" or "not fulfilling your purpose," the message is the same: "Don't kill yourself." Generally, people don't approve of suicide and tell others not to do it.

Suicide as both moral and psychological. Whatever your theology, suicide most often occurs within the brokenness of a mental health problem. While the focus of this chapter has been on various theologies of suicide, it's important to return to the paradox that a suicidal person may ask moral questions about suicide and experience disease at the same time. Plantinga argues, "Sin makes us guilty while disease makes us miserable. We thus need grace for our sin but mercy and healing for our disease."[69] Suicidality involves both moral as well as emotional aspects. Lewis Smedes says it this way: "As Christians, we should worry less about whether Christians who have killed themselves go to heaven, and worry more about how we can help people like them find hope and joy in living. Our most urgent problem is not the morality of suicide but the spiritual and mental despair that drags people down to it."[70] Because suicide is both moral and psychological, theology may not always function as a deterrent. One Anglican priest I interviewed said, "I don't think [discussing theology is] going to help the conversation. . . . My issue right now is trying to keep them alive and if I thought [theology] would help, I would interject it. But at that stage, I'm just trying to keep them from jumping."[71] It is important for each pastoral caregiver to reflect on how he or she weighs the paradox of morality and mental despair.

SUMMARY

For a suicidal person, the hell inside him or her might be feared more than an eternal hell. Pastors, chaplains and pastoral counselors need to carefully reflect on the panoply of theological and historical views on suicide, sin, forgiveness and eternal security, because these views affect what they do for the suicidal person. The similarity that runs through all views is "choose life."

But why do people want to kill themselves? Theories about suicide are important because they drive prevention approaches and organize the vast array of information on suicide. But pastors, chaplains and pastoral caregivers are needed to provide spiritual perspectives and interventions, which theories alone lack. We'll look at various theories next.

DISCUSSION QUESTIONS

1. What are your beliefs about suicide, sin and eternal security?

2. If you believe that suicide is not sin, how would you prevent suicide given that moral objections prevent some people from dying by suicide?

3. If you believe that suicide is sin, how would you prevent suicide given that a suicidal person may fear receiving a moral lesson instead of help in a suicide crisis?

RESOURCES

G. L. Carr and G. C. Carr, *Fierce Goodbye: Living in the Shadow of Suicide* (Scottdale, PA: Herald Press, 2004). There is an entire Fierce Goodbye program with a DVD, so be sure to visit the website www.fiercegoodbye.com.

J. T. Clemons, *What Does the Bible Say About Suicide?* (Minneapolis: Fortress, 1990).

A. J. Droge and J. D. Tabor, *A Noble Death: Suicide and Martyrdom Among Christians and Jews in Antiquity* (San Francisco: HarperCollins, 1992).

SOME RELIGIOUS POSITIONS ON SUICIDE

Note that not all religions or denominations have a central body that determines doctrine.

- The General Council of Assemblies of God (2006)[72]

- Catechism of the Catholic Church (paragraphs 2280-2283)[73]

- The Church Council of the Evangelical Lutheran Church in America[74]

- The Episcopal Church USA Diocesan Resolution on Suicide Prevention[75]

- The Greek Orthodox Archdiocese of America[76]

- An interfaith statement called "A Consensus Statement on Suicide and Suicide Prevention,"[77] which was generated through an interfaith dialogue with Buddhist, Christian, Hindu, Jewish and Muslim faith communities

- The General Assembly of the Presbyterian Church in the United States[78]

- The Union of American Hebrew Congregations[79]

- The United Church of Christ[80]

- The United Methodist Church[81]

- A Moravian church in Anchorage, Alaska, has a statement on the need for prayer and the offer of a pastoral visit to those who are suicidal.[82]

4

THEORIES OF SUICIDE

*No single theory will untangle an act as ambiguous
and with such complex motives as suicide.*

ALFRED ALVAREZ

*But where oh where is the beginning of a death
by one's own hand? When and where does the
notion of self-destruction enter anyone's life?
How does it walk on cat's-paws until it
possesses one's soul? I have never found
the answer nor has any other researcher
in this bitter and arcane discipline.*

IRIS BOLTON

There is no one reason why people kill themselves.

MARK WILLIAMS

Pastoral caregivers can be helped in their ministries by understanding historical and current theories of suicide. These theories will inform pastoral caregiving but will also point out the unique and vital contribution pastors, chaplains and pastoral counselors have to offer—the spiritual perspectives that are sorely needed and often absent in theories.

WHY THEORIES?

A suicide theory is an informed guess about why people kill themselves. Though supported by scientific findings, theories aren't proven by science. They are speculative. So why should we review hypothetical notions? Kurt Lewin has said, "There is nothing so practical as a good theory."[1] And the Roman physician Galen wrote, "It is in vain to speak of cures, or think of remedies, until such time as we have considered of the causes."[2] Theories help us organize the complex details so we can develop prevention strategies. Theories help us think about possible causes and remedies. If we believe that heart disease is related to cholesterol, we may change our diet. Theories drive action. So what theories help explain suicide and structure prevention approaches?

HISTORICAL THEORIES

Historical theories are important because they were instrumental in changing society's attitudes toward suicide.

Richard Burton (1577–1640). People have known about depression since antiquity. For example, Chrysostom describes melancholy as "a cruel torture of the soul, a most inexplicable grief, poisoned worm, consuming body and soul and gnawing the very heart, a perpetual executioner, continual night, profound darkness, a whirlwind, a tempest, an ague not appearing, heating worse than any fire, and a battle that hath no end. It crucifies worse than anything; no torture, no strappado, no bodily punishment is like unto it."[3] However, interest in depression—or "melancholy" or "acedia"—really blossomed during the Renaissance.[4]

Richard Burton, an Oxford scholar described as "the most miserable of men,"[5] published *Anatomy of Melancholy* in 1621. In it he defines melancholy as "black choler" characterized by "fear and sorrow without a cause."[6] He lists the following as potential reasons for melancholy: bad angels or devils, old age, heredity, diet, problems with elimination, bad air, too much exercise, too much or too little sleep, sorrow, shame and disgrace, envy and malice, anger, discontent and misery, ambition, covetousness, addiction, self-love, too much love of learning and study, a bad nurse, bad parenting, seeing terrible things, harsh words, poverty, losses (e.g., death of a friend, loss of one's good name, loss of property and so on), too much work, an unhappy marriage and deformity.[7] He even includes religious despair brought about by apocalyptic sermons and the doctrine of predestination, describing the Calvinist theory of double predestination as a "destructive weapon" that nurtures melancholy and despair.[8] Burton seems to have listed everything he could think of, but his powerful overarching message is that melancholy has causes, and if these causes are addressed, then melancholy can be eliminated.[9]

Burton's work resulted in the more humane treatment of the insane in asylums, and because he recognized that melancholy frequently resulted in suicide, it also resulted in a softening of the legal consequences of suicide.[10] As noted earlier, by the eighteenth century, jurors in England and the American Colonies recognized that melancholy was a disease and therefore not evidence of criminal intent.[11]

Farbes Winslow (1810–1874). From *Anatomy of Melancholy* it was a small step to psychiatrist Farbes Winslow's *Anatomy of Suicide*, published in 1840, which notes, "If we examine attentively the majority of cases of suicide, we shall find that the unfortunate persons have labored, either for some time previously or at the very moment, under depression of spirits, anxiety of mind, and other symptoms of cerebral derangement."[12] Winslow argues that Cato's "whole conduct immediately preceding the last fatal act of his life evinces the extreme mental agitation under which he labored; despair had taken possession of his faculties; the ambition and the hopes of years were prostrated in a moment to the dust, and to escape from a long life of tyranny, he perished on his own sword."[13] Winslow lists all the possible causes of suicide: remorse, disappointed love, jealousy, wounded vanity, false pride, ambition, despair, blind impulse, ennui, speculating in stocks, defective education, socialism, imitation of Goethe's Werther, avoidance of punishment, political excitement, nervous irritation, love of notoriety, heredity, influence of irreligion, and even masturbation.[14] Winslow's approach to suicide prevention was moral and theological:

Teach a man his duty to God, as well as his obligations to his fellow-men; lead him to believe that his life is not his own; that disappointment and misery is the penalty of Adam's transgression, and one from which there is no hope of escaping; and, above all, inculcate a resignation to the decrees of Divine Providence. When life becomes a burden, when the mind is sinking under the weight of accumulated misfortunes, and no gleam of hope penetrates through the vista of futurity to gladden the heart, the intellect says, "Commit suicide, and escape from a world of wretchedness and woe;" the moral principle says, "Live; it is your duty to bear with resignation the afflictions that overwhelm you; let the moral influence of your example be reflected in the characters of those by whom you are surrounded."[15]

A chaplain using these historical approaches might ask a suicidal person, "Are you experiencing any depression?"

Émile Durkheim (1858–1917). Sociologist Émile Durkheim believed that many suicides were not connected with insanity.[16] He argued that because people who died by suicide did not all know each other, the stable suicide rate could be due only to a common cause outside the individual that controlled the individual.[17] He believed people's internal tendency toward suicide was reined in by societal forces.[18] Durkheim was writing in the midst of a great deal of social upheaval.[19] The suicide rate had tripled since the mid-eighteenth century.[20] Durkheim's perspective was that society's failure to regulate or integrate individuals created the vulnerability to suicide.[21] According to Durkheim, people who died by suicide were either not regulated or integrated into society enough (egoistic suicide because of an individualistic focus) or overly integrated (altruistic suicide because the individual was submerged in the duty to the group).[22] A third type of suicide would occur if society experienced upheaval, resulting in morality being regulated differently; people would then tend toward suicide because they were confused (anomic suicide).[23] Durkheim is credited with introducing the idea that social forces affect suicide, resulting in a focus on social reform to prevent suicide.[24] A pastoral counselor with this approach might ask a suicidal person, "Tell me about the groups that you're a part of."

Sigmund Freud (1856–1939). Sigmund Freud believed that the cause of suicide was found within an individual, a result of depression or melancholy.[25] Suicide occurred because of the death instinct and displaced hostility.[26] Freud believed that in melancholy, hostility toward a loved one was shifted away from the other onto the self.[27] Therefore, suicide consisted of "murderous impulses" turned on oneself in a way that overwhelmed the life instinct.[28] Based on his theory, any human being given the right conditions could become suicidal.[29] Suicide prevention for Freud involved treating the underlying melancholy and hostility. A pastor working within this perspective might ask a suicidal person, "What comes to mind when I say *hate*?"

CONTEMPORARY THEORIES

Contemporary theories are notable by the quantity of research which has gone into testing their claims.

Edwin Shneidman (1918–2009). Edwin Shneidman has been called the "father of suicidology."[30] His theory about suicide is based on psychological need: "In almost every case, suicide is caused by pain, a certain kind of pain—*psychological pain*, which I call *psychache*. Furthermore, this psychache stems from thwarted or distorted psychological needs."[31] The psychological needs Shneidman believes are most often associated with suicide are thwarted love, fractured control, assaulted self-image, ruptured key relationships and excessive anger.[32] He recognized that in addition to psychache a person had to develop the ability to harm oneself; he acknowledged that only a small number of people with excessive psychological pain actually took their own lives even though he believed that every suicide resulted from this excessive psychological pain.[33] Shneidman also emphasized ambivalence, the idea that a part of a suicidal person wants to die and a part wants to stay alive, and asserted that a suicidal person experienced a constricted problem-solving strategy, seeing only one option, suicide.[34] Shneidman suggests that the main intervention is to lessen pain by expanding solutions to the presenting problem.[35] A chaplain with this approach might ask a suicidal person, "What is your unsolvable problem?"

J. Mark G. Williams (1952–). Mark Williams sees suicide as a cry of pain resulting from feeling trapped.[36] He gives the following example: "a 12-year-old girl called Agnes Addam who went horse-riding with a girlfriend in 1565 and dirtied her clothes. She started to return home but then became seized with terror over what her father would do to her when he saw she had spoilt her clothes. She rushed into a pond and drowned herself."[37] Suicidal people feel trapped because they are less able to problem-solve, partially because they have selective memories. They remember negative events much more quickly than positive events and also provide half as many ways of solving problems as nonsuicidal people—plus, the solutions they do come up with are less effective.[38] Difficulties with memory and problem solving "undermine the very process by which a person constructs a specific future for themselves, and thereby allows hopelessness to grow and develop without hindrance."[39] Williams suggests that suicide intervention should focus on problem solving.[40] A pastoral counselor with this approach might say to a suicidal person, "What other solutions to your problem can we come up with?"

Cognitive behavioral approaches. The following cognitive behavioral approaches have consistently been found to be helpful to suicidal people and are compatible with each other.[41] What unites these approaches is their focus on cognition (thinking), helping people engage in positive activities (behavioral) and on "the reduction of suicidal behaviors."[42] One of the underlying beliefs of cognitive-behavior theorists is that cognition affects feelings. Negative cognitions such as "I am a hopelessly flawed person" or "My world will always be bleak" lead to feelings such as sadness, which over time might lead to a depressed mood. Thinking (cognition) leads to feeling and mood. Cognitive behavioral suicide prevention approaches are based on the assumption that helping a person change her thinking will improve her feelings and mood, which are assumed to lower suicide risk.

Aaron T. Beck (1921–). Aaron T. Beck believes that suicidal people have two basic ideas that organize all incoming information: hopelessness ("Things will never get better") and unbearability ("I can't take this anymore").[43] Research has found that hopelessness does predict later suicide in many cases.[44] In addition to these ideas, suicidal people's cognitions include "helpless core beliefs (e.g., 'I am trapped'), unlovable core beliefs (e.g., 'Nobody cares for me'), and worthless core beliefs (e.g., 'I am a burden')." Beck also has noted that suicidal people focus on suicide as the answer because of difficulties with problem solving.[45] His research team has noticed that:

> Many patients describe a state of cognitive disorientation in the time immediately preceding their suicide attempt. . . . They experience "tunnel vision," focusing on suicide as the only answer to their problems at the expense of less harmful options. They are mentally consumed or preoccupied by the idea that there is no way out and would do anything possible to end the pain. They report that they are in a state of desperation.[46]

Wenzel, Brown and Beck outline a ten-session cognitive therapy intervention focused primarily on reducing future suicidal acts and increasing cognitive skills for coping and problem solving.[47] Some specific interventions are:

1. Writing down reasons to live.[48]

2. Creating a hope kit, which is a "memory aid consisting of a collection of meaningful items that remind patients of reasons to live and that can be reviewed during times of crisis."[49] It can be a shoebox, a scrapbook, a collage, a painting or web page. Wenzel and colleagues mention a suicidal person who acquired clothing from people important in her life and made a quilt.[50] One of my clients has developed a hope kit with ideas of things to do because when she thinks she has nothing to do in life, this sets her on the path to becoming suicidal.

3. Creating small coping cards with ideas to do or statements to tell oneself in a crisis.[51]

The therapy has been demonstrated to reduce suicide reattempt rate by 50 percent.[52] A pastor using this approach might ask a suicidal person, "What thoughts go through your mind when you feel suicidal?"

Marsha Linehan (1943–). McKeon notes that Marsha Linehan's treatment, called dialectical behavior therapy (DBT), has the most scientific support of all approaches.[53] Linehan believes that suicidal people have too few reasons for living.[54] She believes that the best suicide prevention is "a life worth living."[55] What keeps suicidal people from building a life worth living are limited skills: "The basic premise of treatment is that individuals who wanted to be dead did not have the requisite skills to build a life worth living."[56] In other words, suicidal behaviors develop from the individual's lack of skills and environmental factors that inhibit the use of the skills the individual already has.[57]

DBT is an intensive therapy that includes weekly individual therapy and weekly group therapy focused on teaching four skills: interpersonal problem solving, distress tolerance, emotion regulation and mindfulness. It includes the opportunity to get telephone coaching from one's therapist at any time during the week as well as a weekly therapist team meeting. DBT has been found to reduce suicide attempts by half in addition to several other important outcomes such as fewer hospitalizations.[58] DBT adapted for suicidal adolescents includes family therapy, family coaching and family skills training.[59] A chaplain using this approach might coach a suicidal person, "What skills could you use to make it through this crisis?"

Thomas Joiner (1965–). Thomas Joiner has developed the interpersonal-psychological theory of suicidal behavior, which currently dominates the theoretical landscape. This theory proposes that an individual will not die by suicide unless he or she has both the desire to die by suicide and the ability to do so. The desire to die by suicide occurs if two fundamental "superordinate" human needs are frustrated: the need to belong and the need to "feel effective with or to influence others."[60] Joiner calls the frustrated need for belonging "thwarted belongingness" and the frustrated need to feel effective "perceived burdensomeness." All three of the theory's concepts— ability to enact lethal self-injury, thwarted belongingness, perceived burdensomeness—are necessary as the final common pathway to attempt or die by suicide.[61] Joiner explains thwarted belonging as loneliness or isolation and perceived burdensomeness as lack of purpose.

He cites an elderly Malaysian couple's suicide note: "If we had waited for our death due to sickness, we would have caused much inconvenience to all of you."[62] Perceived burdensomeness "produces the crucial mental calculation that 'my death will be worth more than my life to family, friends, society, and so on.'"[63] This theory has promising research support.[64]

Joiner suggests targeting the desire for suicide by addressing thwarted belongingness and perceived burdensomeness, because "even individuals with the capability for suicide will not engage in suicidal behavior because they do not desire to do so."[65] Also, the ability to kill oneself is fairly stable, either acquired or not acquired, and therefore less easy to change.[66] A key intervention opportunity is to foster belonging. Joiner writes, "My view is that this need to belong is so powerful that, when satisfied, it can prevent suicide even when perceived burdensomeness and the acquired ability to enact lethal self-injury are in place."[67] A pastoral counselor using this approach might ask a suicidal person, "Do you belong to anyone or to any groups?"

IMPLICATIONS

Theories are speculative, but they attempt to create organization from the chaos of the details. Because suicide is complex, each theory may focus on a different aspect of suicide. Theories are like John Godfrey Saxe's six blind men touching an elephant.[68] One blind man touching the elephant's trunk says that the elephant is like a snake. Another blind man touching the elephant's tail says the elephant is like a rope. Each blind man has understood part of the complexity of the elephant, just as each suicide theory captures an important aspect of suicide. And, as we would expect, these theories converge. One possible synthesis of these diverse theories is a bio-psycho-social approach that incorporates the complex triple focus on biology, psychology and social factors. Suicide not only has biological roots in genetic fearlessness but also psychological roots in mental health problems and constricted problem-solving and social roots in isolation. These theories overlap and suggest several strategies for suicide prevention.

- Suicidal people may have an underlying mental health problem such as depression for which they need a referral to a mental health professional.

- They may be ambivalent; a part of them wants to live.

- They may have ineffective problem-solving strategies.

- They need ideas for how to cope with their pain.

- They need life skills to build a life worth living and reasons for living, including hope.

- They need to belong.

- They need opportunities to serve so that they won't feel like a burden.

A Bio-Psycho-Social-Spiritual Approach

Though many of these theories and suggested strategies for suicide prevention are helpful for pastors, chaplains and pastoral counselors, there is one glaring omission: a spiritual approach to suicide prevention. And one key reason spiritual approaches need to be included is that many suicidal people seek help from clergy. Approximately 25 percent of respondents to a large national survey—people who had all types of mental health disorders—said they had contacted clergy for help.[69] Suicidal ideation, plans or attempts were significant predictors of making contact, and suicidal people who sought treatment were as likely to contact clergy as other providers. Ellison, Vaaler, Flannelly and Weaver found in a study that about one-third of their respondents viewed clergy as "first-line helpers" for most mental health problems, including risk of self-harm.[70] And when people contact clergy, they ask them spiritual questions.[71] A second reason to focus on spiritual approaches to suicide prevention is that religiosity is a known protective factor against suicide.[72] Suicidal people use faith practices to cope with suicidal thoughts.[73] And a third reason is that while psychology can deliver empirical findings not contained in the Bible, theology can deliver truths not discoverable through science.[74] Pastors, chaplains and pastoral counselors are needed in the work of suicide prevention to integrate spiritual approaches, resulting in a bio-psycho-social-spiritual approach. I suggest the following theological additions to the theories above.

Life. One's theology of life affects suicidality. Pastors, chaplains and pastoral counselors should address what a "good" life means. How does an individual get a good life and what should the person do if she or he loses the good life? What is a life worth living and preserving? For example, to develop a theology of life, pastoral caregivers might include relevant theological concepts such as God's love for humanity (1 Jn 4:8), his desire to forgive sin (2 Pet 3:9) and his desire to be in everlasting relationship with us (Jn 3:16). Pastors, chaplains and pastoral counselors can teach people how to build a life worth living with meaningful purpose and belonging. Church youth groups can develop hope kits with reasons to live. The Christian life is full of reasons for living, such as God's gifting to every Christian (Rom 12:3-10; 1 Cor 12; Eph 4:1-13; 1 Pet 4:8-11) so that every Christian can contribute to a body of believers. It seems contrary to Scripture that a Christian should feel like a burden (1 Cor 12:21-25) or that a Christian not have a group to which she belongs (Gen 2:18; Heb 10:25). One poignant example for me is a client who is an atheist but believes that he's alive today because he joined a group at his sister's church.

Death. Pastoral caregivers should address theological questions about death. For example: When, if ever, does suffering justify escape from life by death? Are there moral objections to deciding one's time of death? What is the difference between suicide, physician-assisted suicide and euthanasia? What is the difference between martyrdom and suicide? For what or for whom is it worth risking or laying down one's life? What ceases to exist at death and what continues to exist? What is the nature of Christian hope? How should the church minister to those left behind after a suicide? Who in society should own a weapon and develop the ability to enact lethal injury, and what can the church do to support these individuals from enacting their own death? Pastoral counselors might discuss the Christian paradox of living between two worlds where dying can be gain but remaining in the flesh can be more necessary (Phil 1:21-24). Chaplains might discuss the Christian hope both future and present (Rom 8:18-30). Pastors might discuss how Christ's death defeated death and that the dead will rise in Christ (1 Cor 15:3, 26) and that God is a righteous judge (Gen 18:25; Ps 7:11). Clergy have told me about taking steps to remove the means for suicide from someone who was thinking about it and had the ability to enact lethal injury.

Suicide. As argued previously, pastors, chaplains and pastoral counselors need to develop a theology of suicide. Not only do pastoral caregivers need to reflect theologically on whether suicide is a sin that damns one to hell but also on how a Christian becomes suicidal and is restored to health. In addition, pastoral caregivers can help prevent suicide by examining their own beliefs and attitudes. They can engage the issue of suicide directly—stigma-free—when people become suicidal, attempt suicide or die by suicide, as Paul did with the Philippian jailer (Acts 16:28). They can address the myths about suicide in their faith communities by discussing the subject openly without judgment, as the Bible does. Doing so can make it easier for a suicidal individual or someone who has lost a loved one to suicide to get the help she or he needs.

Suffering. In my team's study of fifteen Protestant clergy and their ministry to suicidal people, we found that the most frequent theological question asked of clergy by suicidal individuals was related to suffering: "Why doesn't God give me joy?"[75] Pastoral caregivers need to address why Christians suffer. How is suffering explained in the light of God's power and love? Is suffering a judgment on the Christian? What is the Christian response to suffering? Is suffering undignified? Is it something to be endured or avoided? A theology of suffering ought to be big enough to explain the real challenges of life and provide ideas for how Christians manage suffering. Some ideas on pain management include knowing God is present at all times (Ps 23:4), knowing that we can have hope even though God doesn't eliminate pain (Lam 3:19-22), realizing that he is as concerned about injustice as we are (Lk 18:7-8) and recognizing that lamenting is a very Christian thing to do.[76] Suffering can be redeemed (Gen 50:20; Rom 8:28), and hope, waiting and self-care are Christian responses to pain (1 Cor 13:13; Ps 33:20; Mk 6:31).

Community. Because belonging and having a sense of purpose and influence on others help protect people against suicide, pastoral caregivers should address a community's function in the life of a Christian. Who contributes to the community and how? Who can be legitimately excluded from the community, why and when can this happen, and can an individual exclude herself? Pastors have told my research team that they involve the church community in their suicide prevention work. One clergy person said, "It isn't just me trying to help this person, it is the church's ministry."[77] Church community life is rich with learning. In community, people learn life skills such as how to build enduring relationships through forgiveness (Eph 4:32) and gratitude (1 Thess 5:18).[78] Problem-solving skills are modeled, such as seeking advice (Prov 15:22) and listening carefully to all sides on a matter (Prov 18:13, 17). It is also in community that those touched by suicide can be ministered to; Christians mourn with those who mourn (Rom 12:15).

Pastors, chaplains and pastoral counselors are needed to integrate spiritual approaches with psychological theories, which do not include theologies of life, death and suicide. Theories lack a theology of suffering and God-focused pain management. They lack the theology of community, a place of belonging and purposeful service as well as a place where life's complexities are lived out.

SUMMARY

Theories are important because they drive prevention practices. Nine theories of suicide generate several implications for suicide prevention for pastors, chaplains and pastoral counselors. While cognitive-behavioral perspectives currently dominate the theoretical landscape, spiritual theories and strategies are also needed because people impute on clergy a preventative role when they seek their help, because religiosity protects against suicide and because the Bible may carry a different weight than psychological theories in making claims about how to build a life worth living, when to justify death, what attitudes toward suicide are biblical, how to find meaning in suffering, and how to build a community worth contributing to.

But how do pastors, chaplains and pastoral counselors actually help suicidal people? What steps for assessing suicide risk and intervening at each level of risk can they take? The next chapter will address this process.

DISCUSSION QUESTIONS

1. Are the theories of suicide discussed in this chapter practical or helpful to you?

2. What is your theory of how people get to the point of suicide?

3. Do you agree with the current focus on the link between mental illness and suicide?

4. Does Joiner's theory make intuitive sense to you and fit with your experience? Are belongingness and not feeling burdensome fundamental human needs?

5. What other spiritual approaches need to be incorporated by pastors, chaplains and pastoral counselors in the work of suicide prevention?

RESOURCES

M. G. Hubbard, *More Than an Aspirin: A Christian Perspective on Pain and Suffering* (Grand Rapids: Discovery House, 2009).

T. Joiner, K. Van Orden, T. Witte and D. Rudd, *The Interpersonal Theory of Suicide: Guidance for Working with Suicidal Clients* (Washington, DC: American Psychological Association, 2009).

C. S. Lewis, *The Problem of Pain* (New York: Macmillan, 1962).

A. L. Miller, J. H. Rathus and M. M. Linehan, *Dialectical Behavior Therapy with Suicidal Adolescents* (New York: Guilford, 2007).

A. Wenzel, G. K. Brown and A. T. Beck, *Cognitive Therapy for Suicidal Patients: Scientific and Clinical Applications* (Washington, DC: American Psychological Association, 2009).

5

HELPING SOMEONE IN A SUICIDE CRISIS

As a society, we do not like to talk about suicide.

DAVID SATCHER, MD, PHD, SURGEON
GENERAL OF THE UNITED STATES

Paul's model of suicide prevention is one we can follow today.
He intervened in the jailer's crisis. He stopped him from
harming himself. He gave him a reason to live.
We can do the same.

ALBERT HSU

Sam is a 42-year-old married church deacon who reveals to you that he just broke off an affair he's been having with his secretary over the last six years. Sam's wife of eighteen years is unaware of the affair and presses him to visit his doctor because he's losing weight, is waking at 4 a.m. every morning, and is tearful at home and at work. Sam has missed several golf games with his friends, which is unusual for him. He is spending less and less time with his two children. He tells you that he feels very guilty about the affair and is convinced that God will punish him for his sins. He says he ruminates so much about his guilt that he hasn't been able to concentrate at work.[1]

Do you wonder if Sam is suicidal? I do, but not because he's male. I'm wondering if he's suicidal because he's displaying warning signs. Your first step in gauging whether a person is in a suicide crisis is to look for warning signs. The following steps are offered as an organizing framework for recognizing suicide risk and connecting the person at risk to mental health services. It is important to seek training and consultation from mental health professionals, hospital emergency departments or a suicide crisis line throughout these steps.

STEP 1: SPOT WARNING SIGNS

A warning sign is a noticeable hint that risk for suicide has increased. A person with one or more warning signs may have some risk for suicide, especially if he or she has experienced a recent trigger event (an important loss, legal problems, financial difficulties, unemployment).[2] Some warning signs to watch for include:

- Talking about or writing about death, dying or suicide

- Threatening to kill oneself

- A worsening mental health problem such as depression, especially when accompanied by agitation[3]

- Dramatic brightening of mood after a period of depression[4]

- Seeking access to means, such as hoarding pills

- Reckless behavior, such as increased substance use

- Decreased hygiene, such as not showering

- Social withdrawal

- Preparatory behavior, such as giving away prized possessions

What warning signs do you see in Sam?[5]

At this point, you might hope a good Samaritan will come along and help Sam. The reason you need to take action is that no one else might spot the warning signs. Many teens talk to their friends—not to their parents—about their suicidal thoughts.[6] Adults talk to friends and family.[7] As noted in the previous chapter, many people talk to clergy. Approximately 25 percent of a large national sample of people with all types of mental health disorders contacted clergy for help, and 56 percent of these saw clergy alone. Some of the main reasons for contacting clergy were suicidal thinking, plans or attempts. Suicidal people who sought help were as likely to contact clergy as other providers.[8] It may be up to you to take action. Avoiding your need to take action can negatively affect the suicidal person. Paul Seaman recounts how he awkwardly told his weekly Bible study group that he was contemplating suicide and would appreciate their prayers. No one from the group called or offered him support.[9]

Step 2: Assess for Suicidal Thinking

The next step to helping Sam is to find out if he is experiencing suicidal thinking. And the only way to do this is to ask him directly. One hesitation you might have is that you're afraid asking about suicide might put the idea in Sam's mind. This is highly unlikely. In one study, 2,342 high school students participated in a screening survey over two days. Half the surveys contained questions about suicidality. The students who got the suicide questions did not report more distress or depression or thoughts of suicide after they completed the survey or two days later.[10] In another study, college students were asked to read either the warning signs for suicide or the warning signs for a heart attack. Students who read the warning signs for suicide did not report increased depression, anxiety, hopelessness or suicidal thinking.[11] People who aren't suicidal don't become suicidal because you ask, and most suicidal people are relieved when you bring up the topic for them. Thoughts of suicide are intensely distressing because they are scary, unexpected and embarrassing. Imagine Sam not knowing how to start a conversation about suicidal thinking. And imagine his relief when you bring up the topic for him.

A second hesitation you might have is that you think Sam will probably lie. This also is not usually the case. People are usually able to describe their experience truthfully.[12] Of course, some people may take a while to trust you.[13] To build trust, it's helpful to listen to the person's concerns and avoid making promises you can't keep. For example, Cleo may be wondering if she can trust you not to take her to the hospital. You can't promise that and you can't guarantee you'll never take her to the hospital because suicidal thinking fluctuates.[14] However, you can promise to keep Cleo's best interests at heart. What will you do if Cleo asks you to promise to keep something secret before she talks to you? Avoid those promises. But if you do promise, remember that the higher obligation is to life, not to your promise. To put it bluntly, an angry Cleo is better than a dead Cleo.

Occasionally, some people may be reluctant to disclose suicidal thinking. They display warning signs but are unwilling to collaborate with you.[15] Other people are actively psychotic or intoxicated. These people should be evaluated at a mental health center or hospital emergency department.

A third hesitation people experience is knowing how to ask about suicide. It's important to ask a direct and precise question.[16] Ask directly, "Do you have thoughts of suicide?" or "Are you thinking about killing yourself?" Avoid, "Are you thinking of not being around for much longer?" which is too vague. Avoid, "You don't have thoughts of suicide, do you?" which is like begging the person to answer, "No, of course not!" Take a minute right now to ask the question out loud: "Do you have thoughts of suicide?" One of the hardest parts of helping a suicidal person is getting used to asking this question directly, specifically and out loud.

STEP 3: ASSESS WHERE AN INDIVIDUAL IS ON A SUICIDE CONTINUUM

If Sam says, "Yes, I have thoughts of suicide," your next step is to find out where he is on the suicide continuum (see fig. 1). A suicidal person is on a continuum from slightly suicidal to somewhat suicidal to very suicidal. At the far right end of the continuum, a person is in a suicide crisis with intense thoughts of suicide combined with the belief that he cannot overcome these thoughts and may act on them. As Sam moves closer to the very suicidal end of the continuum, the situation becomes more serious. On the less suicidal end of the continuum, the situation is serious but less so. You need to find out where Sam is because that will affect the help you offer him. Where do you estimate Sam is on this continuum?

You might be hoping a test exists for determining how serious the situation is. Unfortunately there isn't one, certainly not one that predicts suicide accurately every time.[17] Screening instruments can detect mental health problems and suicidality in adults and teens.[18] But using these requires specialized training and follow-up inter-

Figure 1. Suicide continuum

views.[19] What you can do is recognize suicide risk and connect the person at risk to mental health services.

To help you assess how far along the suicide continuum Sam has moved, think about markers along the continuum. These markers are ideation, intent, plan, means and imminence. Imminence refers to how impending a suicide is. Use questions to estimate which markers Sam is near or has passed.

- Ideation: Do you have thoughts of suicide? How many times a day or week do you have these thoughts? How much time do you spend thinking about suicide?[20] How strong are the thoughts? Do you hear voices that tell you to kill yourself? What do you do to resist them? When did you start having these thoughts? What was going on at that time? What is the worst suicidal thinking you've ever had?[21]

- Intent to die: Do you think you will follow through on these thoughts? On a scale from one to ten, how likely do you think it is that you'll act on this thinking?[22]

- Plan: Have you thought about how you would kill yourself? How have you prepared for your death?[23] Are you fearless enough to follow through on your plan?[24]

- Means: Do you have the means to follow through on your plan? (You will need to determine if these means are lethal—i.e., is there a high potential for death associated with the means?[25])

- Imminence: When do you think you might follow through on your plan?

For example, the following is an interview with Jack, who isn't far along on this continuum right now.

PASTOR: Sometimes people who are depressed think about suicide. Jack, do you have thoughts of suicide?

JACK: Not really. Sometimes I think it'd be better not to wake up tomorrow.

PASTOR: How many days this last week did you have those thoughts?

JACK: About once or so.

PASTOR: What is the thought that comes to your mind?

JACK: I wish I didn't have to live another day with my roommate.

PASTOR: What is it about living with your roommate that's hard?

JACK: All the conflict. It can be intense.

PASTOR: How long have these thoughts been going on?

JACK: I'd say about a month or so.

PASTOR: What was going on about a month ago when these thoughts started?

JACK: I started dating my girlfriend. I think my roommate is jealous. We haven't been getting along and it just seems like a pattern with me, having trouble with people.

PASTOR: Was there a time before this that you had suicidal thoughts? For instance, when you were younger?

JACK: When I was 14 and my parents were going through a divorce, I thought about suicide. My mom got me help. I went to counseling for about a year.

PASTOR: The counseling helped. What was helpful?

JACK: Just knowing I wasn't alone.

PASTOR: What do you do with those thoughts now when they happen?

JACK: I usually try to ignore them or I crawl in bed for a nap.

Notice that Jack is toward the left side on the continuum. He has some passive suicidal thinking but he isn't actively suicidal.

Here's an interview with Jill, who is farther along on the continuum.

CHAPLAIN: Sometimes people who are depressed think about suicide. Jill, do you have thoughts of killing yourself?

JILL: Yes, I do.

CHAPLAIN: What thoughts go through your mind?

JILL: I just think it would be better if I were dead.

CHAPLAIN: You wish you were dead?

JILL: Yes, I think about jumping off my balcony.

CHAPLAIN: You have a balcony?

JILL: Yes, I live on the eighth floor.

CHAPLAIN: These thoughts of jumping—do you think you'll follow through on them at some point?

JILL: I'm not sure, but I'm getting those thoughts more and more.

CHAPLAIN: Do you think you'll follow through on them today or the next few days?

JILL: No, but I can't be sure because they might come to me stronger sometime. I'm just not sure.

CHAPLAIN: For now, you're not sure. About how many times last week did those thoughts come into your mind?

JILL: Maybe once or twice.

CHAPLAIN: When you got that thought, what did you do?

JILL: Well, I didn't jump.

CHAPLAIN: You resisted them?

JILL: I think I'm a coward.

CHAPLAIN: You wonder if the reason you didn't follow through is that you're a coward. Any other reason?

JILL: I can't think of any.

CHAPLAIN: Let's keep thinking about reasons, but first let me ask, when did these thoughts start?

JILL: They started just after embezzlement charges were filed against me and I lost my job. Now I might have to file for bankruptcy.

Chaplain: You have a lot that's happened recently. When did all this happen?

Jill: About a month ago.

Chaplain: Earlier we were talking about you not jumping and you wondered if it was because you're a coward.

Jill: I can't think of any other reason.

Chaplain: Well, I wonder if you're thinking about reasons to die like the legal charges and the possible bankruptcy. But I wonder if everything is hopeless.

Jill: It feels like it.

Chaplain: Tell me about a reason that brought you here today.

Jill: I remember helping a friend stay alive when she was in the middle of a hard time.

Chaplain: Tell me more about how this makes you hopeful enough to come talk to me.

Notice that Jill is almost at the dangerous end of the suicide continuum. She has suicide thoughts, a plan and the means. And she's ambivalent. She doesn't intend to act on suicidal thoughts right now, though she's at fairly high risk because the thoughts might intensify at any time.

Step 4: Assign a Level of Risk—Low, Medium or High

The next step is to weigh the information you've gathered and evaluate the level of risk. You will intervene differently depending on your estimate. Risk can be low, medium or high. Examples of the three levels of risk follow.

Low. Linda calls you and says her husband just walked out on her. She is crying hysterically. After you talk with her, she calms down and tells you she was so angry she thought about killing herself just to show her husband. She says she won't act on that thought and wouldn't even know how to harm herself, but she wonders what to do with the hurt and anger.

Medium. Bernice tells you in confidence that she's been depressed since a date rape six months ago. She still feels too ashamed to tell any of her friends or family what happened, and she wonders if God will ever forgive her. She looks depressed and, when you ask, says her primary care doctor started her on an antidepressant last week. She tells you that when she was 12 and her parents were going through a divorce she tried cutting her legs a few times, but she stopped because it didn't help. She goes on to say she has some upsetting suicidal thoughts some days but does not have a suicide plan.

High. David calls you and says he is struggling with his wife's death from breast cancer a year ago today. He wonders why God didn't heal her. As he continues to talk, you realize that he seems depressed and doesn't seem to look forward to the future. He keeps saying, "I can't imagine life without Janet." As you continue to question him, you find out he has a gun next to him and plans to kill himself after hanging up the phone unless you can give him a reason to live.

Risk estimations are based on an informed hunch.[26] I estimate that Linda has a lower risk because she reports one instance of suicidal thinking with no intent. Bernice has medium risk because she is thinking about suicide some days. David has high risk. He has suicidal thinking, intent, an imminent plan and access to a gun. If estimating risk seems confusing, arrange for the individual to be evaluated immediately by a mental health professional or at a hospital emergency department, or call 1-800-273-TALK, the National Suicide Prevention Lifeline, or call 911. Consultation is central to suicide prevention.

STEP 5: TAKE ACTION FOR EACH RISK LEVEL

Each of the vignettes above presents a person in a very different place on the suicide continuum. The next step is to take action based on the risk level. Unfortunately, there is no miraculous human intervention that resolves suicide risk.[27] But there are specific actions you can take to prevent suicide, actions that become more extensive with increasing risk. Following are several ideas for pastoral care, which is different from mental health counseling, an important distinction that argues for referral to mental health services.[28] Whenever there is suicidal risk, it's best to consult with and refer to a mental health professional.

As you intervene, focus on first aid, not surgery. If you're at a park and have a heart attack, you don't want the people around you to perform heart surgery. You want them to perform CPR. Your job with suicidal people is to focus on safety, not on solving the problem that is causing the suicidal crisis. For example, if someone is in a suicidal crisis because she is processing childhood sexual abuse, your job is to keep her safe, not to heal the memories of abuse.

No risk. A person without any risk is a person who has no suicidal thinking and never has had suicidal thinking. The main intervention is to continue to provide this person with all the usual pastoral care.

Low risk. A person with low suicide risk is

- A person with persistent passive wishes to be dead but no intent and no history of suicidal thinking or behaviors, such as Jack.[29]

- A person who experiences brief suicidal thoughts but has no intent or plan and no history of suicidal thinking or behaviors, such as Linda.

Some suggestions for low-risk individuals are consultation, referral to a mental health professional and creation of a safety plan.

Consultation. It is always best to consult with a mental health professional, hospital emergency department or crisis hot line to see if you missed something important, to get help with assessing risk and intervening, and to get support for yourself. No matter how much experience you have, it's best to consult with professionals who have experience working with suicidal people.

Referral for mental health treatment. As we saw in chapter 1, suicidal thinking often occurs in the context of a mental health problem, which requires professional treatment and therefore a referral to a mental health professional.[30] Making referrals sounds straightforward but can be challenging. A pastor my team interviewed told us that lack of known mental health resources was just about the scariest thing he faced.[31] Pastors say they prefer to have a referral list before a crisis, which they develop by talking to trusted people in their community. The second challenge with referral relates to the therapist-client relationship, which is one of the keys to a positive outcome in therapy.[32] If the therapist-client connection isn't positive and trusting, someone like Linda may need help finding another therapist with whom she can connect.

Once you refer, check to see if Linda followed up on the referral.[33] And then stay involved. See yourself as part of a multidisciplinary team; you are providing an important part of the treatment. Stauffacher writes:

> We clergy need to see our role as being part of a larger treatment team that is concerned with the care of a person in Body, Mind and Spirit. As a vital part of that team, it is appropriate to see what we do as different from the work of physicians, therapists and social workers. We represent the sacred within the secular and bring with us both Testament and Sacrament with Covenant.[34]

Being part of the team means you may want to speak with the mental health professional yourself. You are allowed to talk to the therapist, but the therapist is not able to talk to you about the client because of confidentiality laws. The exception is if Linda authorizes the therapist to talk to you about her treatment. Any decision to share confidential information will be carefully discussed between Linda and the therapist. Confidentiality is one of the most important aspects of therapy, but collaboration is also important. If it makes therapeutic sense, Linda will sign an authorization, either limited or unlimited. For example, Linda can limit the sharing to emergency situations or to the fact that she is attending therapy sessions or to spiritual aspects of the treatment. Therapists can also share information with a parent or guardian who makes medical decisions for a minor (under 18 years old), and therapists are usually allowed under state law to break confidentiality when a person is at high risk for suicide.

Safety plan. A safety plan, or crisis response plan, is a short, easy-to-read plan for Linda to implement during a suicide crisis, complete with a list of calming activities and contacts.[35] It is like a life jacket. Its purpose is to keep a person afloat and alive in the midst of a flood of suicidal thinking. Suicidality fluctuates; low risk can turn into medium or high risk quickly. Linda may have no suicidal thinking when she leaves your office but, two hours later, after a call from her ex-husband, she may become suicidal. A safety plan gives her something else to do besides contemplate suicide and tells her what to do when she feels suicidal. Basic content includes:

1. How to cope with distress

- Increase social support (list nontoxic helpers and contact information)

- Manage distress (praying, walking, playing with the dog, listening to music)

2. Emergency numbers (1-800-273-TALK)[36]

The goal of a safety plan is to interrupt the chain of events leading to suicide. One of the messages of a safety plan is that Linda can be successful in battling the thoughts of suicide. Blauner writes, "I've experienced the 'I want to die' moment thousands of times over the last eighteen years, which means suicidal thoughts have passed *just as many times*."[37]

It's important to develop this plan while not in crisis and to put it someplace where it is very accessible. Jane, who had multiple personalities, had an alter ego who would hide the safety plan. So she left a second safety plan in a sealed envelope with her neighbor.

Here's Linda's safety plan:

When my ex-husband calls and I feel hopeless:

- Call my mom or my friend Belinda.

- Pray.

- Go to the gym.

- Get out my hope kit.

- Call my pastor.

- Call my therapist.

- Call 1-800-273-TALK.

Notice that Linda's safety plan includes a hope kit, which will remind her of reasons to live.[38] It can be a memo in her cell phone or a shoebox with keepsakes that will cue Linda to think of her reasons to live. Suicidal people can develop a very personal hope kit by putting in items that remind them of

- A time when someone helped them in the past
- Something they like to do that gives them hope
- A quote that helped in the past to prevent a suicide attempt
- A time when they felt proud of themselves
- A photograph of something or someone that represents hope

Linda's safety plan also includes the number for the National Suicide Prevention Lifeline (1-800-273-TALK). A crisis line is important because you or others may not be available when Linda needs help. Talking to someone may interrupt the spiral to suicide. The National Suicide Prevention Lifeline is a 24-7 line that's staffed by more than 120 crisis centers throughout the United States. When you call the number, your call is automatically forwarded to the crisis center closest to you and therefore the one that knows your local resources. Take time now to visit the website at suicidepreventionlifeline.org. Notice the many resources for veterans, the hearing and speech impaired, and Spanish speakers. In addition to the lifeline, a safety plan could include the phone number of a local suicide prevention center such as the Samaritans (samaritanshope.org), started by an Anglican priest.[39] Or it could include the phone number for emergency services or mobile crisis teams in the community. Current research supports the effectiveness of these crisis lines.[40] Keep in mind that these lines will accept calls from suicidal people and also from caregivers such as you.

Notice that a safety plan is not a safety contract, which is a binding promise that Linda makes not to kill herself. Such a contract, written or verbal, answers the question, "Do you promise to not kill yourself between now and the next time we see each other?" Unfortunately there is no evidence that these are effective.[41] For example, the Minnesota Office of the Ombudsman investigated cases of suicides that had occurred in inpatient acute care facilities and found that a no-harm contract was in place in almost every case.[42] In one study, patients with no-suicide contracts had a significantly higher likelihood of self-harm behavior.[43] Some suicidal people find these contracts unhelpful. A contract doesn't encourage Linda to speak freely about her suicidal thoughts and doesn't tell her what to do, just what not to do.[44] In my experience, suicidal people hesitate to make a promise they aren't sure they can keep.[45] But refusal to sign one is not necessarily evidence of high risk. Let's go back to Linda:

> **PASTOR**: Would you be willing to work with me on a safety plan for if the thoughts come back stronger?
>
> **LINDA**: Sure, but no promises.
>
> **PASTOR**: Fair enough.

Medium risk. A person with medium risk of suicide is someone who

- Has no suicidal thinking but has a past history of suicidal behavior[46]

- Has occasional to daily suicidal thinking without intent, with or without prior history of suicidal thinking or behaviors, such as Beatrice

- Has occasional to daily suicidal thinking with intent but no plan and no imminence

Remember that for each additional point along the suicide continuum, you want to be more extensive in your intervention. For medium risk, do what you do for low risk (consult, refer for mental health treatment and develop a safety plan), and add additional interventions, such as more frequent visits to allow for more frequent monitoring. Keep in mind that suicide risk fluctuates.[47] A person may be at medium risk now but at high risk in an hour. Clergy are in a position to be aware of fluctuation more than some other professionals. Stauffacher and Clark write, "Visiting parishioners is a pastoral tool and skill. Use it."[48] A clergy person's relationships with people are closer than those of some other professionals.[49] Few professionals meet with their clients in their homes or over a potluck supper and discuss spiritual truths. Keep in mind that pastoral visits do not need to be undertaken by clergy alone. Lay people in the church can also be involved. Later in the chapter we'll discuss the importance of these visits.

If a suicidal person with medium risk moves to the right on the suicide continuum, she or he may begin to formulate a suicide plan. If this occurs, be sure to refer the person for an immediate evaluation at a mental health outpatient clinic or hospital emergency department. After this evaluation, you may be called on to help with means restriction. Means restriction involves reducing the availability or taking away the method or means that a person is contemplating using to kill herself. It is best that the suicidal person avoid exposure to the method.[50] For example, take some time to brainstorm how you could help restrict access to these means:

- Aspirin

- Antidepressant medication

- Razor blade

- Gun

- Belt

- Balcony

- Bridge

Here are a few ideas: One of my clients put a big bookcase in front of her balcony door so that she had time to use her safety plan while taking the books out before being able to move the big bookcase. We also worked on her moving to a lower floor. Prescribers of medication can provide weekly or even daily prescriptions or not prescribe certain medicines that are more lethal. (Any unused medication should be flushed down the toilet so that it can't be retrieved from the garbage.) Police can keep a gun for safekeeping, or it can be given to someone else.

One of the concerns you may have about means restriction is that you think the suicidal person will just substitute another method for the one he is currently contemplating. Interestingly, people don't usually do this because of their ambivalence.[51] Not having the means available provides an ambivalent person with enough time to reconsider the decision to die. The best example comes from the United Kingdom, where toxic coal gas was replaced by natural gas in the late 1950s. Not only was there a steady decrease in coal gas suicides, the overall suicide rate decreased by a third.[52] In one study of 515 people who were restrained from jumping from the Golden Gate Bridge, only 4.9 percent, or twenty-five of them, eventually died by suicide. Seven eventually jumped from the Golden Gate and one from the Bay Bridge. Ninety percent did not die of suicide or other violent means.[53] In another US study, each 10-percent decline in household firearm ownership over a twenty-two-year period was associated with significant declines in rates of firearm suicide and overall suicide.[54]

It's important to note that means restriction, while effective, isn't fail-safe. The decision to die remains with the suicidal person. However, even though you can't restrict every means on earth and a person might still substitute an alternate means, it's justifiable to restrict the means.

High risk. A person with a high risk of suicide is someone who

- Has occasional to daily suicidal thinking with intent and plan and may or may not have the means readily available[55]

- Hears voices that tell him to kill himself

- Has imminent intent and the means to follow through on a specific suicide plan

Jill, who thinks once or twice a week about jumping from her balcony, is at high risk. She is at almost the highest risk point on the suicide continuum and could resolve her ambivalence and choose death at any time. David, who calls you with a gun sitting next to him, is at the highest risk point—imminently at risk. Suicide is impending.

For Jill, your focus is facilitating an immediate evaluation with a mental health professional in an outpatient office or in the emergency department. If you're not sure which to do, consult with a crisis line. Transportation-wise, consider whether a trusted friend can drive Jill to the emergency department or whether an ambulance or the police will need to drive her to the hospital. Don't leave her alone.

For David, your focus is keeping him alive. Keep him on the phone. On another phone line, call 911, explain the situation and ask the police to go to his house while you continue to talk to David. You can tell him what you're doing and that you're concerned for his life.

The reason to keep David on the phone talking with you and never leaving Jill alone is that while suicide plans are typically developed over time,[56] suicide decisions can be made impulsively. In one seventeen-country study, most suicidal people (60 percent) took one year to transition from thinking about suicide to making a plan and attempting suicide.[57] But the ultimate timing and final decision to act are often determined in moments.[58]

The emergency department. Unfortunately, when Jill arrives at the emergency department, the wait time might be long because emergency departments tend to be overcrowded.[59] When she is seen, the visit will involve a medical evaluation, then usually a suicide risk evaluation and then a disposition or decision about whether Jill is able to be safe in the community or needs hospitalization.[60] Typically, one of three criteria needs to be met before Jill is hospitalized: (1) she's at high risk of harming herself, (2) she's at high risk of harming others, or (3) she can't take care of herself because of a mental health problem.[61] At least one criterion needs to be met or it's unlikely that Jill will be hospitalized. In fact, during the wait, Jill's will to live may emerge and she might not be at high risk when evaluated.

If David remains at high risk, hospitalization is often viewed as the safest approach because it decreases availability to means, increases monitoring and may allow David to start a medication.[62] Hospitalization can help, but it is not foolproof in preventing suicide.[63] About 3 to 10 percent of suicide deaths in the United States occur during hospitalization.[64]

Hospitalization. You may have some concerns about hospitalization, though my perspective is that none of these should keep a person from being hospitalized. A first concern might be that if the emergency department isn't connected to a hospital, it can take several hours to be transferred to a hospital—the average wait is seven hours.[65] Another concern might be that David shouldn't be exposed to other "mental patients." Keep in mind that mental health problems are not contagious.

A third concern might be that people don't heal in the hospital, and that is somewhat true. As the American Psychiatric Association notes, "Hospitalization, by itself, is not a treatment."[66] Think about hospitalization as a time of stabilization, not healing. A fourth concern is how to care for a person's children or pets, or Jill's car in the parking lot. Make sure you talk through these concerns with the suicidal person. As far as telling children about a parent's hospitalization, Greene-McCreight provides this advice:

> Children need communication at times even as horrible as these, but it must be judicious communication. Do not mention suicidal thoughts or gestures. Just something simple. "Mommy is sick. She is very sad. She needs to go to the hospital. She will get better and be home soon. The doctors will take good care of her." . . . Don't bring in half-truths for the sake of protecting the children. Speak matter-of-factly, quietly, calmly. Stress that the hospital is a good place for those who are sick.[67]

One last concern I hear often is that people don't want to be "locked up forever." Every state has different mental health laws, so learn your state's laws. Someone like David will be offered the least restrictive option possible (which may be voluntary unlocked hospitalization, where David can leave if he chooses, depending on where he is on the suicide continuum). The most restrictive option is involuntary locked hospitalization, where his civil right to leave is taken away for about seventy-two hours (depending on state law) because suicide crises are believed to abate within several days. In some circumstances, David might be kept involuntarily longer than seventy-two hours following reevaluation. State laws protect David's civil rights by requiring reevaluations.

STEP 6: PROVIDE PASTORAL CARE

Pastors, chaplains and pastoral counselors are gatekeepers who identify people at risk and connect them to other professionals. They also provide spiritual care to suicidal people at all risk levels because other professionals don't typically provide this support.[68] Stauffacher writes, "As clergy, we have unique skills and tools that we can offer to people, ones that are different from those offered by physicians and other caregivers."[69] Once pastors, chaplains and pastoral counselors address safety, they provide needed pastoral care.

Prayer. A friend of mine courageously told someone she was thinking about suicide, and her friend told her she'd pray for her. Definitely pray, but address safety first. This does not mean prayer is not important. We pray because God hears and heals (Jas 5:14). Greene-McCreight writes:

> One very important way to help your friends who suffer from mental illness is to pray for them. The assurance that people were praying for me, since I had so much trouble praying for myself, was a salve. My true friends during this time were the ones I knew were praying for me. It can be very difficult to pray for someone day in and day out, over and over again, especially when you see little improvement, when you feel like a scratched CD uttering the same phrases over and over. . . . Even so, this was so vital for me. . . . That many people were knocking on God's door for me strengthened me in putting up with the disease and sped the healing, even though the full healing was years in coming. Maybe it would never have come if people had not been praying.[70]

Belonging. Another type of pastoral care is offering the opportunity to belong. The kingdom of God is about belonging to God and to a faith community (Rom 14:8; Jn 8:35; Rom 7:4; Rom 12:5; Gal 6:10). When God said, "It is not good that the man should be alone" (Gen 2:18), he was speaking about humanity's superordinate human need for belonging.[71] This need is so fundamental that social isolation is a significant risk factor for suicide, "a finding that is among the most robust in suicide prevention."[72] Suicidal people are desperately lonely and estranged from others.[73] Joiner gives the example of his father: "My dad's desire for death, I believe, developed in the context of his losing touch with his professional identity, his marriage, and his church."[74] Pastors, chaplains and pastoral counselors are uniquely able to address people's loneliness.[75] Doty and Spencer-Thomas point out that in our day deep connections with others have been shrinking and that "faith communities provide a connection to one another—a belongingness—that creates a buffer against suicide."[76] David may be a member of a church but not know that he belongs. What could you do to help David know he belongs?

It seems simplistic, but sending a note can make a difference. Jerome Motto studied 3,006 patients who were discharged after a psychiatric hospitalization. He followed three groups: those who got treatment after discharge, those who refused treatment who did not receive letters or calls, and those who refused treatment who received nondemanding letters or phone calls on a set schedule. The call or letter expressed interest in how the person was doing and was signed by the person in charge of the patient's care. The letter might say, "Dear X, It has been some time since you were here at the hospital and we hope things are going well for you. If you wish to drop us a note we would be glad to hear from you."[77] A self-addressed unstamped envelope was enclosed, and if the person wrote back, their letter was answered. The group that received calls or letters had the lowest suicide rate during the first two years after discharge.

Gregory Carter and his colleagues repeated Motto's study without the personal touches.[78] They followed 772 people who had attempted to poison themselves. Among those who received eight nondemanding automated printed postcards during a twelve-month period after discharge, the number of attempts to self-poison was cut in half. Guillaume Vaiva and his colleagues found that calling someone who attempted suicide one month after discharge from the emergency department reduced reattempts by about half.[79] The call provided empathy and reassurance, encouraged compliance with treatment, and provided brief crisis intervention when needed.

Given the power of a note or call, it is intuitive that an in-person visit would also be helpful. Pastors have told us that if a suicidal person gives permission, they connect him or her to lay ministers or deacons and that the ministry to a suicidal person is a churchwide ministry.[80] This fleshly belonging can remind the suicidal person of their belonging to God.

A potential challenge is getting a suicidal person to agree to meet with you. Your job is at least to offer and offer again, keeping in mind that the ultimate responsibility lies with the suicidal person. Susan

Rose Blauner makes the point, "The only person who can 'fix' the suicidal thinker is the suicidal thinker."[81]

Meaning. In addition to belonging, everyone needs meaning. Langer and Rodin demonstrated that nursing home residents given the responsibility to care for a houseplant were happier, more active and lived longer than a control group.[82] Suicidal people also need meaning even more than nursing home residents. A suicidal veteran in one research study said, "[God's] got something else for me to do. I don't know what that is and I become confused with what I should do or what I want to do. But something is there. I've got, you know . . . he's got something for me to do. And I'm going to find it."[83] The second superordinate human need proposed by Joiner is to "feel effective with or to influence others," or not to feel like a burden.[84] Every Christian has spiritual gifting (Rom 12:3-10; 1 Cor 12; Eph 4:1-13; 1 Pet 4:8-11) for use in service to God and the faith community. Christians who perceive themselves as a burden may need teaching from Scripture (1 Cor 12:21-25) and an opportunity to serve. Kaplan and Schwartz point out that God himself "intervenes in the lives of char-acters [e.g., Elijah, Moses] who express some sort of death wish."[85] He helps them return to faithful service. For those who feel they are a burden to their family, McKeon suggests, "The key therapeutic task may be to help the patient recognize that while there may be some burden that is imposed on family by their illness, the magnitude of that burden pales in comparison to the burdens experienced by loved ones following a death by suicide."[86]

Hope. Hope springs eternal in the human breast—but not in those who are suicidal. They live painfully with eroded hope. They do not want to die as much as they want to find relief from the pain of hope-lessness. This is a bitter place to be. But what is hope? Hope can be a wish, like wishing for a Ferrari—"I hope I drive a Ferrari someday." But hope in the Bible is much more. Hsu writes:

> Most people use hope as a verb: "I hope things will turn out better" or "I hoped he wouldn't do this." When hope is a verb, it is usually just wishful thinking on our part. We crank up our feelings and try to generate enough emotional or mental energy to bring something into reality.

Such hope is only a human activity, limited by our finitude. But the Bible uses hope as a noun. . . . Hope, in the Christian sense of the word, is far more than a wish or a dream. It's a tangible thing, as real as any object. "We have this hope as an anchor for the soul, firm and secure" (Hebrews 6:19). Our hope is a noun, as solid as a cast-iron anchor.[87]

Hope in the Bible is as central as faith and love (1 Cor 13:13). It is confidence in a more positive future based in our faithful certainty of God—the God who is present (Ps 34:18; Rom 8:24-27), loving (1 Jn 4:8) and sovereign (Ps 31:15) and who redeems our suffering (Gen 50:20; Rom 5:3-5).[88] In our adversity God may feel hidden (Is 45:15), but we seek him (Heb 11:6) and wait for him (Ps 130:5). He will create a new heaven and a new earth without pain (Rev 21:4).

Sometimes we in the community of faith need to hold on to hope in our God for the person who cannot. In Tolkien's *Lord of the Rings* trilogy, we read that Sam and Frodo held on to hope for each other, repeating the Latin dictum *Dum vita est spes est*, "While there is life, there is hope." Greene-McCreight writes, "Sometimes you literally cannot make it on your own, and you need to borrow from the faith of those around you."[89] In the community of faith, we need to stand as hopeful people for the suicidal person who no longer believes that anything can ever get better again. Hanging on to hope is paradoxical because at the same time you're hanging on to hope you're also acknowledging the suffering of your life.

Lament. Pastors have told my research team that suicidal Christians struggle with theological questions about suffering, asking, "Why doesn't God give me joy?"[90] Greene-McCreight says, "Christians as perennially cheery . . . is a cruel caricature of those Christians who are indeed depressed or otherwise mentally ill. Often they feel guilty on top of being depressed, because they understand their depression, their lack of thankfulness, their desperation, to be a betrayal of God."[91] Pastors, chaplains and pastoral counselors need to teach a full and complex perspective on Christian suffering—that both joy and suffering are normative Christian experiences (1 Pet 4:12; 2 Cor 1:8) and that living a triumphant Christian life means managing suffering, not having a suffering-free life (Phil 2:27-28). In the lament psalms, which make up nearly half of all psalms, God gives us the words to express our suffering to him.[92] God himself is acquainted with suffering (Is 53:3), cares about our suffering (Ps 56:8) and walks with us through it (Ps 23:4), though he hates the sin at the base of all suffering (Mal 2:16; Rev 2:6). Suffering is not inherently good.

Self-love. Self-hate is a centerpiece belief for many suicidal people with depression, who feel worthless, like a poison on the planet.[93] As much as some Christians may view self-hate (or at least self-disregard) as a Christian virtue, it is not. According to the Great Commandment, Christians are to love themselves as much as they love their neighbors (Mt 22:37-39). Beck and Demarest specify:

> Does self-denial as taught by Jesus require us to hate ourselves? (See Matthew 16:21-28 and parallel passages in Mark 8:31-38 and Luke 9:21-27.) Does Jesus literally require of His disciples that they hate their own lives? (See Luke 14:25-27.) Is God honored when we regard ourselves with loathing and disparagement? The answer to each of these questions is an unqualified no. . . . The three self-denial passages in the Gospels come in the context of warnings Jesus was giving His disciples about His upcoming death in Jerusalem. Jesus warned them that they too needed to be prepared to take up a cross and follow him by denying themselves (giving up their own personal agenda for their lives and becoming cross-bearing followers of Jesus).[94]

Pastoral caregivers need to teach a full perspective on appropriate self-love.

The truth in love. As we intervene with a suicidal person, it can be easy to lapse into platitudes: "Don't worry. It'll get better. God is in control." Platitudes are trite statements, true in one sense. God is sovereign and suicidality ebbs and flows. But platitudes don't acknowledge the real suffering of a suicidal person. Job replied to his friends, who were full of platitudes, "Do you think that you can reprove words, as if the speech of the desperate were wind?" (Job 6:26). Pastors, chaplains and pastoral counselors need to speak the truth, inviting their parishioners gently into Christian disciplines without offering simplistic solutions or judgment. Townsend calls platitudes "easy answers" that "often alienate a depressed person who cannot make the 'magic' work."[95] Pastoral caregivers should avoid simplistic beliefs that may crumple like a house of cards.

Summary

Sam, Jack, Jill, David, Linda and Beatrice all need pastoral care. They need pastors, chaplains and pastoral counselors to be gatekeepers, recognizing their various levels of suicide risk and connecting them to other professionals. They also need the vital spiritual interventions of prayer, opportunities for belonging and meaningful service, and teaching about hope, suffering and appropriate self-love.

But what do pastoral caregivers do for someone who has attempted suicide? How do pastors, chaplains and pastoral counselors evaluate how serious an attempt is? How do they help prevent future attempts? We'll take up these questions in the next chapter.

Discussion Questions

1. How confident do you feel about being a gatekeeper—identifying suicidal people and getting them help? How could you increase your level of confidence in this role?

2. Have you ever talked to a suicidal person? What happened?

3. What would you put in a hope kit?

4. Which would you use to prevent suicide: a safety plan, a no-suicide contract or both?

Resources

P. G. Quinnett, *Counseling Suicidal People: A Therapy of Hope*, 3rd ed. (Spokane, WA: QPR Institute, 2009).

Gatekeeper Trainings
- ASIST (Applied Suicide Intervention Skills Training), www.livingworks.net.
- Connect Suicide Prevention Project, www.theconnectprogram.org.
- QPR (Question, Persuade and Refer), www.qprinstitute.com.

6

HELPING A SURVIVOR
OF ATTEMPTED SUICIDE

*When I first awoke in intensive care in the hospital
near my home I thought to myself, It didn't work.
I can't even kill myself right.*

A PERSON WHO ATTEMPTED SUICIDE,
AS REPORTED BY EDWIN S. SHNEIDMAN

Albert Alvarez attempted suicide. When he did not die, he felt disappointed, cheated and ashamed.[1] It is undeniable that "an attempted suicide is a deeply emotional event."[2] Everyone involved, from the survivor of the attempt to the pastor, chaplain or pastoral counselor, is profoundly affected. Seven steps may help us as we come alongside those who have attempted suicide.

STEP 1: PROCESSING OUR FEELINGS

One of the first steps we need to take in helping a suicide attempt survivor is to recognize our own feelings about the attempt. If we are unaware of our feelings or leave them unprocessed, they may come out in unhelpful ways. For example, when Iris attempted suicide for the second time, her pastor felt anger toward her and never found the time to visit her in the hospital. When Bob attempted suicide, his pastoral counselor (whose mother had attempted suicide) became so anxious that he began calling Bob daily, even after the crisis had passed. Awareness of our feelings and the effort to manage them will allow us to be more helpful to an attempt survivor. There are four types of feelings we may experience.

Guilt. Caregivers may feel guilty of being human, unable to control another person's choices, of not being clairvoyant. We may unreasonably hold ourselves responsible for not having picked up on warning signs, whether or not the person wanted to share her pain, and whether or not he invited our influence over his choice.

Some might take refuge in the belief that anyone would attempt suicide under the same circumstances, a perspective that may grow out of guilt that a suicide attempt happened "on our watch." This is a myth because many people suffer through terrible trauma without attempting suicide. A complex interplay of elements affects a person's decision to take his life, not just circumstances and not just our actions.[3]

Anxiety and worry. We may feel anxiety after someone's suicide attempt. We may constantly worry that we may not be so "lucky" next time. Our thoughts and our sleep may be uneasy.

Feeling overwhelmed and burdened. Pastoral caregivers shoulder heavy helping roles, which can feel overwhelming and burdensome at times. One pastor my team interviewed expressed these sentiments well: "How do you regroup . . . when you engage a lot of suffering? And particularly when you don't feel like you're making much progress against the suffering?"[4] Pastors we interviewed told us that self-care strategies such as practicing faith, participating in supportive relationships, engaging in recreation, setting boundaries, taking time for reflection and having a counselor were all helpful approaches. If we find that self-care is inadequate to balance out our profound engagement with human suffering, we would do well to increase our level of collaboration with other professional caregivers or seek support ourselves.

Anger or outrage. In interviews, clergy have described emotional reactions to suicidal people that include "anger, frustration, fear, grief, or feeling overwhelmed."[5] A suicide attempt can seem like a personal rejection of all the help we have poured into a person, which can make us feel angry. We might also feel outrage that this person has made a choice we think is incomprehensible, as when a person attempts suicide with children at home. A trusted person can help us process these emotions.

STEP 2: RESPONDING TO THE FEELINGS OF THE PERSON WHO ATTEMPTED SUICIDE

Attempt survivors are flooded with a confusing mix of emotions. We'll discuss three types.

Mixed feelings. Survivors of a suicide attempt can simultaneously experience both relief and a sense of failure. Ambivalence is the common cognitive state of suicidal people.[6] A part of a suicidal person wants to die but another part wants to live. For example, Susan Rose Blauner writes, "Every time I overdosed I eventually picked up the phone and called for help because my feelings changed. I started to feel afraid; the suicidal thought passed, and I no longer wanted to die."[7]

Therefore, the part of a suicidal person that wanted to live may feel relieved. The part that wanted to die may feel like a failure.[8] It's important for pastoral caregivers to be able to listen to this confusing mix of feelings. It helps to realize that everyone experiences opposite feelings at times, like "love-hate" feelings toward one's job. It's human to experience opposite feelings; understanding this can help us listen to the ambivalence of the attempt survivor.

Guilt. Some Christians believe they are beyond God's acceptance and forgiveness for their suicidal thinking and their attempt. William Cowper, an eighteenth-century poet and hymnodist, believed after his suicide attempts that he was beyond God's forgiveness.[9] "[Cowper] felt a contempt for himself not to be expressed or imagined. Whenever he went into the street, it seemed as if every eye flashed upon him with indignation and scorn. He felt as if he had offended God so deeply that his guilt could never be forgiven, and his whole heart was filled with pangs of tumultuous despair."[10] Cowper's pastor, Rev. Martin Madan, sat by his bedside and shared repeatedly about Jesus' forgiveness. It is said that because of Madan's ministry, "some hope dawned in the heart of the sufferer, and the wounded spirit within him, though by no means healed, was less troubled."[11] William Cowper needed to hear about God's forgiveness (Ps 103:10-12).

God's forgiveness is on display in our own nonjudgment. Christians ought not judge others (Mt 7:1). Let's remember that God works only through weak, sinful instruments. Clemons writes, "God was able to use an attempted suicide [Jonah] as the means of accomplishing a great salvific task and revealing a profound theological truth."[12]

Weakness. Many people believe they should be able to handle life's problems on their own.[13] As a result, a person who has attempted suicide might be filled with self-disgust: "How could I let myself get to that point?" Like the imperceptible change a frog experiences in a slowly heating water bath, so the descent into suicidal thinking can be slow and hard to perceive.

An attempt survivor may feel vulnerable that his "weakness" and "inability" to manage pain has been exposed. For men this can be particularly difficult. Canetto has argued that the reason men use firearms and die by suicide more than women is that to do otherwise would appear weak and unmasculine.[14] An alternate perspective is that it is not weak to be human and to reach out to others for help (Gen 2:18; Eccles 4:8-12; Prov 15:22, 23, 31-32).

These feelings can be confusing both to the caregiver and the survivor. Knowing that they are typical can help us avoid the temptation to tell the person to "stop feeling that way!" It's important to accept the feelings of the person who attempted suicide as valid and then to gently invite him or her into an alternate perspective. There is a vast difference between these two approaches: (1) telling Carol to stop feeling like a failure, and (2) listening to Betty's feeling of failure, accepting failure as a valid emotion, and gently inviting her to lean into hope. Here are examples of both types of responses.

"Stop feeling that way!"

CAROL: I failed. I can't even kill myself.

CAREGIVER: What do you mean you failed? You're talking like a crazy person. No one wanted you to die. How can you say that?

CAROL: I don't know. I just feel like that. I don't know why.

CAREGIVER: Well, stop it. Everyone is just so relieved that you pulled through. And you should feel relieved too.

CAROL (unconvincingly): OK.

Gentle invitation into a new perspective

BETTY: I failed. I can't even kill myself.

PASTORAL COUNSELOR: Pulling through feels like a failure?

BETTY: Yes. I so badly wanted to die, to escape the pain. Now I still have to face all of it.

PASTORAL COUNSELOR: Your pain didn't go away.

BETTY: Right.

PASTORAL COUNSELOR: Some people who attempt suicide feel a sense of failure but also a sense of relief. Do you feel any relief?

BETTY: A little. A small part of me feels a little relieved, but not much.

PASTORAL COUNSELOR: Not much. Would that little part of you want to find some hope?

BETTY: Maybe.

PASTORAL COUNSELOR: What if we problem-solved some of the things that are causing you pain—would that help?

We may also be tempted to tell an attempt survivor that she was being manipulative or selfishly trying to get attention. Most people who attempt or die by suicide are suffering from intense psychological pain from which they want to escape—not selfishly, but because they have convinced themselves that others would be better off without them, that their death would be a "blessing to others."[15] It's difficult but important to hear this perspective.

PASTOR: When you attempted suicide, your kids were in the next room. What was going on for you?

MARY: I just felt like such a bad mom, like my kids would be better off without me.

PASTOR: You felt it would be in their best interests for you to die? Do you still feel that way?

MARY: Yes, to some extent. They are such great kids and they deserve a healthy mom.

PASTOR: They are great kids, but I don't agree suicide is the solution.

Would you be willing to read a book about a child who lost his mother to suicide?

MARY: Well, I'm not sure I want to, but there are books like that?

We may also be tempted after a suicide attempt to scrutinize or dissect the survivor's every word for underlying suicidal messages. Don't stop scrutinizing; attempt survivors are now at greater risk for suicide, so it's important to remain vigilant. But we also need to be aware that the person who attempted may feel that he or she is living in a fishbowl of negative assumptions and expectations. We need also to know that a parent who attempts suicide with her children in the house may be investigated by social services.

YOUTH PASTOR: You had an unspoken request during prayer time. Is there anything you want to talk about?

MAX: No, it's unspoken.

YOUTH PASTOR: Are you feeling suicidal?

MAX: Why does everyone think I'm going to try to attempt again? That was last year.

YOUTH PASTOR: Does it feel like you're living in a fishbowl? Like everyone is checking up on you?

MAX: I can't sneeze without my mom wondering if I'm going to attempt suicide!

YOUTH PASTOR: You have a lot of people who care about you.

In this scenario, Max and his youth pastor were able to process the increased scrutiny.

STEP 3: DETERMINING WHETHER THIS WAS A SUICIDE ATTEMPT

After processing feelings, decide if this was indeed a suicide attempt. Some suicidal behaviors are not attempts. By definition, a suicide attempt involves self-inflicted injury with some evidence of intent to die but is nonfatal.[16] What makes a suicide act an attempt is the intent to die, not the physical damage that occurred. The potential for physical injury, the injury itself or the medical lethality of the act (which refers to the likelihood that the injury will result in death) does not determine whether an act was a suicide attempt. Here are several examples of suicidal behaviors; the first two are suicide attempts.

Suicide attempt: High medical lethality with nonfatal injury, with clear intent to die. Larry had been unemployed for seven months and became depressed. When his wife and children were away visiting relatives, he purchased a handgun, leaving a suicide note on the kitchen counter and a note on the door to call 911, warning visitors against going into the house. A neighbor heard the gunshot, came to the door and called 911. Larry survived and feels both disappointment and relief.

Suicide attempt: Low medical lethality with nonfatal injury, with clear intent to die. When Louise told her boyfriend she was pregnant, he broke up with her. She told her friend Denise that she was too nervous to tell her parents and then swallowed five of Denise's mother's anti-anxiety pills on impulse. Denise called 911. Louise says she wanted to die but she is relieved she didn't.

Undetermined suicide-related behavior: Low medical lethality with no injury, with unclear intent to die. Sally had yet another fight with her husband of thirty years. She felt hurt. She alternated between ignoring him and snapping at him. When he drove off, she took four sleeping pills. When she woke up, she said she wasn't sure she meant to attempt suicide and she would never kill herself because of her Christian beliefs.

Sally engaged in suicidal behaviors to try to communicate to her husband, "How could you leave me?" It may be that Sally's intent to die was masked by her desire to get back at her husband for driving off.[17] While her behaviors might not qualify as a suicide attempt, they should be taken seriously because Sally's intent to die may emerge.

Self-harm: Low medical lethality with no injury, with no intent to die. Julie cuts her fingers with razor blades whenever she is upset because it calms her. The pain reminds her that she is still alive. When her youth pastor asks her about the bandages, she denies any thoughts of suicide or intent to die. Self-mutilation, burning or cutting is not usually a suicide attempt. Where suicide is an escape from pain, self-mutilation is usually a way of managing pain, many times without intent to die.[18]

Keep in mind, however, that people who self-mutilate and people who attempt suicide aren't mutually exclusive groups of people. Some people who self-mutilate also intend to die.[19] It's best to ask the person if she has suicidal thoughts or wants to die.[20]

CHAPLAIN: You cut your arm. Did you expect you would die?

BARB: Yes. I thought I would.

CHAPLAIN: You survived. Do you still want to die?

BARB: It's funny, but the minute I started losing consciousness, I wanted to live. But I thought it was too late.

STEP 4: TAKING THE ATTEMPT SERIOUSLY

A prevalent myth is that people attempt suicide to get attention and should be ignored like a two-year-old having a tantrum. However, suicide attempts should always be taken seriously, not only because people intend to die but also because

- People who attempt may attempt again.[21]

- With each attempt, a person develops greater ability to harm herself using increasingly more lethal methods.[22]

- Individuals who have made a previous suicide attempt are thirty-eight to forty times more likely to die eventually by suicide than would be expected otherwise.[23] A prior suicide attempt is the single strongest risk factor for death by suicide.[24] This is also true for adolescents.[25]

Though most people attempt suicide multiple times before dying, groups differ.[26] Among young adults ages 15 to 24 years old, there is one suicide for every one hundred to two hundred attempts, but among adults ages 65 years and older, there is one suicide for every four attempts.[27] Women attempt more than men.[28] In other words, older adults and men make fewer attempts before dying by suicide.

After one attempt, a person has crossed a threshold into a "a highly vulnerable group with an excessive suicidal risk."[29] Even if this is the survivor's hundredth attempt, take it seriously. Fortunately, suicide is not inevitable after an attempt.[30] In a study that followed 3,690 people who attempted suicide for ten years, 28.1 percent of those who had been admitted for a suicide attempt were readmitted for a further nonfatal suicide attempt, and 4.6 percent died by suicide.[31] Because we can't predict what any person will do, take all attempts seriously.

Suicide threats. Should threats be taken seriously too? Someone might say, "If I don't get that job, I'll have to kill myself!" We all know some threats aren't serious. Other threats obviously are serious. Some threats, though, are hard to figure out. Wilkerson tells the story of a 15-year-old young woman who told her parents, "I had nothing left to live for and was going to kill myself. They laughed. They said it was just puppy love and someone else would come along to take his place. My minister told me it takes time to heal a broken heart." When Wilkerson tried to contact this young woman, his letter was returned with this note on the back: "Send no more mail. Janet is no longer with us. She took her life."[32] This story illustrates the need to take talk of suicide seriously. The default should be to take threats seriously, even when a person has threatened multiple times. A suicide threat requires a focus on the person's safety.

> **BART**: Well, I'll just kill myself!
>
> **PASTOR**: Are you saying that if I don't meet with you now you'll kill yourself?
>
> **BART**: Yeah. You can reorganize your schedule. I need your help.
>
> **PASTOR**: If you are going to kill yourself, I will need to take steps to get you to the emergency room. Shall we get that process started?
>
> **BART**: No, I just want to meet with you.
>
> **PASTOR**: As I said, I have a funeral today and can't meet with you but I could meet with you tomorrow.
>
> **BART**: OK, what time?
>
> **PASTOR**: We can meet at 8:30 a.m. Can you keep yourself safe till then?
>
> **BART**: Yes.
>
> **PASTOR**: OK, what will you do to keep yourself safe till then?
>
> **BART**: I have my safety plan on the fridge and my hope kit.

Step 5: Understanding the Seriousness of the Attempt

No matter how serious or seemingly trivial, all suicide attempts should be taken seriously because people who intend to die are more likely to attempt again—and thus more likely to die.[33] But because some people aren't forthcoming about their intent to die, we might need to examine the circumstances surrounding the attempt, which can inform us about the risk of a reattempt. We might expect medical injury or lethality to help in the determination. Surprisingly, medical lethality is not always related to suicidal intent.[34] Some people want to die but don't know how to do it. And some people injure themselves without intending to die. Williams summarizes circumstances that inform levels of risk.[35] People with greater intent

- Choose to harm themselves in a place away from people
- Time the act so that intervention is unlikely
- Take precautions against discovery
- Are less likely to have second thoughts and do something to get help during or after the attempt
- Prepare for death, such as writing a will
- Write a suicide note
- Take action they believe will kill them
- Intend to die
- Premeditate the act
- Are sorry to have recovered[36]

Even if only one of these criteria is met, the attempt should be taken seriously.

Step 6: Hospitalization

If you discover that a person has attempted suicide or meets even one of the criteria above, and if the person is not yet at a hospital, that person needs to be evaluated in the emergency department immediately. This is not the moment for anything but a focus on safety. The primary decision at this point is whether a family member or friend can drive the suicidal person to the emergency department and can be trusted to get there or whether an ambulance or the police will need to take the person to the hospital.[37]

After the attempt survivor is checked in, there will be an evaluation. Unfortunately, the wait time can be long because emergency departments tend to be overcrowded. Often there is a medical evaluation, then usually a suicide risk evaluation and finally a decision or disposition.[38] In some cases, the person who attempted will have sat for hours in the emergency department and no longer intends to kill herself, because suicidal thinking and intent fluctuates. In these cases the person may not be hospitalized.

Voluntary vs. involuntary hospitalization. The emergency department's decision might be to hospitalize and, depending on state law, the person who attempted will be offered voluntary hospitalization first. A voluntary hospitalization means the person is admitted but can leave when he wants. If the evaluator does not believe that the person can be safe with a voluntary hospitalization or if he refuses voluntary hospitalization, the person may be involuntarily hospitalized. An involuntary hospitalization means the person is admitted to a locked unit from which he can't leave. In many states, involuntary hospitalization can't exceed seventy-two hours without ongoing reviews by a psychiatrist. If the disposition is hospitalization and the emergency department isn't connected to a hospital or the hospital doesn't have available beds, it can take several hours to be transferred.[39] All of this waiting can be frustrating for the attempt survivor and for pastoral caregivers.

In the hospital. We might be surprised to learn that hospitalization doesn't prevent suicide in all cases.[40] About 3 to 10 percent of suicide deaths in the United States occur in the hospital.[41] One research team in England and Wales that studied 2,177 suicides found that 358 (16 percent) were psychiatric inpatients at the time of death, 21 percent of whom were under special observation in the hospital.[42] Hospitalized people who kill themselves might look "normal" just before suicide; they may deny suicidal thinking or plans right before suicide and seem to the medical staff like they're clinically improved.[43]

If we suspect that a hospitalized person is not safe, we should tell the hospital staff. After Kenneth Nally died by suicide, his parents filed a wrongful death action against Grace Community Church of the Valley. While the California Supreme Court ruled in 1988 in favor of the church and refused to impose a duty on pastoral counselors to refer suicidal people to appropriate medical care, it behooves pastors to do so—not as a duty but as a suicide prevention measure. This short note appears in the court record: "On the afternoon of March 12, Pastors MacArthur and Rea visited Nally at the hospital. Nally, who was still drowsy from the drug overdose, separately told both pastors that he was sorry he did not succeed in committing suicide. Apparently, MacArthur and Rea assumed the entire hospital staff was aware of Nally's unstable mental condition, and they did not discuss Nally's death-wish comment with anyone else."[44]

Though hospitals don't guarantee safety, the hospital is the safest place for an attempt survivor because hospitals prevent access to suicide means. Hospital personnel typically go through a person's belongings at admission, removing anything dangerous. Suicide attempts tend to be impulsive even though people think about the act for a long time. Not having the means available gives people the opportunity to choose life.[45]

Hospitalization goals. The primary goal during a hospitalization is stabilization. The hospital team wants to help the person to resolve their intent to die. The team usually wants to identify and address the trigger to the attempt. The hospital staff might begin treatment, such as family meetings or medication. The choice to begin medication will depend on the presence of an underlying mental health disorder such as depression. Medications will be locked up and closely monitored because some people's suicide attempt method of choice is overdose on medication.[46]

Pastoral goals. Pastoral caregivers provide critical resources during hospitalization.

Spiritual resources. To cope with suicidal thinking, people rely more frequently on family, friends, peers and faith as sources of hope and support than on mental health professionals.[47] One pastor my team interviewed said it well: "The church itself has enormous healing resources.... [It's important] to see those in partnership with whatever medical and psychological resources."[48]

Involvement. It's hard to contact a parishioner in the hospital because (1) hospital stays are brief, (2) hospital staff members are bound by confidentiality, (3) the patient phone on the unit is often busy, and (4) hospitalized patients are often in treatment sessions. Despite these challenges, persevere. One of my clients felt deserted when she never heard from me. Visits are appreciated, especially brief ones. Greene-McCreight writes, "Visitation should be kept to a maximum of ten to fifteen minutes. . . . While people may think that the hospital is a boring place and that the patient needs conversation, in fact hospitals can be exhausting."[49]

Means restriction. During hospitalization someone close to the individual can go through the attempt survivor's home and remove all means, including medications, razor blades, guns, rope and alcohol.[50] Firearms can be left with local police departments. Means restriction is an effective way to prevent suicide because a person is typically ambivalent about dying, so one small delay allows the reasons to live to emerge; most people do not substitute other methods.[51]

While hospitalization is crucial in helping prevent suicide, stays are short (twenty-four to seventy-two hours), often because of insurance limits and state laws governing involuntary hospitalization. Hospital staff will make recommendations, because much of the work will continue outside the hospital on an outpatient basis.

Discharge. The primary goal after discharge is to help prevent future attempts. To accomplish this goal, an attempt survivor needs help—lots of it, and more than she previously was receiving. Though this may mean meeting with the survivor more often, it usually also means involving more caregivers. If you have been providing spiritual guidance only, the individual will most likely be referred for mental health treatment. If you have been providing counseling, the hospital staff may refer the individual for partial hospitalization or day treatment after discharge. The attempt survivor needs more care.

The main reason for an increase in services is that the period right after discharge is a highly risky time.[52] The research team in England and Wales mentioned earlier found that 519 (24 percent) of the 2,177 suicides they studied occurred within three months of hospital discharge, the highest number occurring in the first week after discharge. Most people who died by suicide were thought to have been at no or low immediate risk at the final contact.[53] Another research team followed 3,690 people who had been hospitalized for a suicide attempt and found that while the risk of reattempt remained high for ten years, the risk is greatest in the first two years after discharge.[54]

Jamison suggests a possible reason for this increase in risk: "Often caught in the dilemma of being too well to be in the hospital but not well enough to deal with the realities and stresses of life outside, as well as having to contend with the personal and economic consequences of having a serious mental illness, patients sometimes feel utterly hopeless and overwhelmed, and kill themselves."[55] Pastoral and mental health care can help a person manage the realities and stresses of life outside the hospital.

Mental health care. Mental health care is crucial because it's a known way to prevent suicide. Welu demonstrated a significant reduction in suicide reattempts associated with increased mental health treatment after a suicide attempt.[56] In fact, hospitals don't usually discharge unless the attempt survivor has an outpatient mental health appointment "within 48 hours if possible, but always within a week."[57] The problem is that only 20 to 40 percent of individuals who attempt suicide follow through with outpatient treatment after discharge from the hospital.[58] Collaborating with the hospital to make sure the follow-through happens is vital. Though some people are more motivated to get help at this time, follow-up with mental health treatment can be challenging, especially for young people who want nothing to do with treatment and the stigma of being different.[59] Of adolescent attempters, 50 percent fail to receive follow-up mental health treatment.[60]

One reason it's crucial to make sure follow-up happens is that some people stop taking their medication after discharge.[61] People stop because it can take many weeks before medication attains full efficacy and they don't think it's working, or because the medication helps and the attempter thinks she no longer needs the medicine.[62] Mental health care increases compliance with medication.[63]

Step 7: Ongoing Pastoral Care

Pastoral caregivers can come alongside someone who has attempted suicide not just during the crisis but in the long term as well.

Monitoring. Part of ongoing pastoral care is monitoring medication and substance use. This may feel intrusive, but medication can be an important part of treatment and can also be used to reattempt suicide. Alcohol and illegal drug use can undermine the effectiveness of psychiatric medication and can worsen sleep, impair judgment and increase risk for another attempt. Here's an example of what this monitoring might be like:

Youth pastor: I think it's been a month since you were in the hospital. You seem a bit down. How are you doing?

Abby: I'm doing OK.

Youth pastor: When you were in the hospital, they started you on an antidepressant. Are you still taking that?

Abby: I stopped taking it after a week. I started to feel better.

Youth pastor: Do you have the pills at home?

Abby: Yes, I'm keeping them for when I might need them.

Youth pastor: That concerns me. Have you talked to your mom about this?

Abby: No. I don't want to make a big deal out of this.

Youth pastor: Medications are serious business. Let's call your mom.

Abby: No! Don't do that. She has enough to worry about. You never told me you were going to tell my mom!

Youth pastor: I'm not going to tell your mom everything we talk about but some things are serious. Your mom would want to know. Let's call your mom together.

Abby (reluctantly): OK.

If pastoral caregivers are concerned about a treatment issue, they can contact the treating professional despite confidentiality laws such as HIPAA.[64] Generally speaking, all health information is confidential unless an adult patient or parent or guardian of a minor authorizes its release by signing a release of information form. (See your state laws for situations that mandate a professional to break confidentiality.) But because clergy aren't usually under HIPAA law, they can provide information to other professionals—even if those professionals are unable to provide information back to clergy.[65] For example, if a pastor alerted a psychiatrist about his concern surrounding a person's medication, the prescriber could prescribe another medication, or smaller quantities in order to prevent an overdose, without necessarily informing the pastor she had done so.

Suicide prevention measures. All attempt survivors need a safety plan and a hope kit in the case of relapse. Also, we need to increase support and belongingness. This may be particularly important for older white men. Joiner writes, "It is the tendency of [older white men] in particular not to replenish their social connectedness as they age. US men in general and white men in particular seem to form some close friendships in childhood and early and late adolescence, but the forming of new and deep friendships in adulthood is relatively rare."[66] In addition, we need to continue to build the person's faith, which protects against suicide and provides hope and reasons for living.[67]

Instilling courage. One Christian discipline we don't hear much about is courage. But the Christian life requires courage (Josh 1:6-7; Ps 27:14; 31:24). Think about the many courageous things we pastoral caregivers have done in our lives: learning to preach when public speaking was petrifying, facing a conflict when we wanted to avoid it or standing up for an unpopular opinion. Survivors of a suicide attempt need the courage to face their pain. After an attempt, that person is again facing the painful life from which she was trying to escape.[68]

CHAPLAIN: You've been waiting for God to cure your cancer, and when you lost hope, you attempted to kill yourself.

DINAH: Yeah, I think I just gave up.

CHAPLAIN: It seemed like God wasn't doing anything?

DINAH: Yeah. I just couldn't take it anymore.

CHAPLAIN: And is that how you see it now?

DINAH: Well, I still wonder if God is doing anything. I'm still not cured.

CHAPLAIN: I don't know what God has in mind but I know that his people have been wondering at his slowness for a long time.

DINAH: So is that supposed to give me hope?

CHAPLAIN: Hope and courage to face the difficulties of life.

DINAH: Courage isn't something I've thought about.

CHAPLAIN: Dinah, have you ever been courageous, like standing up for something you believed in?

DINAH: Well, I did have to go speak to my son's teacher when he was being treated unfairly. That took a lot of courage!

CHAPLAIN: Absolutely. Tell me about another time you were courageous.

Problem-solving. Attempt survivors also need help with solving their problems.[69] Suicidal people have limited problem-solving abilities—an inability to see any solution other than suicide.[70]

CHAPLAIN: So your husband's criticism is a problem.

DINAH: Yes, he can't seem to find anything good about me.

CHAPLAIN: Do you ever stand up to him? And is it safe for you to do that?

DINAH: I did once and it seemed to help. He has never hit me.

CHAPLAIN: You said you were able to stand up to your son's teacher, do you think you could stand up to your husband more often?

DINAH: I'm not sure I could do that. I've only done it once before.

CHAPLAIN: At the hospital here we have a class on assertiveness. Would it help to practice?

DINAH: Well, I suppose. I don't really like groups.

CHAPLAIN: You could go to one group and see what it's like. Maybe going once would give you some ideas.

DINAH: OK, I'll try it once.

Problem-solving can also include referring a husband and wife for couples counseling or a youth and his parents for family counseling to reduce conflict. And as the church would in any crisis or hospitalization, offer help with the basics, such as food, laundry or childcare.

SUMMARY

Coming alongside suicide attempt survivors requires that pastoral caregivers process their own emotions in order to be available to process the survivor's emotions. Providing pastoral care means taking an attempt seriously and supporting engagement in mental health services while also helping the survivor to reflect theologically on courage and build problem-solving skills.

In addition to concern for the attempt survivor, pastors, chaplains and pastoral counselors must also give attention to those directly affected by the suicide attempt. Family members are the unsung heroes of the work of suicide prevention and they need our support. How can pastors, chaplains and pastoral caregivers support family members? We'll look at this next.

DISCUSSION QUESTIONS

1. What reactions would you have or have you had to a suicide attempt?

2. Give examples of ambivalent feelings such as love-hate.

3. Do you agree that all suicide attempts should be taken seriously?

4. Why can't hospitals guarantee safety? Do you agree that hospitals are the safest place for someone who has attempted suicide?

5. Why is discharge from the hospital after an attempt such a risky time?

6. How is self-mutilation different from a suicide attempt?

7. How would you deal with a person who made suicide threats or engaged in multiple attempts?

RESOURCES

Books about people who have attempted suicide

A. Alvarez, *The Savage God: A Study of Suicide* (New York: Random House, 1972).

DeQ. Lezine and D. Brent, *Eight Stories Up: An Adolescent Chooses Hope over Suicide* (New York: Oxford University Press, 2008).

T. Wise, *Waking Up: Climbing Through the Darkness* (Oxnard, CA: Pathfinder Publishing of California, 2003).

Resources for people who have attempted suicide

National Action Alliance for Suicide Prevention Suicide Attempt Survivors Task Force, http://actionallianceforsuicideprevention.org/task-force/suicide-attempt-survivors.

Suicide Anonymous, www.suicideanonymous.net.

American Association of Suicidology Suicide Attempt Survivors, www.suicidology.org/suicide-survivors/suicide-attempt-survivors.

HELPING THE HELPERS

I put people through the wringer before I finally "got it."

SUSAN ROSE BLAUNER, WHO
ATTEMPTED SUICIDE THREE TIMES

*In supporting the family of a suicidal person, we must
first recognize that they do live under constant fear.*

JOHN T. MALTSBERGER, MD;
THOMAS JOBE, MD;
REV. DAN G. STAUFFACHER, DMIN

Early in my career I worked with Hazel, who had attempted suicide several times. Her mother and sisters requested a meeting with me. I was not prepared for their intense emotions, their anger at Hazel, their frustration at feeling ineffective at helping Hazel, their fear that Hazel would kill herself, and their sense of being overwhelmed. Family members labor on behalf of suicidal people, but sometimes they get lost in the crisis. The focus tends to be on the suicidal person—as well it should be—but the family may not get the support they need. And the less help they receive, the less energy they have for helping the suicidal person. The airline safety message reminds us, "Secure your own mask first before helping others." Family members need a chance to be supported, to breathe and to regroup. These unsung heroes are especially deserving of support because they never signed up for this duty. They were drawn into it.[1]

Friends, too, get caught up in suicide prevention. For example, Styron wrote about a friend who helped him: "His support was untiring and priceless. It was he who kept admonishing me that suicide was 'unacceptable' (he had been intensely suicidal), and it was also he who made the prospect of going to the hospital less fearsomely intimidating. I still look back on his concern with immense gratitude."[2]

The other person who can get lost is you. The challenge for pastoral caregivers is that you are not only a helper; you are also a member of the community, and sometimes part of the family that is affected. This chapter is focused on caring for the caregivers. One way to care is to listen to and process the emotions of family and community members.

EMOTIONS

Emotions can affect people's thinking, memory, attention, problem solving and planning.[3] Giving people an opportunity to process their emotions is important so people can be aware of them instead of overcome by them.[4]

Guilt and blame. Families and communities want to protect their vulnerable members and can feel intense shame and guilt in the perceived failure of not being able to do so.[5] One pastor told my research team that guilt surrounding suicide is more intense than that in any other kind of crisis and the main question on caregivers' minds is, "What else could I have done?" She reminds them, "If you could have done something to prevent it, you would have."[6] This pastor's advice reminds us that we can help prevent a suicide crisis, but the ultimate choice belongs to the suicidal person. Helpers take the responsibility to care but they are not to blame for the person's choices. Help others be a fair judge of themselves—to take responsibility to care but not for the other person's choice.

Because these emotions are intense, some people manage their distress by blaming others. Blame is not helpful. One priest point-blank told his congregation during a suicide funeral, "You will not judge this family." Resist the urge to assign blame. Help family and community members on the receiving end of blame to remember that not everyone is going to be able to help them, not everyone can be a skilled helper for them. They need to choose carefully those who will walk with them on their journey. Pastors, chaplains and pastoral counselors need to help a faith community negotiate the dangerous quicksand of blame so that family and community members stay connected to the faith community. Help the community avoid blame because "a poor or troubled relationship with one's pastor or congregation correlates significantly with lower ability to cope with life stressors."[7]

Fear and powerlessness. Constant fear that a loved one will re-attempt and die by suicide—and feeling powerless to prevent it—are central emotions of family and community members. One pastor told my research team about two mothers to whom she provided care.

> With both of the moms who had teenage boys was this huge burden just feeling such love for their child and this deep, deep desire to protect them at all costs and this deep feeling of helplessness, just wanting to talk about that horrible feeling of helplessness. How to know when they have done enough, because they never felt like they did enough. And the mom whose son did kill himself . . . that was her greatest fear in life [that her son would die by suicide.] . . . I didn't get asked questions about hell . . . it was more what will I do? Or how do I manage this burden, how do I figure out the right thing to do?[8]

This pastor provided these two mothers with hours of listening. Susan Rose Blauner's companion wrote about her suicide attempts, "What comes back to me now is how powerless I felt."[9]

Hostility. Susan Rose Blauner's sister-in-law writes, "I began to sense a barrier between us. I felt awkward and ineffective, not knowing what to say or how to respond. Also at this time I experienced some hostility toward you. I could see the effects your condition had on my husband, whom I love deeply. I was angry at you for causing him so much anxiety and stress. Being a parent, I could identify with the anguish your father felt."[10] Family and community members can feel overburdened to the point of feeling angry and hostile.

Pastoral caregivers are called to listen to and process these intense reactions caregivers experience. In addition, pastors, chaplains and pastoral counselors can support caregivers in providing care to their family or community member.

Supporting Family and Community Members

Family and other helpers own many tasks following a suicide attempt, and pastoral caregivers can support them in these tasks.

Follow through on treatment. Some helpers might be tempted not to follow through with mental health treatment after a suicide crisis. They may say, "Maria learned her lesson. She won't do it again. I don't have time to take her [to therapy]."[11] Research tells us that many people like Maria never attend any follow-up sessions and fail to complete a full course of treatment.[12] We also know that it's vital that Maria get treatment in order to reduce the risk of further suicidal behavior.[13] Pastors, chaplains and pastoral counselors can help by identifying the barriers. Does Maria's mom understand how crucial follow-up treatment is? Does Maria need a ride?

Get education. One of the most important tasks for the family and community to undertake once a suicide crisis has occurred is to get education about the warning signs, especially Maria's specific signs, so they can recognize future risk.[14] The general warning signs of suicide are helpful and the mental health treatment team can provide information about specific warning signs for Maria.[15] This information is often found in the safety plan. It's important to encourage family and community members to request a copy of the safety plan because they might be part of it. Pastoral caregivers can let them know that the law allows parents and guardians of minors to obtain this information without a release of information and allows an adult patient to give written permission for the treatment team to release confidential information. Pastors, chaplains and pastoral counselors can also check to see if safety plan steps are clear, specific and include how to contact the treatment team during and after office hours. Preferably, the instructions are written and understood by all.

Pastoral caregivers can clarify for the family or community the importance of a hope kit with reasons to live.[16] Asarnow and colleagues provide this example of a hope kit, which included:

> Pictures of her friends and family (reminders that there were people who loved her and whom she loved), her journal (a cue to write in her

journal, a coping strategy on her safety plan), coping cards listing [helpful thoughts], her gym membership card (a reminder that exercise was on her safety plan), her parents' and friends' phone numbers (cues to call and seek social support), a washcloth (a cue to use the coping strategy of placing a cool washcloth on her face and focusing on the cool sensations), and the location and telephone number of the nearest emergency department (an emergency coping strategy).[17]

Knowing the appropriate warning signs will help family and friends avoid a tendency to overpathologize normal behaviors or underpathologize suicidal behaviors. Miller and colleagues have noticed that:

> Parents' judgments of what behaviors are "dangerous" or "abnormal" have become steadfastly colored by the shadow of past suicide attempts or hospitalizations. . . . [One] parent realized that kids miss school on occasion because of illness, but feared that her daughter's asking to stay home one day because of a migraine signaled a depression relapse; the previous depressive episode had begun with her daughter's finding reasons to stay home (and had ultimately led to a suicide attempt and hospitalization).[18]

When Agnes, who recently attempted suicide, wants to stay home from Bible study one night to clean her house, her friends might fear she's isolating, a precursor to suicide. But Agnes might honestly desire to catch up on some cleaning. Knowing Agnes' specific warning signs will help family and friends to negotiate this challenge.

Pastoral caregivers may need to help family members educate themselves about a school's suicide attempt policy. Help parents who are selecting a school remember not only to check into the school's graduation rate, classrooms, library and fitness center, but also into the school's suicide attempt policy. As a result of high-profile suicides occurring on college campuses and related lawsuits, colleges and universities now contend with potential liability for suicide.[19] Parents need to know this because some institutions of higher learning don't let students return to school after a visit to an emergency department or after a hospitalization. Parents should familiarize themselves with the student counseling center.[20] Developmentally, first episodes of mental health problems often emerge in young adulthood.[21] The busy lives of students can exacerbate mental health problems: some students are away from home for the first time; some experiment with alcohol and drugs and they don't sleep enough.[22] Aware parents can be proactive.

Advocate. Sometimes professionals don't communicate well together. In a study of thirty-six therapists who all lost a client to suicide, one of the issues was poor communication among the therapists themselves.[23] Family and friends need to be advocates for the treatment of their loved one and help ensure well-coordinated treatment. Also, family and community members need to provide input into treatment. Families and community members should think of themselves as consultants.[24] Family and friends know Agnes in ways that professionals never will.

Decrease conflict. A common trigger to a suicide attempt for adolescents and adults is interpersonal conflict.[25] In fact, 70 percent of suicidal adolescents report that some form of interpersonal conflict precipitated their suicidal behavior.[26] Pastors, chaplains and pastoral counselors may be asked to provide marital or family therapy to reduce conflict and therefore suicide risk. Reducing conflict may increase a sense of belonging and contribution (decreased burdensomeness), both of which Joiner believes to be bedrock human needs.[27] Pastoral caregivers want the suicidal person to know, "My family or community loves me no matter what and I am not a burden to them."

One way to increase belongingness and decrease perceived burdensomeness is to create safety in relationships. One possible goal is to encourage the identification of positive attributes of the suicidal person among family members or the spouse to remind them of the love they feel for the individual.[28] Another goal is to develop a sense of nonjudgmental empathy for the pain that drives the desire for suicide.[29] It may be that parents or spouses who were not validated themselves by their caretakers never learned to validate their children's or spouse's emotional displays.[30] Blauner gives this advice:

> Whenever you feel exasperated by the situation (and you will), try to remember that the suicidal thinker is living on an internal battlefield in addition to navigating everyday stress. . . . The goal is to accept the

suicidal thinker—suicidal thoughts and all—rather than judge or try to fix him. What you can offer is non-judgmental compassion as he stumbles down the road to freedom. You can be there when he trips and falls, and when he finds relief. You can embrace him with out-stretched arms, saying, "I love you. I am here for you." As long as he isn't hurting himself or anyone else, let him fumble his way into the light without trying to convert him to your way of thinking; each per-son's reality is different.[31]

Help family and community members to expect ups and downs, improvements and setbacks. Help them stay connected especially when there is no suicide crisis so that having a crisis doesn't reinforce the idea that the only way to get a family's or community's attention is to have a suicide crisis.

One key strategy is to help the family or community develop direct communication in a way that avoids escalation. Escalation occurs when the discussion begins small—about putting dishes in the dish-washer, for example—and ends up big—about running away or suicide. An effective approach to preventing escalation is using the speaker-listener technique, which is a structured way to commu-nicate safely and clearly.[32] This technique involves taking turns be-tween being the speaker who talks and the listener who reflects back the speaker's meaning. This technique is used in marital counseling and has been adapted for use in a variety of human relationships, including parenting.[33]

One of the questions I am asked by parents most is whether to dis-cipline their suicidal child and continue to hold him or her to the house rules. Every child needs limits. However, as with all good par-enting, leniency and authoritarianism need to be balanced.[34] Leniency is what happens when parents are held hostage by the child's suicid-ality. "I know the stakes are too high if I say no and get her angry, so I just let her stay home from school."[35] Or "I feel like I'm always walking on eggshells, so I let him go out with his friends until all hours, because it's better than the consequences of telling him he can't go."[36]

Authoritarianism is swinging to the opposite end. "You are grounded till the end of the school year."[37] Or "You'll have to move out of the house this minute." One approach that balances these two extremes is called authoritative parenting.[38] Help parents enforce reasonable limits and allow reasonable freedoms, keeping in mind that children may have to earn back their parent's trust.[39] Parents need to walk the middle between keeping Sally safe and helping her to grow into a contributing member of society. One of the ways to do this is to stay focused on safety issues. Miller and colleagues provide these examples:

> SALLY: If you don't let me go to see Johnny, I'm gonna swallow these pills right now!
>
> PARENT: Oh, really? You're planning to take those pills? Do we need to get you to the emergency room? I'll call an ambulance.[40]
>
> Or,
>
> PARENT: How can we discuss such a mundane topic as visiting Johnny when your life is in danger? I'm really concerned about you. Do you think I should call an ambulance?[41]
>
> Or,
>
> PARENT: I didn't realize you were so upset! We've got to do something immediately if you are so distressed that you might kill yourself. What about hospitalization? Maybe that is needed.[42]

Help parents to focus on safety in order not to cave to suicide threats.[43]

Another matter with which pastoral caregivers can help parents is the balance between fostering dependence and forcing autonomy. Sometimes parents might jump in and solve an adolescent's problems at school, which the adolescent should learn to negotiate himself or herself. But the parent might also try to force autonomy out of frustration: "Well, then, find a way to pay for therapy yourself!" "Fine, then don't come home at all!" and "You call up the principal and explain this!"[44] It's important to help parents find a balance.

CARING FOR HELPERS: A SUMMARY

Pastors, chaplains and pastoral counselors provide necessary care to families and communities, helping them to negotiate the challenges of life with suicidality. One pastor we interviewed describes this well:

I spent a lot of time just sort of befriending [the husband of a suicidal woman] at church. I would go out of my way to include him with things at church that I was doing. I didn't really need his help at the church, but I knew he was hurting, so he would just sort of use me as a release valve with concerns about his wife . . . wondering . . . if she was ever going to be well or not. . . . He needed coping help and I think his experiences of his wife's counseling [made him say], I am not going to go to counseling. So I was the closest thing he had to a counselor. I was his, his ear.[45]

Pastoral caregivers provide a ministry of presence to family and other helpers.[46]

SUPPORTING YOURSELF: SELF-CARE IS CRUCIAL

Working with suicidal people and their family and community members without a self-care plan is a recipe for burnout. Working with people who have experienced a major tragedy can affect clergy negatively.[47] Weaver and his colleagues found that among clergy groups, "Protestant clergy had the highest overall work-related stress and were next to the lowest in personal resources to cope with the occupational strain."[48] Robert Wicks writes, "The self is limited. It has only so much energy. If it is not renewed, then depletion will take place."[49] One study of 480 caregivers found that those who worked with people with current suicidal thinking or with at least one suicide attempt in their history reported lower health scores than caregivers who did not work with people with suicidal thinking or at least one suicide attempt in their history.[50] Pastors, chaplains and pastoral counselors are at risk of burnout because they care. Wicks stipulates, "Because the seeds of burnout and the seeds of enthusiasm are in reality the same seeds, anyone who truly cares can expect that they will need to ride the waves of burnout—and occasionally get knocked down by a wave they missed."[51]

Some signs of burnout include

- Making derisive comments about people to colleagues

- Making more mistakes

- Lacking energy

- Becoming anxious or afraid

- Losing the wonder of what it means to be part of the clergy

- Using alcohol or food or pornography to manage your emotions

Read up on burnout and increase your self-care.[52] Burnout happens when self-care is not adequate to balance out your profound engagement with human suffering.[53]

Self-care is biblical. Just as God worked and then took a sabbath rest (Gen 2:2-3), so he commands us to practice sabbath rest (Ex 20:8-11) and invites us to come apart from the bustle of life (Mk 6:31). We come apart to pray, as Jesus did regularly (Lk 5:16). The Bible assumes that we love ourselves (Mt 22:39) and that we care for our bodies. Paul tells us, "After all, no one ever hated their own body, but they feed and care for their body, just as Christ does the church—for we are members of his body" (Eph 5:29-30 NIV). Paul also tells the Ephesian elders, "Keep watch over yourselves and over all the flock, of which the Holy Spirit has made you overseers" (Acts 20:28). It's biblical to pay attention to yourself, not to the detriment of others but in order to care for others.

Effective self-care needs to be individualized, so take a trial-and-error approach to find what works for you. Here is a menu of options that pastors tell us they use:

- Practicing your faith. When we asked one pastor about how he regroups after working with a suicidal person, he said, "Sometimes you don't. For me, my habit is to go into the sanctuary and pray by this large cross. We have this large cross in the sanctuary with kneelers around it. And I spend a lot of time in there."[54]

- Reducing isolation through supportive relationships.

- Maintaining your health (exercise, sleep, diet).

- Relaxing through recreation, leisure or hobbies.

- Remembering your call into your vocation.

- Reducing your load by setting boundaries; saying no. Pope and Vasquez remind us, "The focus must remain on the amount of work that we can do well, not the amount that we feel we should do, or used to be able to do, or that some of our colleagues can do."[55] Maltsberger and colleagues add, "We need to be mature enough to know what we can handle and what we cannot."[56] Ray Anderson emphasizes the need to make decisions about your ministry apart from "insatiable" human need:

> Human need is an insatiable and unforgiving slave master, as many pastors have found. Those who seek help from ministers as well as from other Christians will inevitably create a burden too great for any one person to bear. The double bind in using need to define one's ministry as a servant is complicated by the concept of a "calling," or vocation. My own sense of calling to be a minister was directly linked with a pastoral role that I understood as being available and on call for any person who had expressed need for counsel, comfort, advice, or simply a listening ear.[57]

- Regular self-debriefing. One of our pastor interviewees said, "I have to process every encounter I have and whether it's suicide or any other counseling situation or any other. Process it, trying my best to be sure that my emotions are not tied up in it."[58] Another clergy interviewee emphasizes why it's important to process meetings with suicidal people, because the next suicidal "person comes up fresh to you and expects you to relate to him or her as if you were a clean slate."[59]

- Regular debriefing with peers. One pastor we interviewed told us, "The longer I am at this job the more time I put into supervision. It's all peer supervision, but it's so important. It has become life-giving for me."[60]

- Managing your thoughts about your perceived failures. A pastor whose congregant killed herself was helped by a fellow colleague: "I had a wonderful, wonderful pastor who worked me through that, and taught me a lot about suicidal people."[61]

- Seeing a counselor. One pastor told us how he regroups: "I probably didn't regroup, which is probably not a good thing, but I know now that [some pastors] have a therapist that they will see regularly so there's the protection of accountability to make sure that they are not sinking."[62]

- Partnering with other professionals. Pastors have told us that they do not consider themselves front-line mental health workers and that their work is complementary to mental health services.[63] This healthy boundary argues for collaboration.[64] Pastors have told us that they consult with therapists in their congregation or in the community, or with lay ministers or deacons.

Self-care is important, and difficult experiences can result in growth for some people in some areas of their lives.[65] The human spirit created in the image of God is resilient and some people grow through challenge. In the field of psychology, this is called posttraumatic growth.[66] It can result in a renewed appreciation for life, new possibilities, enhanced personal strength, improved relationships with others and spiritual change.[67]

SUMMARY

After a suicide attempt, family and community members—including pastoral caregivers—are the unsung heroes of the work of suicide prevention, and they need support. They need to process their intense emotions and need a map to help them deal with the labyrinth of a suicide crisis. Self-care for them and for pastors, chaplains and pastoral counselors is crucial.

But what about a suicide death? Suicide death is excruciatingly hard, especially for a Christian, so how do pastoral caregivers minister to those left behind? How do pastors, chaplains and pastoral counselors minister to children survivors? We'll look at these issues next.

DISCUSSION QUESTIONS

1. How do you balance your roles of pastor, faith community member and family member?

2. How would you manage blame in a faith community? How would you help the family or community member who is being blamed stay connected to the faith community?

3. What would you say to a parent who refuses to bring her suicidal daughter to treatment for faith reasons?

4. Have you experienced burnout? What is your self-care routine? What barriers do you experience to regular self-care?

RESOURCES

D. C. Clark, *Clergy Response to Suicidal Persons and Their Family Members* (Chicago: Exploration Press, 1993).

S. D. Govig, *In the Shadow of Our Steeples: Pastoral Presence for Families Coping with Mental Illness* (Binghamton, NY: Haworth Pastoral Press, 1999).

After an Attempt: A Guide for Taking Care of Your Family Member After Treatment in the Emergency Department (Arlington, VA: U.S. Department of Health and Human Services, 2005).

PREP Inc. has numerous relationship curricula for learning effective communication: www.prepinc.com.

E. F. Torrey, *Surviving Schizophrenia: A Manual for Families, Consumers, and Providers*, 4th ed. (New York: HarperCollins, 2001).

HELPING SUICIDE SURVIVORS

We won't use terms like "victors versus victims" or other trite phrases that imply that if you have the right kind of faith, or courage, or resilience, or whatever, you should be able to rise above this trial and somehow leave it all behind.

DR. DAVID B. BIEBEL AND SUZANNE L. FOSTER

Even if there is still general disapproval of suicide on theological grounds, that should not prevent us from providing a full ministry of care to those who survive.

DR. HERBERT ANDERSON

Barbara Rubel's father, a retired New York City police officer, killed himself three weeks before she gave birth to her triplet sons.[1] She writes, "I was traumatized by this horror, this unbelievable loss."[2] All death is hard. A suicide death is excruciatingly hard.[3] Suzanne Foster, whose daughter died by suicide, writes that suicide brings with it "chaos and heartache and pain you thought would never end—hurt so intense that at times you may have considered joining your loved one."[4]

UNIQUE ATTRIBUTES OF SUICIDE

Let's review what makes a suicide death so uniquely difficult because one study found that about one third of clergy experienced a suicide death in their congregations.[5]

Shock. All deaths are characterized by shock. C. S. Lewis describes the shock of death as "like being mildly drunk, or concussed. There is a sort of invisible blanket between the world and me. I find it hard to take in what anyone says."[6] But suicide has an even larger shock effect, because it is unexpected, because it is often gruesome, especially for the person who discovers or identifies the body, and it raises innumerable unanswered questions. Jamison writes, "The core of this journey has been described as an agonizing questioning, a tendency to ask repeatedly why the suicide occurred and what its meaning should be for those who are left."[7] Fine explains, "The challenge of surviving is to mourn without understanding; with pain and grief, yes, but with the awareness that we will never know why we have been left by those we have loved."[8]

Fear. Survivors fear the next suicide, sometimes irrationally. Polly gives this example:

> Recently, a friend came over for dinner and asked to use the bathroom to wash up. She was in there for what seemed a very long time and I became convinced that she must be killing herself. I started pounding frantically on the door, certain she was dead. My friend came running out of the bathroom, looking at me as if I were crazy. . . . It happened once, and I keep waiting for it to happen again.[9]

Parents may worry that their children will kill themselves. Marie, whose husband killed himself, says, "I worry about my children. When they get upset, like teenagers do, I'm terrified that they might want to kill themselves."[10] This worry can intensify when the brother or sister reaches the age an older child in the family was when he killed himself.

Children may irrationally fear that they are doomed to suicide.[11] Catlin wrote, "If it's true [that my father and grandfather killed themselves], then I feel there's really no hope for me."[12] However, it's also important to note that some people have said that a sibling's suicide acted as a deterrent to suicide and that a parent's suicide has acted as a deterrent to their children.[13]

Investigations. Police often investigate for a possible homicide until they find evidence of suicide. And because about three-quarters of people who die by suicide don't leave a suicide note, the investigation can take time.[14] Survivors are dealing with their shock at the same time that they are being questioned as suspects. All this occurs while strangers gawk. Fine writes, "There is no dignity or privacy in suicide. The police, the [building superintendent], the dog walkers, the gawkers all found out that my husband killed himself at the same exact time it was confirmed to me."[15] Reporters may become intrusive. Iris Bolton describes her experience: "A suicide in a home is a surprise package. It is a bomb tossed through a transom, that rips your door off its hinges and admits an army of invaders including newspaper reporters, TV cameramen, the curious, the sensation seekers, cemetery salesmen, undertakers, and tombstone promoters."[16] In addition, most life insurance policies exclude suicide for a specified period after the purchase of the policy. If the suicide occurs within that specified time period, the company may investigate.

Stigma. Suicide is stigmatized. Iris Bolton, whose son died by suicide, felt that her car had a huge sign on it reading, "My son committed suicide. I am a failure."[17] Suicide is a difficult death to grieve because survivors fear being ostracized like lepers. Some people believe that suicide can taint a family or is a mark of shame. Erving Goffman states that a stigma is an undesirable attribute that makes a person different or tainted or inferior.[18] Stigma can also be a mark of shame or infamy, like a yellow Star of David, which Jews were forced to wear throughout Nazi Germany's Third Reich. Stigma can also more generally be the experience of social disapproval. Stigma can result in ostracism, such as banishing the lepers from villages in Bible times (2 Kings 7:3). To avoid that stigma, some families may try to keep the suicide a secret or keep some of the details a secret. In one study, about half of those with a relative who had died by suicide concealed the fact at least some of the time.[19] It can be exhausting to keep up the secrecy and it can be exhausting trying to remember who knows which details. The secrecy can go so far as denying suicide. Jamison gives this example:

> A colleague of mine, an eminent scientist who suffered from manic-depressive illness, killed himself a few years ago. His wife, understandably distraught, refused to believe that he had committed suicide.

She made it clear that suicide was not to be mentioned at his funeral or memorial service and, unknowingly, made it very hard for his fellow professors, graduate students, and laboratory staff to deal with his death and move on with their lives.[20]

Family and community response. People may or may not respond to a suicide death with the same level of consolation that other deaths elicit.[21] People don't know if a suicide should be dealt with differently from other deaths, and this may keep them from doing what they normally do after a death. They may respond with silence. Jerry, whose wife killed herself, wrote:

> When I came back to work after the funeral, no one even mentioned that my wife had died. Colleagues whom I had known for years would avert their eyes when they saw me; if we did talk, our conversation would be about the latest sales figures or basketball scores. I wanted to stand on my desk and scream: "My wife is dead. Please, someone, acknowledge it."[22]

Silence denies a person's life. Iris Bolton spoke these words at Julie's funeral: "Speak freely of her to her family and friends and share your remembrances with them. To speak not of her tends to deny her existence; to speak freely of her tends to affirm her life."[23]

Some family or friends may respond with blame. Gina says, "All of a sudden, it seemed as if everybody was blaming me for [my husband's] death."[24] All of the aspects of the survivor's relationship with the deceased may get dragged out and hashed over and used to apportion blame for the death. Freud wrote about a friend who hanged himself, "What drove him to it? As an explanation, the world is ready to hurl the most ghastly accusations at the unfortunate widow."[25]

Guilt. Unfortunately, some survivors accept the blame. One mother whose daughter died by suicide said, "My child's blood is on my hands."[26] Denise, a survivor whose daughter killed herself, says:

> Her death was reported in the newspaper, with the article quoting a neighbor as saying that she had heard screaming in the apartment right before my daughter jumped. I felt so exposed. The whole spotlight of my daughter's suicide immediately focused on me: What kind of

mother was I? What had I said to her to make her want to kill herself? . . . My own guilt was so immense that I accepted the judgment that my daughter's suicide meant something was wrong with me, not her.[27]

Guilt is corrosive.[28] It takes away the safety needed for grieving. Foster writes, "I was plagued by memories of times when I had been a less-than-perfect parent. I would ask myself if that particular incident was the cause of Shannon's decision [to kill herself]. I wondered what I could have done differently that could have changed the course of events. This was a continuing question. I blamed myself for her decision."[29] Guilt can be based on unrealistic expectations, such as being able to protect children from their choices. Foster adds, "What kind of mother would let these things happen to her children?"[30] Guilt can also be based on the unrealistic expectation of being omniscient: "My sister [died by suicide] after breaking up with her boyfriend. . . . The night she died, there was a message from her on my answering machine asking me to call. I was tired and decided to phone back in the morning."[31] How could this woman know omnisciently that her sister was considering suicide?

Survivor guilt. Survivor guilt is feeling that we should have been the one to die. A related feeling is guilt when we enjoy the pleasures God gives us. It can feel disloyal or like a betrayal to enjoy the life that the loved one lost. Iris Bolton describes this guilt: "If I don't feel rotten, it's like I'm betraying [his] memory."[32] As another example, a woman whose son killed himself wrote, "Emotionally, I was numb. I didn't want to be touched sexually. My husband and I had previously enjoyed a very good sexual relationship, which gave us great joy. How could I allow myself to experience joy? It was inconceivable. I remember it took months before our first failed attempt. Failed because I responded and then felt guilty for responding."[33]

Family dynamics. We assume that grief throws people together but in fact it can pull them apart. Any preexisting problem can get worse. Donald, whose wife killed herself, wrote, "It's really a myth that people pull together in a crisis. My wife's suicide exposed all the problems that already existed between me and my children."[34] Marital problems that were underground can be exposed.

Conflicted emotions. Conflicted emotions like grief and anger are common. Hsu writes, "Suicide is particularly traumatizing because we do not know how to resolve our hurt and outrage. If it had been a murder, we could grieve for the victim and vent our rage at the murderer. But in the case of suicide, the victim is the murderer. And so we are conflicted."[35]

A surprising emotion may be depression and thoughts about suicide, surprising because the suicide of the loved one is also detested. One in four siblings and one in five mothers become clinically depressed within six months of a suicide.[36] The suicide death of an adult child increases suicide risk in mothers.[37] Iris Bolton reveals she was "secretly wishing" for her own death.[38] Suicidal thinking is common among survivors.[39] Death offers a way out of the pain.[40] It is reassuring to know that having those thoughts does not mean the survivor will act on them. If the survivor begins to think about her own suicide, help her seek mental health services.[41]

SUICIDE AND CHRISTIAN SURVIVORS

Surviving suicide is indeed a complex journey, one that is different from other types of grieving, and especially for Christians.

Why, God? A suicide death can be even more excruciating for a Christian because all the whys are also directed to God. Foster writes:

> Surely a good God wouldn't allow such a thing to happen. How could he? Children don't die before their parents; it's not right. Didn't he know that Shannon was to graduate from college, get married, give me grandchildren, and bury me at a ripe old age? This was senseless. You knew, God, before time began that this was going to happen. Why her? Why us? Why me? Why did you give me this child only to take her away?[42]

Baffling unanswered questions such as these can produce a crisis of faith.

Dashed expectations. Survivors might expect pastoral care but not get it. Elizabeth expected more from her minister than she received when her father killed himself two hours before Thanksgiving dinner:

> I spoke with the minister about plans for the funeral. He explained that while there was no official church position on suicide, he, personally,

would not be comfortable conducting the services at my father's funeral. He added that it would be possible, however, for my father to be
buried in the main section of the cemetery. I was stunned. Maybe I was
naïve, but I never even considered that there would be any question
about the religious arrangements. Everything I was doing was related
to my father's suicide; the fact that he had died seemed to be lost along
the way.[43]

Whatever his theology, it's unfortunate that this minister was unable
to care in some way for Elizabeth and her family. Biebel and Foster
write about a survivor whose pastor wrote them "a horrible letter,
saying the church wasn't there to minister to us, but we were to minister to them. We left there and didn't return to church for three
years."[44] What pastoral caregivers do in these moments matter.

Surviving

How does one survive the suicide of a loved one? Many difficult tasks
await a suicide survivor.

Telling a child. It's a myth that children shouldn't be told about a
suicide. For example, George's suicide note requests, "Please don't tell
[little Joe] what happened. Tell him I went far away and will come back
one of these days."[45] Contrary to George's request, it's best to tell
children as much truth about the suicide as they are able to understand
at their age. If you don't tell them, they may find out from someone
else when a caregiver is not present. They might find out from neighbor
kids or from other students at school or from the news. Annie, whose
mother killed herself, was told her mother died in a car accident. She
found out through the newspaper: "The local newspaper ran a story
on the front page with the headline CAR ACCIDENT RULED
SUICIDE. It included all the gory details about my mother's suicide."[46]

A second reason is that children know something is going on. A survivor of her father's death writes, "The very important message I would
like to emphasize is: never shield young children from the truth. If you
do, you are causing them more harm than good. Young children do
know what is going on and should be included in the grieving process."[47]

A third reason to tell children is that finding out later can feel like a betrayal. John, whose father killed himself when John was five months old, says, "I asked [my mother] if my stepbrothers and step-father had known about [my father's] suicide all along and she said yes. I felt totally betrayed that I had grown up in a family with everyone knowing something and my not knowing it. I only knew that some-thing was wrong but not what was wrong."[48]

A related reason is that if you don't tell children now, when will you? The Carrs describe giving a workshop and being asked by a woman in the back, "How can I tell my 30-year-old son that his father committed suicide twenty-five years ago? . . . I have never even been able to say the S-word until just now."[49] A fourth reason some expla-nation is needed is that children may fill the vacuum with misconcep-tions about death. They might fear they could die unexpectedly or that the suicide is their fault. It's not unusual for young children to think that they are at fault for a death.[50] This misconception needs to be corrected. A last reason is that suicide can be an important part of mental health history. For example, when one man found out that his mother had killed herself, he had more understanding about his and his brother's long history of depression.[51]

Some possible explanations. It is important to talk to children about suicide according to their developmental ability. For example, children under seven think death is miraculously reversible.[52] They think the deceased will come back or they can go to heaven, visit the deceased and return to earth. Or they worry they could die at any moment. Young children also may think that the death is their fault. Assure them that the death is not their fault. Biebel and Foster suggest the following explanation:

> Remember how our doggie Rusty got sick and died last year? After we buried him, we didn't have him to play with any more. We were so sad for a long time, but after a while, we were happy and sad at the same time when we remembered him. Well, Mommy was sick too. None of us knew how sick she was until it was too late, and we couldn't keep her from hurting herself. She died, and we can't bring her back. So now we will be sad again for a while and we'll miss her a lot, but later when we think of her, we'll be sad and happy at the same time.[53]

Another possible explanation is, "Your uncle was so sick he got very sad and he didn't want to live anymore. I'm very sad that he chose to die this way because there are better ways to handle sadness."

Helping children grieve. Parents can connect children to children's grieving groups at the local hospice. Also, the local library has children's books on grief and suicide. Allow young children to play out the story over and over. That's their way of processing the event and grieving. Keep in mind that with each developmental stage, the child may have to re-grieve with the new knowledge they gain about death and suicide. If the child doesn't seem to be moving past grief, he or she should receive professional mental health services.

Stages of grief. Kübler-Ross theorized a model of end-of-life grieving through five stages: denial, anger, bargaining and depression, ending in acceptance. Many people expect this process to be linear through each stage, but research hasn't supported this.[54] While the grief eases, it may never end, and it is more typical to cycle and re-cycle through the stages in unique ways. C. S. Lewis writes, "In grief nothing 'stays put.' One keeps on emerging from a phase, but it always recurs. Round and round. Everything repeats. Am I going in circles, or dare I hope I am on a spiral? But if a spiral, am I going up or down it?"[55] The end point is being able to manage grief, not eliminate it, as Elizabeth Jennings writes:

> Time does not heal,
> It makes a half-stitched scar
> That can be broken and again you feel
> Grief as total as in its first hour.[56]

The majority of survivors make a good adjustment.[57] Some of the most passionate, dedicated people I have met in the suicide prevention field are survivors. However, the journey can take years. Adjustment involves facing the suicide. Iris Bolton, whose 20-year-old son died by suicide, writes, "Experience had taught me that the only way to face the horror of suicide was to face it."[58] For some, the process includes individual therapy. For many, it involves a peer support group. Countless survivors have told me that the key to their adjustment has been a support group. Bereavement hospice groups may be helpful, but many suicide survivors express a preference for suicide survivor support groups because of the uniqueness of suicide. Another resource is books for survivors. The goal for the survivor is to realize she is not alone.[59] Resources, including books and websites that list survivor groups, are listed at the end of the chapter.

Refusing guilt. One of the tasks of survivors is to grant the deceased responsibility for his or her choice. Carla Fine, whose husband died by suicide, writes, "In order to forgive not only him but also myself, I had to accept that, ultimately, it was Harry's own choice to kill himself. All I can do is disagree with his decision."[60] Iris Bolton adds, "I struggled with guilt—what had I done or not done that I should have or should not have? I finally realized that I gave my son my humanness. . . . What he did with that was his responsibility . . . not mine. I could give him total responsibility for his own actions. I could let the guilt and the anger go."[61]

Avoiding toxic helpers. Another task of suicide survivors is finding the right helpers for their journey. The average person feels awkward around death and even more so around suicide. This awkwardness can produce toxic helpers. The way to tell if a person is a toxic helper is that she will offer platitudes or will tell the survivor how to feel.[62] God says to Eliphaz the Temanite, one of Job's toxic helpers, "I am angry with you and your two friends, because you have not spoken the truth about me, as my servant Job has" (Job 42:7 NIV). Job's cold-comfort friends give him "folly" (Job 42:8) or pat answers to his pain. They say he has lost his family, his livelihood and his health because of sin in his life. One of the problems with pat answers is that while they may be true in some ways, they tell only one part of the truth, not the whole truth. Telford Work notes another reason to avoid platitudes—they add to the suffering:

> Theistic accounts of suffering and evil have fared relatively poorly. Indeed, they have become infamous, especially when they take the form of prooftexts that wound rather than heal. . . . Well-meaning pastors and apologists deliver these one-liners like Job's friends, intending to comfort the afflicted, but instead ratifying injustice in the

world and distancing sufferers from the God they thought was compassionate. For the sufferers, these apophatic responses are insults added onto injury. They are white flags raised in the face of theodicy's epistemological crisis, responding to the problem of evil only by intensifying it.[63]

Platitudes not only are part falsehood but they also do not acknowledge suffering before inviting hurting people into the discipline of hope.

> Like vinegar on a wound
>   is one who sings songs to a heavy heart. (Prov 25:20)

Christians hope in God but we also acknowledge true suffering. Hsu (whose father died by suicide) writes that the wounded "don't need pat answers to incomprehensible questions."[64] Each of the following platitudes contains a solid kernel of truth, but the falsehood in each can cause pain to the one who suffers.

"She is in the Lord's hands." She is. Her times are in God's hands (Ps 31:15). Sinful Israel was engraved on the palms of God's hands (Is 49:16). However, C. S. Lewis, after his wife's death, argues that this is no comfort because

> She was in God's hands all the time, and I have seen what they did to her here. Do they suddenly become gentler to us the moment we are out of the body? And if so, why? If God's goodness is inconsistent with hurting us, then either God is not good or there is no God; for in the only life we know He hurts us beyond our worst fears and beyond all we can imagine.[65]

At these times, the comfort of the person we've lost being in God's hands may not be a comfort.

"It must have been God's will. God is in control." It is true that God is sovereign (Is 14:26-27; Job 1–2). What this statement does not recognize is that God doesn't will affliction (Lam 3:33). God doesn't will suicide but rather the destruction of death through Christ's resurrection: "The last enemy to be destroyed is death" (1 Cor 15:26).

"God will work it all out for good." We know that God is able to make good come out of evil (Gen 50:20). However, the fact that something

good can come out of evil does not minimize pain. We do not suffer "in the abstract."[66] God's own response to death is tears. Jesus wept even though he knew he was about to raise Lazarus to life again (Jn 11:35). God's ability to work all things together for good (Rom 8:28) does not deny a person the right to bitterly grieve a death.

"God wanted your loved one more than you did." Indeed, God wants to be in relationship with people. He loved us first (1 Jn 4:19) and made us his people (1 Pet 2:9-10). But because God fills both heaven and earth (Jer 23:24), he is already not far from each one of us (Acts 17:27). Because God is not confined to heaven, God does not need to remove someone from this world to be near to him or her.

"I know how you feel." We are all human; we all have feelings and we know how feelings feel. But suffering is very personal. We suffer in different ways in response to the same event. You don't really know how someone else feels. Wolterstorff writes, "We say, 'I know how you are feeling.' But we don't."[67] Iris Bolton adds, "Don't make comparisons, like saying, 'I know how you feel because my own baby (or father or mother or best friend) died and I . . . ' No comparisons, please."[68]

"You have to get over this and get on with your life." True enough. Suffering is all around us and we need to manage it and get on with the business of life. However, as Biebel and Foster note, "You can't 'just get over it,' no matter how much you try or how much others want you to. You must go through it to get beyond it."[69] Ted, whose son killed himself, explains that grief involves many layers:

> I don't think people want to keep hearing about it. It's like they are saying, Why are you still reliving what happened after all this time? Get a life, already. But it feels as if I'm speaking about something different now. For the first two years, I was explaining what it was like to lose a son to suicide. Now, I'm describing what it's like to no longer have a son.[70]

"Be strong. God doesn't give us anything we can't handle." It's true that we need to be strong in the Lord (Eph 6:10) and that God does not give us more temptation than we can handle (1 Cor 10:13). However, the apostle Paul writes he was overwhelmed beyond his ability to

endure (2 Cor 1:8-11). Paul says that God intervened, not that he gave Paul only what he could endure. Hsu's reaction to this platitude was fully justified anger. "What are the implications of this? According to this kind of thinking, my dad wasn't strong enough to handle what God had given him, so it killed him."[71]

"It's not so bad." This platitude denies the fact that we live in a world marred by sin. Wolterstorff writes, "But please: Don't say it's not really so bad. Because it is. Death is awful, demonic. If you think your task as comforter is to tell me that really, all things considered, it's not so bad, you do not sit with me in my grief but place yourself off in the distance away from me."[72]

"You have other children." While a parent may have other children, the death of a child is an agonizing and heartbreaking loss no matter how many more there are. Iris Bolton points out, "Children are never interchangeable."[73]

"Take your troubles to God; he will make it better." Though God in fact is our ever-present help and comfort in our times of trouble (Ps 46), the writer of Hebrews points out people who went about destitute, who were mocked, flogged, imprisoned, tortured and killed (Heb 11:35-38). Hubbard notes that God isn't in the business of taking away our pain the way that aspirin takes away a headache.[74]

Obliterate these platitudes from your language. Replace them with a ministry of presence or statements that acknowledge pain. Wolterstorff writes, "If you can't think of anything at all to say, just say, 'I can't think of anything to say. But I want you to know that we are with you in your grief.' Or even, just embrace. Not even the best of words can take way the pain."[75] You could also just say, "I'm sorry." Joiner writes that he was on the receiving end of inept responses to his dad's suicide, but one person's words felt supportive: "I'm just so sorry about what happened to your dad."[76]

Pastoral Care

In the place of platitudes, pastoral caregivers have many opportunities to help suicide survivors. Here are concrete ideas for ministry to the wounded.

A listening ministry of presence. Offer presence. Iris Bolton says, "It was never words alone that comforted. It was simply being with the person."[77] Just as you have shown up for weddings to rejoice with those who rejoice, show up now to mourn (Rom 12:15; Eccles 3:4). It is not good for people to be alone (Gen 2:18), especially in times of sorrow. The faith community can provide this ministry of presence. In the process of sitting with the family, listen to the story again and again. Hubbard tells us, "Our need for listeners grows out of the odd human fact that what happens to us is not finished until the story is told."[78] And retold. And include the siblings and the children of the deceased, who may get lost in the chaos following suicide. Biebel and Foster caution, "The focus of attention after the horribleness and chaos of a suicide tends to be on the parents of the deceased."[79]

Nonjudgment. In your offer of your presence, be nonjudgmental. Bolton advises, "Survivors (particularly parents) are plagued by feelings of doubt and guilt, without needing help from their relatives or friends."[80] Do not judge (Mt 7:1). We are all sinners (Rom 2:1). Foster "received a letter, unsigned but claiming to be from someone in my church, telling me what a horrible mother I'd been and that it was no wonder my daughter did what she did, that I was the cause of her death."[81] If a survivor is intent on taking the blame for something, make sure he or she is being fair. The ultimate decision and responsibility for suicide belongs to the deceased.[82] Much guilt is unfair, and no matter how much survivors castigate themselves, they will never atone because it's not their guilt to atone for. Some guilt might be valid but all actions can be repented of and forgiven.

Faith. Allow Christians to ask the hard questions about God and faith. Wolterstorff writes, "Faith is a footbridge that you don't know will hold you up over the chasm until you're forced to walk out onto it."[83] Though it is hard to listen to, doubt may be the stepping stone to a broader picture of who God is. And pray. "Carry each other's burdens, and in this way you will fulfill the law of Christ" (Gal 6:2 NIV). Pastors, chaplains and pastoral counselors bring their brothers' and sisters' pain to God, to Jesus who was "a man of suffering and aquainted with infirmity" (Is 53:3).

Lament. Survivors begin to reconcile with God through lament, through deploring the suicide. Lament is asking, "Why my loved one? Why me, Lord? What have I done to deserve this?" The first step of lament is to allow emotion, avoiding the urge to block emotion with alcohol or medication or the belief that Christians don't experience pain.[84] Most Christians have no problem with "positive" emotions such as hope and courage but some struggle with "negative" feelings such as despair. But almost half the psalms are psalms of lament. We Christians don't live in a soap bubble; reality touches us and we experience feelings in response to harsh circumstances. Mature people of God mirror these emotions for us in the Bible, emotions such as anguish and bitterness (1 Sam 1:10), sorrow (Ps 6:7; Jer 20:18), grief (2 Sam 19:4), despondency (Ps 42:5, 11; 43:5), distress (1 Sam 22:2; 2 Sam 22:7; 2 Kings 4:27), longing (Ps 38:9; Prov 13:12), anxiety (Ps 6:7; 2 Cor 7:7; Phil 2:26-28), fear (Mt 14:26-30), guilt (Mt 27:3), anger (Ps 7:11; Mk 3:5; Jn 2:15-16; Eph 4:26) and indignation (Ps 137). When we're told we don't grieve as those without hope (1 Thess 4:13), we are not told we do not grieve.[85] And when we can't navigate our intense emotion, God provides us a map with the lament psalms. Hubbard writes, "When we can find no words to carry our suffering and confusion to God, it is encouraging to find that God himself has provided words for us."[86] Using, for example, Psalm 13 or Ann Weems's psalms of lament, help the survivor write a lament to God complete with protest, petition and praise.[87]

Practical help. Jesus said the sheep and the goats will be divided based on the practical service we render to others (Mt 25:31-46). Pastors, chaplains and pastoral counselors can fight the stigma of suicide by making sure the faith community provides suicide survivors with everything it provides to any mourner, such as meals, visits, babysitting and help with financial matters.[88] Survivors have said they get tired of asking for help, so encourage the faith community to offer help and follow through. Bolton writes, "Don't repeat over and over your offers to run errands, sweep the driveway, or call mutual friends. Just DO it!"[89] But make sure the deceased's space is not altered. Bolton cautions, "Don't alter the loved one's room. Do not pick up clothes, or clean the room. When the family members are ready, they will take care of the matter in their own way, or ask for help if it is needed."[90]

Long-term help. Be there for the long term. It's hard to be there in the middle of the night in the crisis, but it's even harder to be there six months or a year down the road. In one study, three of ten study participants noted that clergy did not provide long-term support.[91] Because grieving is a very long-term process, commit to remain with the survivor once all the other mourners have returned to work.[92] The Carrs describe it like this: "Suddenly there was nothing more that 'had to be done,' and the gray, empty days closed in."[93] Be ready for anniversary dates, especially the days leading up to the anniversary. The survivor will dread falling apart on the anniversary date. This can make the days leading up to the anniversary worse than the actual day.

SUMMARY

Suicide death is excruciatingly hard, perhaps more so for a Christian. Survivor tasks, such as telling a child about the death, can be terrifying and painful. Pastoral caregivers have many opportunities to come alongside to minister, not as "toxic helpers" like Job's friends but as ministers of God's grace.

Interestingly, the friends and family survivors are not the only ones touched by a suicide. Everyone in a faith community where a suicide has occurred is a suicide survivor. How can pastors, chaplains and pastoral counselors provide pastoral care to an entire faith community? How can pastoral caregivers help prevent suicide contagion and suicide clusters? Look to the next chapter for this discussion.

DISCUSSION QUESTIONS

1. What makes a suicide death so excruciating for Christians?

2. What is your reaction to negative emotions like sorrow, grief, guilt, or anger?

3. How awkward do you feel around people grieving a death?

4. Have you ever been on the receiving end of a platitude?

Resources

Books for adults

D. B. Biebel and S. L. Foster, *Finding Your Way After the Suicide of Someone You Love* (Grand Rapids: Zondervan, 2005).

I. Bolton with C. Mitchell, *My Son... My Son...: A Guide to Healing After Death, Loss or Suicide* (Roswell, GA: Bolton Press Atlanta, 2005).

A. Y. Hsu, *Grieving a Suicide: A Loved One's Search for Comfort, Answers and Hope* (Downers Grove, IL: InterVarsity Press, 2002).

Books for children and adults helping children

D. Cammarata, *Someone I Love Died by Suicide: A Story for Child Survivors and Those Who Care for Them* (Jupiter, FL: Limitless, 2009).

M. Requarth, *After a Parent's Suicide: Helping Children Heal* (Sebastopol, CA: Healing Hearts, 2006).

B. Rubel, *But I Didn't Say Goodbye: For Parents and Professionals Helping Child Suicide Survivors* (Kendall Park, NJ: Griefwork Center, 2000).

Survivor support groups

American Foundation for Suicide Prevention, www.afsp.org.

American Association of Suicidology, www.suicidology.org.

National Alliance for Grieving Children, www.childrengrieve.org.

Samaritans, www.samaritansusa.org.

The Compassionate Friends, www.compassionatefriends.org.

HELPING THE FAITH COMMUNITY

An ounce of prevention is worth a pound of cure.

Benjamin Franklin

On January 14, 1995, Bishop David E. Johnson, who had recently retired as head of the Massachusetts diocese of the Episcopal church,
killed himself. His suicide affected an entire faith community. How
do you handle such a public suicide? Bishop Shaw, who succeeded
Bishop Johnson, says that after talking with the deceased's widow regarding her desires, he focused on "transparency" in order to help the
larger community process this suicide.[1] He set the example. *The New
York Times* quotes Shaw as saying, "This devastating time is filled with
pain, anger and questioning for all of us who knew, worked with,
loved and were loved by Bishop Johnson."[2] A day was offered to clergy
and lay leaders with a panel and open mike where people could engage
intentionally in processing Johnson's suicide.[3] Shaw helped begin the
healing process.

Helping the Community Heal

Let's review the ways pastors, chaplains and pastoral counselors can
help a faith community begin to heal after a suicide.

*Speak openly: "No lying, no tiptoeing around the subject, no
whispering."*[4] Stigma can affect survivors and entire faith communities. One pastor who lost her mother to suicide told us:

> When my mother died, when she committed suicide . . . I called up our
> district superintendent to tell him, and the first thing he said to me . . .

was, "Well, we'll be careful not to tell anyone how your mother died."
And I was kind of taken aback. . . . Right then and there the big word
"shame" was written across the whole situation, including my life. So I
said to him, "You know, no, that's what happened." . . . They didn't want
to acknowledge that that's what had happened. And the church has to
be better at that.[5]

Stigma is anchored in stereotypes and tends to thrive in secrecy.[6]
Think about some of the stigmatized problems in our society such as
AIDS, imprisonment, addiction and mental illness. Now think about
the secrecy that has fueled misinformation and stereotypes about each.
Less secrecy and more information about, for example, AIDS trans-
mission have decreased stereotypes and the stigma associated with the
disease.[7] In the same way, less secrecy about suicide will make more
information about suicide available and reduce stereotypes and stigma:
"Knowledge counteracts shame and embarrassment."[8]

Pastoral caregivers can fight the stigma of suicide in faith communities by speaking more openly about it. One pastor we interviewed
said, "When we stop talking about [suicide] that's when it goes underground and it gets dangerous."[9] After a suicide death, the decision to
talk about suicide openly is ultimately a family's decision. Don't share
information if it was shared in confidence. But if a family agrees, if the
community already knows about the suicide, if it would benefit the
congregation's healing, the pastoral caregiver can engage suicide
openly by including the words "suicide" or "taking one's own life" and
"depression" in the funeral, while emphasizing other ways of handling
despair. One pastor we interviewed said that to omit a mention of
suicide in a funeral is "to deny people the opportunity to process their
own pain, anger, anguish." The sermon preached at Albert Hsu's father's funeral included a reference to the tremendous pain and anguish Terry suffered:

Answers never come easy after a death, particularly when the death
resulted from the person taking their own life. Depression was the
enemy Terry battled against after he suffered his stroke in November.
He fought an enemy that was as real to him as this casket is to us.
This silent enemy exhausted all his courage and strength. Only God

knows what he was suffering in his soul. For those who saw Terry's struggle, you wonder what you could have done differently. To receive the comfort God offers we need to resist the regrets and the "only if I would haves." We want to resist the regret and realize that Terry's life should not be measured by how it tragically ended, but in how it was lived.[10]

So be open about the suicide death if the family permits, but remember also the deceased's life. Suicide is not the sum total of the deceased person. Acknowledge the person's accomplishments and struggles, but do not celebrate their choice of death. The more pastors, chaplains and pastoral counselors are able to be open about suicide, the more a community can begin the healing process and the more the stigma of suicide can be challenged.

Prevent contagion and suicide clusters. Being open about suicide must be balanced by the pastoral caregiver's awareness of the risk of contagion and suicide clusters. The U.S. Centers for Disease Control and Prevention define a suicide cluster as "a group of suicides or suicide attempts, or both, that occur closer together in time and space than would normally be expected in a given community."[11] A suicide cluster doesn't require a specific number of suicides or suicide attempts as long as they occur closer together than one would expect. For example, in one Native American tribe, seven young people aged 13 to 28 on a single reservation killed themselves by hanging in a forty-day period.[12] The fact that these suicide victims belonged to a bounded age range, were from the same reservation, died within a delimited time frame and used the same methodology suggest a suicide cluster.

A great deal of evidence exists that suicides do sometimes cluster. In the second century A.D., Plutarch writes about an epidemic of young women in Miletus who hanged themselves.[13] Durkheim provides the example of "fifteen patients who hung themselves in swift succession in 1772 from the same hook in a dark passage of [a] hospital. Once the hook was removed there was an end of the epidemic."[14] Kiyoko Matsumoto, a young woman of 19 years, jumped into the Mihara-Yama volcano in Japan in February 1933; 143 people followed her example that year. A policeman was permanently stationed at the crater's edge and is credited with stopping 1,208 attempted suicides in the following two years.[15] In another example, 124 people jumped from the Beachy Head cliffs in Sussex between 1965 and 1979.

Clusters are believed to occur because of a trend toward imitation called suicide contagion, the copycat effect or the Werther effect, after the main character in Goethe's *The Sorrows of Young Werther,* who kills himself.[16] After the novel's publication in 1774, young European men began to dress in blue frock coats and yellow waistcoats, and some killed themselves with the novel nearby.[17] More evidence for contagion exists. Alfred de Vigny wrote a drama in 1835 about Thomas Chatterton's life and suicide. The play was charged with doubling the annual suicide rate in France.[18] A 56-year-old man read about a Beachy Head suicide while he was in the hospital recovering from a suicide attempt by overdose, and said, "Fancy putting something like that in the paper for people like me to see." Two weeks later he jumped to his death from the cliffs.[19] Joiner believes that contagion may be related to habituation, getting used to the idea of suicide. Joiner suggests this reasoning: "My friend did that and she is like me; that means that I can do it too if I want."[20]

Contagion is an apt word because it focuses on exposure. It is defined as "exposure to suicidal behavior of others through the media, peer group, or family."[21] The word *contagion* reminds us that just as exposure to measles is needed for a vulnerable person to get the measles, so exposure to someone's suicide is needed for a vulnerable person to imitate suicide. This exposure can occur during wakes, memorial services and funerals if suicide is spoken of openly, so clergy must keep contagion in mind. David Phillips found that more exposure to suicide results in higher suicide rates. He discovered that monthly suicide rates in the United States from 1947 to 1968 were higher just after news broadcasts of suicide deaths and after fictional portrayals of suicide in soap operas.[22] Phillips and Bollen found a relationship between the number of suicide-focused news bulletins and the number of suicides.[23]

This relationship between exposure to someone's suicide and suicide rates is fairly well established. For example, in Germany, a fictional six-week TV show broadcast in 1981 and again in 1982 depicts a 19-year-old male dying by jumping in front of a train. Up to seventy days after the first episode, the number of railway suicides increased most sharply among 15- to 19-year-old males (up to 175 percent).[24] As another example, in 1998, during the Asian financial crisis, the Hong Kong media widely, explicitly and graphically publicized a suicide by charcoal burning. "The media linked charcoal burning with personal financial despair and portrayed suicide by this method as a painless, peaceful solution to such stress. Within the year charcoal burning had become the third most common method of suicide in Hong Kong, and by 2004 it was the second most common method, after jumping from high places."[25] Undoubtedly, imitation occurs.[26]

But it is also undoubtedly true that how people talk about suicide matters. Evidence of this comes from the Vienna, Austria, subway, where nine suicides occurred from 1980 to 1984. After the press dramatically reported on a suicide in 1986, thirteen suicides occurred that year and nine others occurred in the first few months of 1987. After this epidemic of suicides, members of the media consulted with suicide experts and stopped sensationalizing suicide.[27] Suicides in the underground decreased to three in 1989 and four in 1990.[28] While imitation occurs, talking about suicide in less sensational ways decreases imitation. In wakes, memorial services and funerals, clergy need to be aware of not sensationalizing suicide. Several resources for clergy that provide guidelines for public memorials include the Suicide Prevention Resource Center's white paper titled "After a Suicide: Recommendations for Religious Services and Other Public Memorial Observances" and the CDC's collaborative effort "Reporting on Suicide: Recommendations for the Media."[29] These resources emphasize the need for the following:

Avoid detailed descriptions of the suicide, the method and the location. For example, after the publication of *Final Exit* in 1991, in which Derek Humphry describes suicide by several methods—including suffocation by plastic bag—suicide deaths by asphyxiation by plastic bag increased by 31 percent.[30]

Avoid romanticizing or idealizing the person who died. This helps protect vulnerable people who might view suicide as a way to garner recognition in death.[31] For example, in 1839 a young woman died by suicide at a monument to the great fire of London.[32] This was followed by a young boy's suicide attempt. He explained later, "I wished to be talked of, like the woman who killed herself at the Monument!"[33]

Avoid oversimplifying the cause of suicide. This includes presenting suicide as "the inexplicable act of an otherwise healthy or high-achieving person."[34] It is best to include mention of mental health problems, if applicable, to say that it's sad that the person wasn't able to reach out for help, and to emphasize that no problem is so great that it's not possible to work toward a solution.[35] As one pastor pointed out to us, it's also best to check with the people giving the eulogy. In one case a eulogy included, "Well, you can't blame him for what he did." The pastor found himself having to rebut this justification for suicide during the funeral.

Avoid emphasizing that the deceased is now at peace from their problems. Vulnerable people might view suicide as a viable option to their problems. One pastor we interviewed told us that he preached on the assurance of salvation at a funeral for a congregant who died by suicide. Immediately after the funeral and in the following days, "there was one person after the other who said, if that's the case, then I'm ready to go now." The pastor's experience argues for an emphasis on a full understanding of salvation, which is about more than reaching the afterlife. Salvation is also about living as a faithful disciple of Jesus in the here and now.

While being open about suicide, clergy need to choose their approach carefully. Not everyone exposed to the flu catches it, only those who are vulnerable. This is also the case with suicide contagion. Vulnerable individuals can include anyone, but the group that seems to be at greatest risk is adolescents and young adults.[36] Nearly all suicide clusters occur in this age group.[37] Using data from a nationally representative sample of US high school students, Cutler and colleagues found that teenagers who knew friends or family members who had attempted suicide were about three times more likely to attempt suicide than teens who did not know someone who had at-tempted suicide.[38]

The adolescents and young adults who are especially at risk tend to be those with small, intense social networks, those who have grouped together around shared characteristics that create vulnerability to suicide, and those who may acquire pro-suicide views from others or the ability to kill themselves.[39] Of course, some adults can be vulnerable to suicide, especially those who are already inclined toward suicide or are suggestible.[40] After a suicide, pastoral caregivers should focus resources to adolescents and young adults and those adults who may be particularly vulnerable.[41]

Here are some suggestions for young people after a suicide to prevent suicide contagion and clustering:

- Make sure members of the deceased person's social network and their parents are informed as soon as possible. In the absence of information, people make up their own stories. Go to the individual's Sunday school class or youth group, provide the basic facts about the suicide (omitting details such as methodology and location) and allow the group members to process the loss and their guilt ("I should have done something to prevent the suicide!") and their anger ("How could she do this!"). Help the group develop plans for managing and coping with their distress. Instead of planting a tree, which romanticizes the death, the group might write letters to the deceased. Encourage the young people to watch each other for signs of distress or suicide. Tell them not to keep someone else's or their suicidal thoughts a secret but to get help from a trusted adult.[42]

- Decide who the most vulnerable small groups in the faith community are, such as fringe adolescents, adolescents with depression or adolescents who would identify with the deceased in some way. Evaluate how they are doing and make sure to provide them with support and resources.

- During a wake, memorial service or funeral, suggest to the young people that they look around and choose adults they can contact if they need help.[43]

- Mention other ways of finding constructive solutions to problems in the midst of depression.[44]

Additional suggestions for adults in the faith community include:

- Decide who the most vulnerable adults in the faith community are, such as fringe individuals or people who are depressed, have attempted suicide or have lost someone to suicide. Evaluate how they are doing and make sure to provide them with support and resources. One pastor we interviewed said, "If you sense something with people, just put it on the table and talk about it. If you're off base and it's not an issue for them or [they] can't deal with it yet, that's OK. At least I've said, 'If this is an issue, let's talk.'"

- Consider providing a "listening circle" or holding an open forum for the faith community to process grief, guilt and anger.

- Continue to provide support to the family as discussed in the previous chapter, even at church. Designate someone in the faith community to be a resource the family member can turn to when upset during church. A favorite Sunday school teacher might be designated for a child or teen and a small group member might be designated for an adult member of the family.[45] Grieving family members will be reassured that church is indeed a safe place. One pastor we interviewed said he gives people handouts because he believes, "They're not going to hear what I'm saying. Maybe at some point they'll read this and it may provide some comfort."

- Consider volunteering for or donating to a cause represented by the deceased's death. For example, if the person was a veteran, volunteer at a veterans organization or make a donation.

- Be ready for the fact that each death or suicide in the faith community or in the news may bring up the last suicide. Distress from the current death or suicide may be compounded and intensified by the unfinished grief.

Response Protocols

Clergy can take these steps after a suicide, but they can also be ready by proactively developing response protocols before a suicide ever occurs. Doty and Spencer-Thomas suggest developing "standard operating procedures" for what to do in an acute suicidal crisis or following a suicide.[46] These include a plan for disseminating information, because in a vacuum rumors proliferate. Information reduces the likelihood of inaccuracies. Doty and Spencer-Thomas suggest these steps for informing a faith community about a suicide:[47]

- Verify the information before disseminating it.

- Tell the leaders of the faith community first. Expect that their reactions will be intense and that they will need an opportunity to deal with their own feelings before informing the rest of the community.

- Set up a system so that each person in the faith community will hear about the suicide from a familiar person, for example, the youth pastor.

- Make a brief statement to the faith community as a whole with known facts of the suicide without the details such as method and location.

- Send a letter to community members to alert families to be sensitive to potential reactions to the suicide, including suicide warning signs. Include known facts without the details of method and location. The letter should encourage individuals and families to bring their concerns to the faith community and should tell community members how to get help, such as contacting the National Suicide Prevention Lifeline at 1-800-273-TALK.

Procedures such as these tend to be easier to develop ahead of time instead of on the spot during a crisis. "The wisdom of the prudent is to give thought to their ways" (Prov 14:8 NIV). It would seem wise and prudent to give thought to these procedures before a crisis occurs.

Ministry to the Community: Managing the Ripple Effects

In our interviews, clergy have made it clear that a suicide affects the entire faith community. One pastor told us, "[Suicide] ripples out and affects so many people." What are these "ripple effects"?

Illusions. One ripple effect is the shattering of the illusion that suicide could never happen in this faith community. This illusion is even more brutally destroyed when the deceased is a member of the clergy. One pastor told me about a church where the pastor killed himself in the church sanctuary. She said, "It was a horrible violence done to the church." This illusion may be even more difficult to release for those who are dealing with death for the first time, as is often the case—a chaplain we interviewed said, "For many of them it is a first time to deal with a death."

Judgment. One chaplain told us that after a suicide, family members are sometimes shunned. As noted in an earlier chapter, Biebel and Foster write, "Within two years of a suicide, at least 80 percent of survivors will either leave the church they were attending and join another or stop attending church altogether. The two most common reasons for this are (1) disappointment due to unmet expectations and (2) criticism or judgmental attitudes and treatment."[48] The stigma on the family is a large ripple effect that a pastoral caregiver must address. As mentioned in an earlier chapter, one priest told his congregation during a funeral, "You will not judge this family."

Leaving the faith community. Survivors do leave the faith community following a suicide. One reason given by a pastor we interviewed is that a survivor may need space to grieve. He gives the example of a woman who was reminded of her sister's suicide each week when her pastor was preaching because her pastor helped officiate at the funeral. "[Survivors] find it very difficult to be with you because you represent so much pain." This woman attended another church for a while as she grieved. The pastor emphasized not taking this personally and added, "I knew that the best way for me to pastor her was not to be her pastor. I needed to see that she was pastored." He remembers having to encourage the faith community that they did not do "a bad job" supporting this woman. He encouraged the church to "continue to pray and support her and support her husband."

Guilt, anger, betrayal. Suicide provides little opportunity for understanding and closure, and a faith community will struggle with a sense of communal failure. One pastor told us that after a suicide his church experienced a shared sense of "How did we fail here?" The faith community will also wonder what else they could they have done. One pastor we interviewed said it is important for a church community to understand that if they had known how serious the situation was, they would have intervened. It's helpful to remember that some suicidal people do not invite others into their pain. Pastors, chaplains and pastoral counselors can help people to judge themselves fairly and to find God's mercy for acts of omission or commission. The following prayer by Canon J. W. Poole of Coventry Cathedral may be a helpful reminder of the deceased's responsibility for his decision and the willingness of God to extend forgiveness:

> Remember, O Lord, in thy compassion
> Those whose courage fails them
> In the moment of despair;
> When they begin to lose heart,
> Renew their hope;
> When they are beaten to the ground,
> Raise them up again;
> If they die by their own hand
> Forgive them, and forgive us all;
> And assure them, both of thy love
> And of their own worth;
> through our Redeemer Jesus Christ.[49]

Greater awareness of pain. After a suicide, people start to talk about their own experience with suicide—that of a parent or sibling or relative or roommate. Members of the community gain a greater awareness that Christians indeed struggle painfully. One pastor told us about the ripple effect of looking at others through this new perspective: "Who else in our midst might be feeling this way? And who else should we have an eye on now? . . . Or just the sense of 'Wow, we didn't realize things were that bad for that exuberant young man, so what does that mean about other people here?'" Another pastor told us, "People certainly suddenly had much more compassion for people who were hurting, not to turn their back to them, and to really reach out and come alongside of people and say 'Are you OK?'" Another pastor organized a potluck supper after a suicide to buttress connections between members of the faith community.

The "one another" statements in the New Testament suggest many ways to build connections in a faith community: love one another (Jn 13:34; 1 Jn 3:11, 23; 4:7, 11), be devoted to one another and honor one another (Rom 12:10), live in harmony with one another (Rom 12:16), stop passing judgment on one another (Rom 14:13), accept one another (Rom 15:7), instruct one another (Rom 15:14), greet one another (Rom 16:16), agree with one another (1 Cor 1:10), serve one another in love (Gal 5:13), bear with one another in love (Eph 4:2), be kind and compassionate to one another (Eph 4:32), sing to one another with psalms (Eph 5:19), submit to one another (Eph 5:21), teach and admonish one another (Col 3:16), encourage one another (1 Thess 4:18; 5:11; Heb 3:13; 10:25), spur one another on toward love and good deeds (Heb 10:24), do not slander one another (Jas 4:11), live in harmony with one another (1 Pet 3:8), offer hospitality to one another (1 Pet 4:9), clothe yourselves with humility toward one another (1 Pet 5:5), confess your sins to one another (Jas 5:16) and wash one another's feet (Jn 13:14).

One last word on self-care. The challenge for the pastoral caregiver is that he or she is not only managing the suicide and the ripple effects in the community but also his or her own reactions. A pastor said, "It's a really great time to [get] the kinds of support that we all need all the time. To get a little bit more of it. And to know that you need it. And to realize that the suicide is affecting [you] and everyone's response to the suicide is also deeply affecting [you]. . . . So you're actually managing not just the single event but everything that comes from it." A chaplain added, "I think clergy have to go through and work out their own grief before they do a funeral because working out one's grief during the service is not the time to do that. So I think that clergy, no matter what the death is . . . need to be able to pull away to have time to yourself, to have time with God, to talk with whoever you need to talk with to work it through yourself because every death brings back a memory of another death, or two or three."

Suicide Prevention Training

Another type of preparation for suicide prevention in a faith community is training. Institutions such as schools and the military have begun to implement suicide prevention training of two types. An educational program informs an entire community about suicide and how to access help. For example, a training might be delivered to all high school freshmen in health class or to a youth group. A gatekeeper training targets those who are in a position to recognize the warning signs of suicide and help people who may be suicidal. Gatekeepers are specific people "whose jobs, roles or personalities give them special insight and access into the lives of others . . . the kind of people others confide in and turn to for advice"—for example, school counselors, military chaplains, youth pastors, youth workers and pastoral counselors.[50] Some communities combine the two types. If your faith community is interested in gatekeeper training, one way to evaluate if a program is a good fit is to complete the Suicide Prevention Resource Center (SPRC) online training called "Choosing and Implementing a Suicide Prevention Gatekeeper Training Program" (training.sprc.org). This training will also provide invaluable implementation tips. Both types of trainings have advantages and disadvantages.

Some evidence indicates that "trained adults are the last to know when a person is in trouble."[51] Because adolescents tend to talk to their peers about their suicidal thinking, it's important that students recognize suicide risk and know how to access help.[52] An educational program casts a wide net so that everyone in the community is prepared to recognize warning signs and knows how to take action. For example, Signs of Suicide (SOS; www.mentalhealthscreening.org/programs/youth-prevention-programs/sos) is a school-based curriculum that includes education and screening and uses a video and discussion guide. Students are taught ACT, which stands for acknowledge (notice suicide warning signs), care (tell the at-risk person you care) and tell an adult. SOS has been found to increase knowledge about suicide, increase more adaptive attitudes about depression and suicide, and reduce suicide attempts.[53]

Though there is not enough evidence about other suicide awareness curricula to either support or not support them,[54] Joiner and colleagues write, "There are almost certainly ways that this material can be disseminated safely."[55] Another way to educate a group is to invite a suicidology expert to deliver an educational program on suicide prevention and include an educational video. Not all videos are useful. If you choose to pursue this route, make sure that the video is focused on preventing suicide, that you follow the video with discussion, and that someone is available for answering questions and identifying and helping students in distress. See the American Association of Suicidology (suicidology.org) for reviews and recommendations of educational videos.

A gatekeeper's role is to recognize warning signs of suicide and get the suicidal person help. One advantage of a gatekeeper training is that it can be more efficient and more cost-effective to train fewer people in greater depth. Two examples of gatekeeper trainings include QPR, which has the advantage of being brief, and ASIST, which has the advantage of being in-depth.

QPR (qprinstitute.com) is a one- to two-hour training and stands for question, persuade and refer. It's an emergency mental health intervention that teaches lay and professional gatekeepers to recognize and respond to suicide warning signs and behaviors. Like CPR, QPR helps the gatekeeper learn to recognize early suicide warning signs, then to *question* their meaning to determine suicide intent or desire, *persuade* the person to accept or seek help and *refer* the person to appropriate resources. It has been found to help adults ask about suicide risk in students.[56] It has been delivered to faith leaders and is available online.

ASIST (livingworks.net), Applied Suicide Intervention Skills Training, is a two-day training in suicide first aid to help a person at risk stay safe and seek further help as needed. Participants learn to use a suicide intervention model to identify people with thoughts of suicide, seek a shared understanding of reasons for dying and living, develop a safe plan based on a review of risk, be prepared to do followup and become involved in suicide-safer community networks. ASIST is an in-depth training and has been delivered to faith leaders.

Consider implementing educational or gatekeeper training in your faith community. Having someone in your faith community trained in suicide prevention could save lives. And because ministerial formation often focuses on referral, additional suicide prevention training could be helpful to pastoral caregivers.

PARTNERING

Pastoral caregivers tell us that having partners in the community is important in preventing suicide. Partnering also prevents burnout, which happens when pastors, chaplains and pastoral counselors shoulder alone the weight of working with people in crisis. Dr. Thomas Jobe and his colleagues write, "Functioning in isolation is one of the greatest risks of ministry. Responding to the threat of suicide is not something pastors should do alone."[57] Partnering helps manage the risk of burnout and provides a larger safety net for the person at risk and for those touched by suicide. One of the ways to begin to develop partnerships is to be trained in the National Alliance on Mental Illness's Connect program (theconnectprogram.org).

In this six-hour program participants not only learn about suicide and how to help, they also learn how to work across systems to create a safety net for people at risk for suicide. Specific best-practice protocols have been developed for gatekeepers, social services agencies and mental health/substance abuse support providers, as well as those working in education, law enforcement, emergency medicine and other disciplines. Connect provides a training tailored to faith leaders and faith communities.

Who are the other professionals that pastors, chaplains and pastoral counselors need to work with before or during a suicide crisis or after a suicide? Countless community professionals are involved in prevention, intervention and postvention, including law enforcement, the fire department, the emergency department at the local hospital, medical providers, school personnel (teachers, school counselors and coaches) and funeral directors. Another group of professionals involved in this work with suicidal people are mental health professionals. Because of the confusion regarding how these providers differ from one another, let's review the specialty of each.

A psychiatrist is a medical doctor (MD) who has completed several years of training beyond his or her medical degree. A psychiatrist's specialty is prescribing medications (though many also provide talk therapy), so a psychiatrist is usually the best medical professional to work with a person taking several medications. Psychiatrists are sometimes booked up. If an individual is taking only one medication, it's possible to refer to a primary care provider, keeping in mind that primary care providers, while MDs, don't have the level of training in mental health issues and mental health medications that psychiatrists have. Licensed clinical nurse specialists can also prescribe medications and have less training than psychiatrists.

Other mental health professionals generally cannot prescribe medications, though in some states psychologists are trained to prescribe. The focus of these other mental health professionals is on talk therapy, and they differ primarily in the level of education and training they have received and their focus. Because mental health law differs by state, the titles (and therefore the letters behind a name) could be different in your state. Keep in mind that a licensed professional has met the requirements of the state board that manages the practice of mental health professionals in your state.

- Licensed psychologists have a doctorate in psychology (PhD or PsyD) and specialize in psychological assessment or testing.

- Licensed independent clinical social workers (LICSW) have a master's degree in social work and specialize in improving a person's resources.

- Licensed mental health counselors (LMHC) or licensed professional counselors (LPC) have a master's degree in counseling and focus on counseling.

- Licensed marriage and family therapists (LMFT) have a master's degree in marriage and family therapy and specialize in working with couples and families.

- Substance abuse counselors have a bachelor's degree with a specialty certification in helping people with substance abuse and addictions.

It's important to find out which of these professionals are accepting referrals or to provide someone in need of professional help with several referrals, knowing that some providers are unable to accept new clients or patients. Keep in mind that one of the most important aspects of mental health treatment is the relationship with the provider. It's ideal to monitor how the relationship with a provider is progressing. An unsatisfying relationship most likely will result in the person leaving treatment.

One important way to partner in suicide prevention activities is to join your local suicide prevention coalition. For information about suicide prevention efforts in your local area, see SPRC's state suicide prevention information pages online (sprc.org/states). Your local coalition might be involved with veterans, schools, Rotary clubs, workplace employee assistance programs, older adults, social services or corrections facilities. These organizations may be looking for opportunities to include faith communities in their suicide prevention efforts. Doty and Spencer-Thomas write, "Many systems are often needed to collaborate in order for deep and sustained change to be realized, and faith communities are a critical piece of the prevention puzzle."[58] The 2012 *National Strategy for Suicide Prevention: Goals and Objectives for Action* report views the role of faith communities as vitally important to suicide prevention efforts.[59] One objective is for faith communities to "participate in local coalitions of stakeholders to promote and implement comprehensive suicide prevention efforts at the community level."[60]

SUMMARY

Suicide affects not only the family of the deceased. It affects the entire faith community. Pastoral caregivers face numerous complexities in a faith community after a suicide, such as how to balance talking openly about the death and respecting the family's desires while managing suicide contagion and clusters. Plus, pastoral caregivers manage the ripple effects in the community while dealing with their own reactions to suicide. Helping a faith community after a suicide is no small order. Getting training and partnering with others in the community decrease the pastoral caregiver's burden. If pastors do partner in community suicide prevention efforts, what contributions to these efforts might the pastoral caregiver expect to make? We'll look at this question next.

DISCUSSION QUESTIONS

1. For each of the following, discuss the stereotype or secrecy that has fueled the stigma: AIDS, imprisonment, addiction, unemployment and mental illnesses.

2. Why is suicide so stigmatized? What could you do to help destigmatize it?

3. What would your message be at a suicide wake, memorial service or funeral?

4. How would you prevent suicide contagion and clusters?

5. How do suicide prevention trainings help save lives?

6. Who could you partner with in your community in order to save lives?

RESOURCES

Centers for Disease Control and Prevention, "CDC Recommendations for a Community Plan for the Prevention and Containment of Suicide Clusters," *Morbidity and Mortality Weekly Report* 37, no. S-6 (1988): 1-12.

Children and teens
Boys Town hotline, www.boystown.org/national-hotline.
Kids Help Phone Canada, www.kidshelpphone.ca.
Kristin Brooks Hope Center/National Hopeline Network, www.hopeline.com.
Samariteens, www.samaritanshope.org.
Trevor Project for LGBTQ youth, www.thetrevorproject.org.

College students
The Jed Foundation, www.jedfoundation.org.

Seniors

Institute on Aging Center for Elderly Suicide Prevention Friendship Line, 1-800-971-0016, www.ioaging.org/collaborations-elder-protection/center-for-elderly-suicide-prevention/friendship-line.

People of color

National Organization for People of Color Against Suicide (NOPCAS), www.nopcas.org.

Spanish speakers and veterans

Kristin Brooks Hope Center/National Hopeline Network, www.hopeline.com.
National Suicide Prevention Lifeline, 1-800-273-TALK, www.suicidepreventionlifeline.org.

Suicide sermon resources

J. T. Clemons, *Sermons on Suicide* (Louisville, KY: Westminster John Knox, 1989).
Mennonite Media, Fierce Goodbye, "Help for Pastors," www.fiercegoodbye.com.
Suicide Prevention Resource Center, *After a Suicide: Recommendations for Religious Services and Other Public Memorial Observances* (Newton, MA: Education Development Center, 2004).

CONCLUSION

People ask me all the time whether working in suicide prevention is depressing. I don't find it depressing at all. For me, suicide prevention is focused on the hopeful prospect of ministering God's grace to those he loves, those who have lost their way. Suicide prevention is about saving lives and about witnessing human resilience. Human beings are unbelievably buoyant in the face of great suffering and challenge. Every day that I observe this resilience, I see validation that people are created a little lower than the angels (Ps 8:5), and it leads me to worship the Creator.

My faith informs my hope. For me, faith has a place at the center of the work of suicide prevention. Pastors, chaplains and pastoral counselors are needed in suicide prevention because of their unique and vital contribution of faith. This book has been focused on helping pastoral caregivers recognize their unique competencies in coming alongside those touched by suicide and in contributing to the suicide prevention efforts in their community.

WHAT PASTORS, CHAPLAINS AND PASTORAL COUNSELORS CAN DO TO PREVENT SUICIDE

This book has proposed a number of ways pastoral caregivers can help prevent suicide; here is a summary.

Discuss theology. Practical theology is a core discipline of pastors, chaplains and pastoral counselors, and it shapes how pastoral caregivers interact with people touched by suicide. Clergy minister in ways that are unique compared with other caregivers, which is presumably why some people see clergy as firstline helpers for most mental health problems, including risk of self-harm.[1] Many theological issues emerge when pastoral caregivers minister to people touched by suicide. As noted in chapter 4, such issues include a theology of

- *Life.* What does a "good life" mean? How do you get a good life? What should people do if they lose the good life?

- *Death.* Who has the right to decide time of death? Is a "sad life" equivalent to a "dead life"?

- *Suicide.* How does a Christian become suicidal? How is a suicidal Christian restored? Is suicide a sin? What circumstances, if any, legitimate suicide? If suicide is a sin, is the sin forgivable? Do people who kill themselves go to hell? If not, is suicide morally objectionable?

- *Suffering.* Do Christians suffer? How do we explain suffering in the light of God's power and love? Is suffering a judgment on the Christian? What is the Christian response to suffering?

- *Community.* What is a community's function in the life of a Christian? Who contributes to the community and how? Who can be legitimately excluded from the community, and why and when?

Grapple with suffering. In my team's interviews with clergy, we have found that the primary issues suicidal people discuss with their pastor are their lack of Christian joy, their suffering and their theodicy—the attempt to resolve the anomaly of suffering with a loving God. Christians often seem puzzled by their suffering. They expect to turn trials into triumph; they expect to be "too blessed to be depressed, too glad to be sad, too anointed to be disappointed, too elated to be agitated, too grounded to be confounded."[2] And yet Christians suffer. Our faith is full of paradoxes.[3] For example, Jesus incarnate was both fully God (Tit 2:13) and fully human (1 Jn 4:2). Christians have been "predestined" for adoption (Eph 1:5 NIV) but "everyone who believes" will not perish (Jn 3:16-18). Christians are saved by grace (Eph 2:8), and faith without works is dead (Jas 2:17). The Bible tells us, "If you are angry with a brother or sister, you will be liable to judgment" (Mt 5:22) and yet, "Be angry but do not sin; do not let the sun go down on your anger" (Eph 4:26). Emphasizing one aspect of these paradoxes to the neglect of the other will result in the people of God getting off balance. Pastors, chaplains and pastoral counselors are needed to teach a balanced perspective on Christian suffering, that both prosperity (Deut 5:33; Prov 21:5) and suffering (Rom 12:12; 2 Cor 1:8; 1 Pet 4:12) are normative Christian experiences, that Christians experience both joy (Phil 4:4) and sorrow (Ps 6:7), that living a triumphant Christian life means managing suffering, not having a suffering-free life (Hab 3:17-19; Phil 2:27-28).

Engage suicide openly. As leaders in faith communities, pastoral caregivers have the opportunity to engage the issue of suicide directly at three crucial moments: before suicide is a concern, when people become suicidal and after they attempt or die by suicide. These three phases can be referred to as prevention, intervention and postvention. Prevention is hindering the development of suicide, just as a measles vaccination hinders getting the measles. Intervention is getting involved to thwart a possible adverse outcome, just as performing a Heimlich maneuver thwarts choking. Postvention is providing support and assistance to those left after a suicide. If suicide is like drowning, prevention is doing what you can to prevent drowning, like building a fence around a swimming pool and providing swimming lessons. Intervention is doing what you can once a person falls in the pool, like performing CPR. Postvention is doing what you can for the family after a drowning.

Pastors, chaplains and pastoral counselors engage the whole suicide gamut. They prevent suicide by helping people build lives worth living with belongingness, meaningful service and reasons for living. They intervene with suicidal people, those who survive attempts and their family members, by acting as gatekeepers; they recognize suicide risk and connect the person at risk to help. Pastoral caregivers also intervene in the midst of crisis, brokering referrals, providing pastoral counseling, discussing theology, guiding moral decisions, developing hope and hope kits, taking guns or pills out of a home, monitoring progress, and providing a ministry of presence and practical assistance. They provide postvention after a suicide death by offering support and assistance to those who have lost a loved one to suicide. They officiate at wakes, memorial services and funerals. And they simultaneously return to the prevention phase; they focus on preventing suicide by directing community efforts to contain suicide contagion and clusters. And during all of these phases—prevention, intervention and postvention—pastors, chaplains and pastoral counselors challenge the stigma of suicide by talking openly about it and providing accurate information. Pastoral caregivers are unique in that, as leaders of their communities, they have the influence to make a community-wide difference.

Build lives worth living. Religion protects against suicide. Pastors, chaplains and pastoral counselors play a unique role in teaching people to protect themselves from suicide by building lives worth living, with meaningful purpose and belongingness, because these protect against suicide. In addition to encouraging people's involvement in religious activities, pastoral caregivers also help strengthen people's reasons for living by offering them a place to belong and serve and teaching them to build enduring marriages, strong cohesive families, and identities and esteem founded on God's everlasting love. Here are seven factors that protect against suicide that underline the unique roles pastors, chaplains and pastoral counselors play:

1. *Support by family, friends and significant others protect against suicide.*[4] Pastoral caregivers teach Christians to support each other. The "one another" passages in the Bible emphasize support of others. In fact, the mark of a Christian community is love for one another: "By this everyone will know that you are my disciples, if you have love for one another" (Jn 13:35). Being a Christian means caring about others: "Do nothing from selfish ambition or conceit, but in humility regard others as better than yourselves. Let each of you look not to your own interests, but to the interests of others" (Phil 2:3-4). Pastors, chaplains and pastoral counselors not only emphasize love for one another but also

provide the methods to maintain support from family, friends and significant others. The Bible is replete with strategies for how to maintain good relationships—for example, by not gossiping (Prov 20:19) and forgiving each other's sins (Col 3:13). Among adolescents, family cohesion (a feeling of togetherness in the family) and parental support protect against suicide.[5] The Bible teaches strategies for maintaining family cohesion by honoring parents (Ex 20:12; Eph 6:2) and not exasperating your children (Eph 6:4).

2. *The presence of an intimate partner protects against suicide.*[6] Pastoral caregivers are in the unique position of teaching God's ideal for the permanency of marriage (Mal 2:16). When two people are joined in marriage they become one flesh (Gen 2:24). Although the field of psychology encompasses numerous strategies for how to manage intimate partner conflict, the Bible informs some of these strategies—for example:

> So then, putting away falsehood, let all of us speak the truth to our neighbors, for we are members of one another. Be angry but do not sin; do not let the sun go down on your anger, and do not make room for the devil. . . . Let no evil talk come out of your mouths, but only what is useful for building up, as there is need, so that your words may give grace to those who hear. And do not grieve the Holy Spirit of God, with which you were marked with a seal for the day of redemption. Put away from you all bitterness and wrath and anger and wrangling and slander, together with all malice, and be kind to one another, tenderhearted, forgiving one another, as God in Christ has forgiven you. (Eph 4:25-27, 29-32)

Pastoral caregivers help prevent loss of interpersonal relationships and therefore increase protective factors against suicide.

3. *Church attendance protects against suicide.*[7] McCullough and Willoughby suggest that church attendance provides social support, encourages health-promoting behaviors and discourages health-compromising ones. They add that religion does more; it promotes self-regulation and self-control, "reining in socially non-

normative behavior and promoting socially normative behavior."[8]
It's important to note that self-control is a fruit of the Spirit (Gal
5:23) and people who are conscientious do not engage in many
health-risk behaviors, including attempted suicide.[9] Pastors, chaplains and pastoral counselors can encourage church attendance,
which protects against suicide, because church attendance promotes many other protective factors such as self-regulation and
self-control.

4. *Religion promotes effective coping with stress.* Religious coping
   practices—including prayer, worshiping God, meditation, reading
   Scriptures and meeting with a spiritual leader—protect against
   suicide.[10] This makes sense because prayer and spiritual practices
   affect physical health positively, and people actively use spiritual
   practices to cope with suicidal thinking.[11] For example, in one
   study people more frequently relied on family, friends, peers and
   faith as sources of hope and support than on mental health professionals.[12] Using faith to cope fits with the message of the Bible;
   encounter with almighty God (Gen 17:1), the risen Christ (Lk
   24:52) and the Holy Spirit (Acts 2:4) is life-changing. God's Word
   refreshes the soul, makes one wise, and gives joy to the heart and
   light to the eyes (Ps 19:7-8). Pastoral caregivers have the opportunity to connect suicidal people to God and spiritual practices
   because these help people cope with stress.

5. *Coping strategies focused on solving and managing a problem and
   regulating one's emotional responses protect against suicide.*[13] The
   Bible abounds with teachings on regulating one's emotional responses, including "a soft answer turns away wrath" (Prov 15:1).
   Life problems are approached with prudence, shrewdness and in-
   dustry, and careful planning balanced with waiting on God (Prov
   31:13-27; 16:9; Jas 4:13-15). For example, Jesus teaches the use of
   a regulated process for resolving conflict when someone sins
   against you (Mt 18:15-17). Pastors, chaplains and pastoral counselors can teach biblical approaches to problem-solving and
   emotion regulation.

6. *Having reasons for living protects against suicide.*[14] Several projects along these lines can be found on YouTube—for example, videos titled "100 Reasons to Live." Youth groups can be involved in similar projects, developing a hope kit for each student containing that individual's reasons for living. Corporately, Christians have many reasons for living: God's love for us, hope in the midst of suffering, the beauty of the creation, the blessings of family and friends, and moral objections to suicide. But two of the most important reasons for living are related to what Joiner calls bedrock human needs: belongingness and a sense of competency.[15] Christians are gifted to serve in the church in some capacity (Rom 12:6-8; 1 Cor 12; Eph 4:11-13; 1 Pet 4:10-11), giving each Christian belonging ("Individually we are members one of another" [Rom 12:5] and "You are the body of Christ and individually members of it" [1 Cor 12:27]) and a place of meaningful service ("We have gifts that differ" [Rom 12:6] and "To each is given the manifestation of the Spirit for the common good" [1 Cor 12:7]). Pastoral caregivers can ensure that all Christians are aware of their gifting and have the opportunity to utilize their gifting in meaningful service.

7. *Among adolescents, healthy self-esteem protects against suicidal thinking and behaviors.*[16] While clearly teaching humanity's sinful nature, the Bible is also unequivocal that human beings are made in the image of God (Gen 1:27; 9:6), are fearfully and wonderfully made (Ps 139:14) and are deeply loved by God (Jn 3:16). Christians are "God's own people" (1 Pet 2:9). All people including adolescents need to understand that they bear the stamp of God's imagination and his love. They need to be taught to love themselves as they love others. Pastors, chaplains and pastoral counselors can teach these truths.

Pastoral caregivers help people build beliefs and behaviors in their lives that protect against suicide; they help people build lives worth living.

Develop community. Pastors, chaplains and pastoral counselors have noted that they don't work alone; the faith community helps suicidal people, those who survive attempts, their family members and those affected by a suicide death. Pastoral caregivers provide leadership but the community also does its own teaching. The faith community teaches skills, such as how to build enduring relationships, to protect against suicide. These skills are learned, practiced and lived out in community. In a small group, people might learn listening skills, self-awareness and empathy, as well as spiritual practices such as prayer and meditation. In the same small group, people will learn belongingness. At a potluck people might learn problem-solving, decision-making and negotiation skills—for example, how to reach consensus in a divided committee. Organizing coffee hour might teach people how to cope with stress and about meaningful service. Attending church services might help a person develop spiritual practices such as worship and reading Scripture. A discussion in a youth group meeting might help develop skills for resisting peer pressure. It's also in community that people discover how destructive stigma can be.

Community is also where those who need support can get it. It is the faith community that can write letters to people touched by suicide. Sending a note can make the difference for anyone touched by suicide and a visit from a lay minister or deacon can help. It is the faith community that can come alongside someone touched by suicide and offer concrete acts of service such as meals, help with laundry and child care.

Partner. Countless community professionals are involved in suicide prevention, intervention and postvention, including law enforcement, the fire department, the emergency department at the local hospital, medical providers, school personnel, coaches, mental health professionals and funeral directors. As leaders in faith communities, pastors, chaplains and pastoral counselors can partner with these professionals in their efforts. A pastoral caregiver can also join the local suicide prevention coalition. Partnering with others makes sense because it shares the heavy burden of helping others and because involving more professionals creates a wider safety net for those touched by suicide.

A WORKABLE TASK

There are two primary reasons why suicide prevention is a workable task for pastoral caregivers. The first is that suicide already exists in the faith community. The fact is, most pastors, chaplains and pastoral counselors will engage suicide at some point in their ministries. In one study, 84 percent of clergy had been approached by a suicidal person for help.[17] Many people turn to clergy for support and guidance, especially during challenging times.[18] In another study, about a third of respondents viewed clergy as "first-line helpers" for most mental health problems, including risk of self-harm.[19] Yet another study found that clergy are equally likely to be contacted for help by a person with a major mental health diagnosis as a mental health professional, and suicidal ideation, plans or attempts are significant predictors of making contact with clergy.[20] Suicide is part of the faith community.

The second reason suicide prevention is a workable task for pastoral caregivers is that they are using competencies they already possess to build many of the factors that protect people against suicide. Pastors, chaplains and pastoral counselors teach theologies of life, death, suffering and community. Whether they are aware of doing so intentionally or not, they teach people reasons for living. They teach and model hope, use of spiritual practices, and skills for creating enduring relationships. Though suicide prevention may seem like a huge task, it is an achievable task, one in which pastoral caregivers are already involved. The purpose of this book has been to encourage pastors, chaplains and pastoral counselors dealing with suicide so they can engage this work more effectively using the skills they already have.

SUMMARY

Pastoral caregivers have unique competencies necessary in suicide prevention. They offer their primary discipline of practical theology as well as faith beliefs and behaviors that protect against suicide. Pastors, chaplains and pastoral counselors need to be prepared to be involved in suicide prevention, intervention and postvention because suicide already exists in the faith community.

DISCUSSION QUESTIONS

1. What do pastors, chaplains and pastoral counselors have to offer to suicide prevention that is unique?

2. Given the heavy burdens that pastors, chaplains and pastoral counselors already shoulder, what makes suicide prevention workable?

3. Have any of your perspectives on suicide changed over the course of reading this book? If so, how have they changed?

4. What is your current perspective on suicide?

NOTES

INTRODUCTION

[1]While all of the stories and examples in this book are based on real people and events, names and identifying details have been altered to protect the privacy of the individuals involved.

[2]Not all mental health professionals believe suicide is preventable or should be prevented, although these perspectives represent a minority opinion (see T. Szasz, "Suicide as a Moral Issue," *The Freeman* 49 [July 1999]: 41-42).

[3]S. Stack and B. Bowman, *Suicide Movies: Social Patterns 1900-2009* (Cambridge, MA: Hogrefe, 2012).

[4]R. H. Fazio, "How Do Attitudes Guide Behavior?" in *Handbook of Motivation and Cognition: Foundations of Social Behavior,* ed. R. M. Sorrentino and E. T. Higgins (New York: Guilford, 1986), pp. 204-43. J. A. Krosnick and W. A. Smith, "Attitude Strength," in *Encyclopedia of Human Behavior,* ed. V. S. Ramachandran (San Diego: Academic, 1994).

[5]H. R. Fedden, *Suicide: A Social and Historical Study* (London: Peter Davies, 1938), p. 19.

[6]Ibid., p. 19.

[7]Ibid., p. 18.

[8]E. Stengel, *Suicide and Attempted Suicide* (Harmondsworth, UK: Penguin, 1964), p. 57.

[9]Fedden, *Suicide,* p. 48.

[10]J. R. Watt, *Choosing Death: Suicide and Calvinism in Early Modern Geneva* (Kirksville, MO: Truman State University Press, 2001), p. 70. Also, Fedden describes Regulus's suicide as "the finest of the Roman suicides," Fedden, *Suicide,* p. 60.

[11]Josephus, *The Jewish War* 7, as cited in L. Carr and G. Carr, *Fierce Goodbye: Living in the Shadow of Suicide* (Scottdale, PA: Herald Press, 2004), p. 149.

[12]Stengel, *Suicide and Attempted,* p. 57.

[13]R. F. Worth, "How a Single Match Can Ignite a Revolution," *New York Times,* January 21, 2011, www.nytimes.com/2011/01/23/weekinreview/23worth.html.

[14]T. Joiner, *Why People Die by Suicide* (Cambridge, MA: Harvard University Press, 2005), p. 144.

[15]M. Williams, *Cry of Pain: Understanding Suicide and Self-Harm* (London: Penguin, 1997), p. 115.

[16]S. Langdon, *Babylonian Wisdom* (London: Luzac, 1923), p. 80. It's important to note that though Ecclesiastes is similar literature, the conclusion is quite different.

[17]*Mori licet cui vivere non placet.* Fedden, *Suicide: A Social*, pp. 12, 78.

[18]*Itaque sapiens vivit, quantum debet, non quantum potest.* Seneca, *Ad Lucilium Epistulae Morales*, Epistola 70, ed. Richard M. Gummere, Perseus Digital Library, Tufts University, www.perseus.tufts.edu/hopper/text?doc=urn:cts:lati nLit:phi1017.phio15.perseus-lat1:70.

[19]E. Durkheim, *Suicide: A Study in Sociology*, trans. John A. Spaulding and George Simpson (New York: Free Press, 1951), p. 330.

[20]Ibid., p. 89.

[21]R. Burton, *The Anatomy of Melancholy*, vol. 1 (London: Dent, 1964), p. 435.

[22]Fedden, *Suicide*, p. 71.

[23]Ibid., p. 86.

[24]Ibid., pp. 166, 168.

[25]Ibid., p. 203.

[26]Watt, *Choosing Death*, p. 110.

[27]M. Montaigne, "A Custom of the Ile of Cea," in *The Essays of Montaigne* 1.3 (1877), trans. Charles Cotton, ed. William Carew Hazlitt, Project Gutenberg, www.gutenberg.org/ebooks/3600. See also Rousseau, *La Nouvelle Héloïse* (1761), and Montesquieu *Lettres Persanes* (1721).

[28]A. Schopenhauer, "On Suicide," in *The Essays of Schopenhauer*, trans. Mrs. Rudolf Dircks, Project Gutenberg, www.gutenberg.org/cache/epub/11945/ pg11945.html.

[29]William Carlos Williams, "The Descent of Winter," *The Collected Poems of William Carlos Williams* (New York: New Directions, 1986), p. 308.

[30]*Un suicide pose un home. On n'est rien debout; mort on devient un héros. . . . Tous les suicides ont du succès. . . . Décidément, il faut que je fasse mes préparatifs.* L. Reybaud, *Jérome Paturot: Á la recherché d'une position sociale* (Paris: Paulin, 1848), ia600501.us.archive.org/12/items/jromepaturoo1reyb/ jromepaturoo1reyb.pdf.

[31]F. Oyebode, "Choosing Death: The Moral Status of Suicide," *Psychiatric Bulletin* 20 (1996): 85-89.

[32]Albert Camus, *The Myth of Sisyphus*, trans. J. O'Brien (London: Penguin, 1942).

[33]D. Humphry, *Final Exit: The Practicalities of Self-Deliverance and Assisted Suicide for the Dying* (Eugene, OR: Hemlock Society, 1991).

[34]Williams, *Cry of Pain*, pp. 111, 112.

[35]Alexander Leitch, "Van Dusen, Henry Pitney," in *A Princeton Companion*

(Princeton, NJ: Princeton University Press, 1978), etcweb.princeton.edu/Cam
pusWWW/Companion/van_dusen_henry.html.

[36]Sigmund Freud, *Beyond the Pleasure Principle*, trans. and ed. James Strachey
(New York: W. W. Norton, 1961), p. xxii.

[37]Fedden, *Suicide*, p. 64.

[38]Horace Walpole, "Letter to Lady Ossory 15 August, 1776," in *The Yale Edition
of Horace Walpole's Correspondence*, vol. 32, ed. W. S. Lewis, 42 vols. (New
Haven, CT: Yale University Press, 1937–1980), pp. 314-15.

[39]J. K. Galbraith, *The Great Crash 1929* (Boston: Mariner, 1997), p. 128.

[40]Ibid., p. 214.

[41]David Foster Wallace, "Transcription of the 2005 Kenyon Commencement
Address," May 21, 2005, web.ics.purdue.edu/~drkelly/DFWKenyonAd
dress2005.pdf.

[42]A. Alvarez, *The Savage God: A Study of Suicide* (New York: Random House,
1972), p. 210.

[43]C. Fine, *No Time to Say Goodbye: Surviving the Suicide of a Loved One* (New
York: Doubleday, 1997), p. 148.

[44]John Dryden, *All for Love*, Project Gutenberg, www.gutenberg.org/cache/
epub/2062/pg2062.html.

[45]F. Winslow, *The Anatomy of Suicide* (Boston: Milford House, 1972), p. 59.

[46]Ibid., p. 59.

[47]J. W. von Goethe, *The Sorrows of Young Werther* (New York: Vintage Classic,
1971).

[48]Plato, *Phaedo*, trans. Benjamin Jowett, Project Gutenberg, www.gutenberg
.org/files/1658/1658-h/1658-h.htm.

[49]Dante, *Divine Comedy*, trans. Henry Wadsworth Longfellow, Project
Gutenberg, www.gutenberg.org/files/1001/1001-h/1001-h.htm.

[50]Virgil, *Aeneid* 6.433-37, trans. A. S. Kline, Poetry in Translation, www.poetry
intranslation.com/PITBR/Latin/VirgilAeneidVI.htm#_Toc2242932.

[51]Shakespeare, *Hamlet* 3.1. Hamlet also says in 1.2 that God has "fixt His Cannon
'gainst Selfe-slaughter."

[52]Milton, *Paradise Lost* 10.1023.

[53]Fedden, *Suicide*, p. 35.

[54]Winslow, *Anatomy of Suicide*, p. 307.

[55]Fedden, *Suicide*, pp. 37, 140.

[56]Ibid., p. 143.

[57]Stengel, *Suicide and Attempted*, p. 60.

[58]D. B. Biebel and S. L. Foster, *Finding Your Way After the Suicide of Someone
You Love* (Grand Rapids,: Zondervan, 2005), p. 80.

[59]Ibid., p. 169.

[60]D. B. Larson and S. S. Larson, "Spirituality's Potential Relevance to Physical and Emotional Health: A Brief Review of Quantitative Research," *Journal of Psychology and Theology* 31, no. 1 (1987): 37-51.

[61]U.S. Department of Health and Human Services (HHS) Office of the Surgeon General and National Action Alliance for Suicide Prevention, *2012 National Strategy for Suicide Prevention: Goals and Objectives for Action* (Washington, DC: HHS, 2012).

[62]Durkheim, *Suicide: A Study*, p. 44.

[63]A. Wenzel, G. K. Brown and A. T. Beck, *Cognitive Therapy for Suicidal Patients: Scientific and Clinical Applications* (Washington, DC: American Psychological Association, 2009), p. 6.

[64]For additional examples of varying suicide intent, see R. McKeon, *Suicidal Behavior*, in the series Advances in Psychotherapy: Evidence-Based Practice (Cambridge, MA: Hogrefe and Huber, 2009), p. 9.

[65]Wenzel, Brown and Beck, *Cognitive Therapy*, pp. 6, 18.

[66]M. M. Silverman et al., "Rebuilding the Tower of Babel: A Revised Nomenclature for the Study of Suicide and Suicidal Behaviors, Part II: Suicide-Related Ideations, Communications and Behaviors," *Suicide and Life-Threatening Behavior* 37, no. 3 (2007): 264-77.

[67]Wenzel, Brown and Beck, *Cognitive Therapy*, p. 18.

[68]Ibid., p. 20.

[69]Stengel, *Suicide and Attempted*, p. 60.

[70]H. I. Kushner, *American Suicide: A Psychocultural Exploration* (New Brunswick, NJ: Rutgers University Press, 1989), p. 19.

[71]Watt, *Choosing Death*; Kushner, *American Suicide*, p. 26.

[72]*Les lois sont furieuses en Europe contre ceux qui se tuent eux-mêmes. On les fait mourir, pour ainsi dire, une seconde fois; ils sont traînés indignement par les rues; on les note d'infamie; on confisque leurs biens.* Montesquieu, *Lettres Persanes* 76 (my translation).

[73]Kushner, *American Suicide*, p. 26.

[74]Williams, *Cry of Pain*, p. 15. Clemons adds, "Wesley did not feel the need to justify his position. He merely assumed that: (1) [suicide] was an evil deserving the harshest of measures, and (2) that even though there may have been some psychological reason to excuse such a 'madness,' the severity of punishment would be justified in order to serve the common good." J. T. Clemons, *What Does the Bible Say About Suicide?* (Minneapolis: Fortress, 1990), p. 84.

[75]John Donne, *Biathanatos*, ed. William A. Clebsch (Chico, CA: Scholars Press, 1983), p. 40.

[76]*"Le plus cruellement qu'il se pourra, pour monstrer l'experience aux autres."* Winslow, *Anatomy of Suicide*, p. 142.

[77]Burton, *Anatomy of Melancholy*; Winslow, *Anatomy of Suicide*.

[78]Kushner, *American Suicide*, p. 33.

[79]Williams, *Cry of Pain*, pp. 4, 12.

[80]Fedden, *Suicide*, p. 193; Stengel, *Suicide and Attempted*, p. 59.

[81]Fedden, *Suicide*, pp. 261-62.

[82]Williams, *Cry of Pain*, p. 13; Kushner, *American Suicide*, p. 30; Durkheim, *Suicide: A Study*, p. 327.

[83]Biebel and Foster, *Finding Your Way*, p. 122.

[84]Stengel, *Suicide and Attempted*, p. 62; K. R. Jamison, *Night Falls Fast: Understanding Suicide* (New York: Vintage, 1999), p. 18.

[85]Alvarez, *The Savage God*, p. 276.

[86]Silverman et al., "Rebuilding the Tower," pp. 264-77.

[87]E. S. Shneidman, *The Suicidal Mind* (New York: Oxford University Press, 1996), p. 63; Karl A. Menninger, *Man Against Himself* (New York: Harcourt, Brace and World, 1938), p. 87.

[88]Donne, *Biathanatos*, p. 49.

[89]J. D. Carter and S. B. Narramore, *The Integration of Psychology and Theology* (Grand Rapids: Zondervan, 1979), p. 73.

[90]S. Jones, "An Integration Response to Biblical Counseling," in *Psychology and Christianity: Five Views*, ed. E. L. Johnson (Downers Grove, IL: IVP Academic, 2010), p. 279.

[91]A. Holmes, *All Truth Is God's Truth* (Grand Rapids: Eerdmans, 1977), p. 8.

[92]J. D. Wardell and J. P. Read, "Does Cue Context Matter? Examining the Specificity of Cue-Related Activation of Positive and Negative Alcohol Expectancies," *Experimental and Clinical Psychopharmacology* 21, no. 6 (2013): 457-66.

[93]C. Smith, *The Bible Made Impossible: Why Biblicism Is Not a Truly Evangelical Reading of Scripture* (Grand Rapids: Brazos, 2011), p. 5.

[94]E. L. Johnson, "Christ, the Lord of Psychology," *Journal of Psychology and Theology* 25, no. 1 (1997): 11-27.

[95]Elizabeth Barrett Browning, "Aurora Leigh," *The Oxford Book of English Mystical Verse*, ed. D. H. S. Nicholson and A. H. E. Lee (Oxford: Clarendon, 1917), p. 19.

[96]Sigmund Freud, "The Future of an Illusion," in *The Standard Edition of the Complete Psychological Works of Freud* (London: Hogarth, 1927), p. 18.

[97]M. R. McMinn, "An Integration Approach," in *Counseling and Christianity: Five Approaches*, ed. S. P. Greggo and T. A. Sisemore (Downers Grove, IL: IVP Academic, 2012), p. 84.

CHAPTER 1: WHO DIES BY SUICIDE?

[1]World Health Organization (WHO), "10 Facts on Injury and Violence," Fact File, www.who.int/features/factfiles/injuries/facts/en/index1.html.

[2]The latest figures for suicide deaths available from the Centers for Disease Control and Prevention (CDC) are 2010 data. CDC, "Leading Causes of Death," Injury Prevention and Control: Data and Statistics, www.cdc.gov/injury/wisqars/leading_causes_death.html. HIV deaths are from S. L. Murphy, J. Q. Xu and K. D. Kochanek, "Deaths: Preliminary Data for 2010," National Vital Statistics Reports 60, no. 4 (2012), www.cdc.gov/nchs/data/nvsr/nvsr60/nvsr60_04.pdf.

[3]R. McKeon, *Suicidal Behavior*, in the series Advances in Psychotherapy: Evidence-Based Practice (Cambridge, MA: Hogrefe and Huber, 2009), p. 11.

[4]H. I. Kushner, *American Suicide: A Psychocultural Exploration* (New Brunswick, NJ: Rutgers University Press, 1989), p. 104.

[5]Estimates are based on the 1990–1992 National Comorbidity Survey and the 2001–2003 National Comorbidity Survey-Replication. R. Kessler et al., "Trends in Suicide Ideation, Plans, Gestures, and Attempts in the United States, 1990–1992 to 2001–2003," *Journal of the American Medical Association* 293, no. 20 (2005): 2487-95.

[6]K. McCabe, "Teen's Suicide Prompts a Look at Bullying," *Boston Globe*, January 24, 2010, www.boston.com/news/education/k_12/articles/2010/01/24/teens_suicide_prompts_a_look_at_bullying.

[7]CDC, "Leading Causes," www.cdc.gov/injury/wisqars/leading_causes_death.html.

[8]K. R. Jamison and K. Hawton, "The Burden of Suicide and Clinical Suggestions for Prevention," in *Prevention and Treatment of Suicidal Behavior: From Science to Practice*, ed. K. Hawton (New York: Oxford University Press, 2005), p. 189; A. L. Miller, J. H. Rathus and M. M. Linehan, *Dialectical Behavior Therapy with Suicidal Adolescents* (New York: Guilford, 2007), p. 7; E. Baca-Garcia et al., "Suicidal Ideation and Suicide Attempts in the United States: 1991–1992 and 2001–2002," *Molecular Psychiatry* 15 (2010): 250-59.

[9]CDC, "Leading Causes," www.cdc.gov/injury/wisqars/leading_causes_death.html. Durkheim found the same pattern in the nineteenth century. E. Durkheim, *Suicide: A Study in Sociology*, trans. John A. Spaulding and George Simpson (New York: Free Press, 1951), p. 101.

[10]CDC, "Leading Causes," www.cdc.gov/injury/wisqars/leading_causes_death.html.

[11]P. Rosenthal and S. Rosenthal, "Suicidal Behavior by Preschool Children," *American Journal of Psychiatry*, 141, no. 4 (1984): 520-25.

[12]CDC, "Fatal Injury Reports," Injury Prevention and Control: Data and Statistics, www.cdc.gov/injury/wisqars/fatal_injury_reports.html.

[13]Ibid.

[14]J. L. McIntosh and C. W. Drapeau, "U.S.A. Suicide 2010: Official Final Data,"

American Association of Suicidology, September 20, 2012, www.suicidology
.org/c/document_library/get_file?folderId=262&name=DLFE-635.pdf.

[15]CDC, "Fatal Injury Reports, National and Regional, 1999–2010," webappa.cdc
.gov/sasweb/ncipc/mortrate10_us.html.

[16]CDC, "Nonfatal Injury Reports, 2001–2012," webappa.cdc.gov/sasweb/ncipc/
nfirates2001.html.

[17]In 2010 in the United States, 30,277 men died by suicide and 16,962 of them
used firearms; 8,087 women died and only 2,430 of them used firearms. CDC,
"Fatal Injury Reports, National and Regional, 1999–2010," webappa.cdc.gov/
sasweb/ncipc/mortrate10_us.html.

[18]In 2009 in the United States, 19,392 suicide deaths were due to firearms and
16,962 of these were men. Ibid.

[19]Pew Research Center, "Why Own a Gun? Protection Is Now Top Reason: Perspectives of Gun Owners, Non-Owners," Pew Research Center for the People
and the Press, March 12, 2013, www.people-press.org/2013/03/12/why-own
-a-gun-protection-is-now-top-reason.

[20]A. Alvarez, *The Savage God: A Study of Suicide* (New York: Random House,
1972), p. 180.

[21]ABC News, "Man Survives Suicide Jump from Golden Gate Bridge," April 28,
2006, www.abcnews.go.com/GMA/story?id=1900628.

[22]Tad Friend, "Jumpers: The Fatal Grandeur of the Golden Gate Bridge," *The
New Yorker*, October 13, 2003, www.newyorker.com/archive/2003/10/13
/031013fa_fact.

[23]S. Canetto and I. Sakinofsky, "The Gender Paradox in Suicide," *Suicide and
Life-Threatening Behavior* 28, no. 1 (1998): 17.

[24]Substance Abuse and Mental Health Services Administration, *Results from the
2010 National Survey on Drug Use and Health: Summary of National Findings*,
NSDUH Series H-41, HHS Publication No. (SMA) 11-4658 (Rockville, MD:
Substance Abuse and Mental Health Services Administration, 2011).

[25]J. S. Hyde and J. D. DeLamater, *Understanding Human Sexuality*, 10th ed.
(New York: McGraw-Hill, 2006), p. 299.

[26]E. S. Shneidman, *The Suicidal Mind* (New York: Oxford University Press,
1996), p. 15.

[27]S. Fazel et al., "Prison Suicide in 12 Countries: An Ecological Study of 861
Suicides During 2003–2007," *Social Psychiatry and Psychiatric Epidemiology*
46, no. 3 (2011): 191-95.

[28]Males accounted for 87.7 percent, and females accounted for 12.3 percent.
Todd D. Minton, "Jail Inmates at Midyear 2010—Statistical Tables," Bureau of
Justice Statistics, U.S. Department of Justice, April 14, 2011, www.bjs.gov/
index.cfm?ty=pbdetail&iid=2375.

[29]M. Noonan, "Mortality in Local Jails, 2000–2007," Bureau of Justice Statistics, U.S. Department of Justice, July 2010, www.bjs.gov/content/pub/pdf/mlj07 .pdf; L. M. Hayes, "Prison Suicide: An Overview and Guide to Prevention," *The Prison Journal* 75, no. 4 (December 1995): 431-56.

[30]C. J. Mumola, "Suicide and Homicide in State Prisons and Local Jails," Bureau of Justice Statistics, U.S. Department of Justice, August 2005, www.bjs.gov/ content/pub/pdf/shsplj.pdf.

[31]D. Pratt et al., "Suicide in Recently Released Prisoners: A Population-Based Cohort Study," *Lancet* 368, no. 9530 (2006): 119-23.

[32]M. Williams, *Cry of Pain: Understanding Suicide and Self-Harm* (London: Penguin, 1997), p. 125.

[33]K. R. Conner et al., "Reactive Aggression and Suicide: Theory and Evidence," *Aggression and Violent Behavior* 8, no. 4 (2003): 413.

[34]Genes account for 70 percent of fearlessness. T. Joiner, "Lonely at the Top: Why Men Are the Lonely Sex," presentation given for the Massachusetts Co- alition for Suicide Prevention, Northeast Region, September 20, 2012, Bedford, MA; T. Joiner, *Myths About Suicide* (Cambridge, MA: Harvard University Press, 2010), p. 100.

[35]Voltaire, "Cato—On Suicide," in *A Philosophical Dictionary,* vol. 3, in *The Works of Voltaire,* vol. 7 (Paris: E. R. DuMont, 1901), p. 20.

[36]T. Joiner Jr., *Why People Die by Suicide* (Cambridge, MA: Harvard University Press, 2007), p. 67.

[37]E. Harris and B. Barraclough, "Suicide as an Outcome for Mental Disorders: A Meta-Analysis," *British Journal of Psychiatry* 170, no. 3 (1997): 205-28.

[38]Joiner, *Why People Die,* p. 156.

[39]J. Kemp and R. Bossarte, "Suicide Data Report, 2012," Department of Veterans Affairs, Mental Health Services, Suicide Prevention Program, 2012, www.va .gov/opa/docs/Suicide-Data-Report-2012-final.pdf.

[40]D. Woods, "Military and Veteran Suicides Rise Despite Aggressive Prevention Efforts," *The Huffington Post,* September 3, 2013, www.huffingtonpost .com/2013/08/29/military-veteran-suicides-prevention_n_3791325.html. For the entire series on military suicides, see www.huffingtonpost.com/news /invisible-casualties.

[41]McKeon, *Suicidal Behavior,* p. 12.

[42]K. Hawton and L. Harriss, "How Often Does Deliberate Self-Harm Occur Relative to Each Suicide? A Study of Variations by Gender and Age," *Suicide and Life-Threatening Behavior* 38, no. 6 (2008): 650-60.

[43]There is some evidence that men may attempt as much as women, especially when "the behavior is motivated by the intent to die rather than by the intent to communicate something to others." A. Wenzel, G. K. Brown and A. T. Beck,

Cognitive Therapy for Suicidal Patients: Scientific and Clinical Applications (Washington, DC: American Psychological Association, 2009), p. 33.

[44]E. Robins, *The Final Months: A Study of the Lives of 134 Persons Who Committed Suicide* (New York: Oxford University Press, 1981), p. 315.

[45]S. Seedat et al., "Cross-National Associations Between Gender and Mental Disorders in the World Health Organization World Mental Health Surveys," *Archives of General Psychiatry* 66, no. 7 (2009): 785-95.

[46]G. Borges et al., "A Risk Index for 12-Month Suicide Attempts in the National Comorbidity Survey Replication (NCS-R)," *Psychological Medicine* 36 (2006): 1747-57.

[47]R. Campbell et al., "The Co-occurrence of Childhood Sexual Abuse, Adult Sexual Assault, Intimate Partner Violence, and Sexual Harassment: A Meditational Model of Posttraumatic Stress Disorder and Physical Health Outcomes," *Journal of Consulting and Clinical Psychology* 76, no. 2 (2008): 194-207. N. Sedeh and D. E. McNiel, "Facets of Anger, Childhood Sexual Victimization, and Gender as Predictors of Suicide Attempts by Psychiatric Patients After Hospital Discharge," *Journal of Abnormal Psychology* 122, no. 3 (2013): 879-90.

[48]M. I. Oliver et al., "Help-Seeking Behavior in Men and Women with Common Mental Health Problems: Cross-Sectional Study," *British Journal of Psychiatry* 186 (2005): 297-301. K. L. Knox et al., "Risk of Suicide and Related Adverse Outcomes After Exposure to a Suicide Prevention Programme in the US Air Force: Cohort Study," *British Medical Journal* 327, no. 7428 (2003): 1376.

[49]S. Stack and B. Bowman, *Suicide Movies: Social Patterns 1900–2009* (Cambridge, MA: Hogrefe, 2012), p. 6.

[50]CDC, "Fatal Injury Reports, National and Regional, 1999–2010," webappa.cdc.gov/sasweb/ncipc/mortrate10_us.html.

[51]CDC, Nonfatal Injury Reports, 2001–2012," webappa.cdc.gov/sasweb/ncipc/nfirates2001.html.

[52]Stengel, *Suicide and Attempted*, p. 69.

[53]K. E. Jamison, *Night Falls Fast: Understanding Suicide* (New York: Vintage, 1999), p. 31

[54]Durkheim, *Suicide: A Study*, p. 177.

[55]Harris and Barraclough, "Suicide as an Outcome," pp. 205-28.

[56]In the 2001–2003 National Comorbidity Survey-Replication, 4,320 people ages 18 to 54 were interviewed. Kessler et al., "Trends in Suicide," pp. 2487-95.

[57]T. Joiner et al., *The Interpersonal Theory of Suicide: Guidance for Working with Suicidal Clients* (Washington, DC: American Psychological Association, 2009), pp. 21, 44; Harris and Barraclough, "Suicide as an Outcome," pp. 205-28. Rates differ by gender. For example, for major depression 7 percent of men and 1 percent of women have been found to die by suicide. G. W. Blair-West

and G. W. Mellsop, "Major Depression: Does a Gender-Based Down-Rating of Suicide Risk Challenge its Diagnostic Validity?" *Australian and New Zealand Journal of Psychiatry* 35, no. 3 (2001): 322-28.

[58]Joiner, *Myths About Suicide*, p. 89.

[59]U.S. Department of Health and Human Services, *Mental Health: A Report of the Surgeon General* (Rockville, MD: U.S. Department of Health and Human Services, Substance Abuse and Mental Health Services Administration, Center for Mental Health Services, National Institutes of Health, National Institute of Mental Health, 1999).

[60]E. K. Mościcki, "Epidemiology of Suicide," in *The Harvard Medical School Guide to Suicide Assessment and Intervention*, ed. Douglas G. Jacobs (San Francisco: Jossey-Bass, 1999), p. 45.

[61]S. Goldsmith et al., *Reducing Suicide: A National Imperative* (Washington, DC: National Academies Press, 2002), p. 5.

[62]Mościcki, "Epidemiology of Suicide," p. 47.

[63]McKeon, *Suicidal Behavior*, p. 18.

[64]K. R. Conner, M. S. McCloskey and P. R. Duberstein, "Psychiatric Risk Factors for Suicide in the Alcohol-Dependent Patient," *Psychiatric Annals* 38, no. 11 (2008): 742-48.

[65]M. K. Nock et al., "Cross-National Analysis of the Associations Among Mental Disorders and Suicidal Behavior: Findings from the WHO World Mental Health Surveys," *PloS Medicine* 6, no. 8 (2009).

[66]T. R. Goldstein, J. A. Bridge and D. A. Brent, "Sleep Disturbance Preceding Completed Suicide in Adolescents," *Journal of Consulting and Clinical Psychology* 76, no. 1 (2008): 84-91. See also J. H. Bjorngaard et al., "Sleeping Problems and Suicide in 75,000 Norwegian Adults: A 20 Year Follow-up of the HUNT I Study," *Sleep* 34, no. 9 (2011): 1155-59.

[67]N. Sjöström, J. Hetta and M. Waern, "Persistent Nightmares Are Associated with Repeat Suicide Attempt: A Prospective Study," *Psychiatry Research* 170, no. 2-3 (2009): 208-11.

[68]Joiner, *Why People Die*, p. 152.

[69]A. A. Roy et al., "Genetics of Suicide in Depression," *Journal Of Clinical Psychiatry* 60, no. 2 (1999): 12-17. A. Roy, N. L. Segal and M. Sarchiapone, "Attempted Suicide Among Living Co-twins of Twin Suicide Victims," *The American Journal of Psychiatry* 152, no. 7 (1995): 1075-76.

[70]J. A. Egeland and J. N. Sussex, "Suicide and Family Loading for Affective Disorders," *Journal of the American Medical Association* 254, no. 7 (1985): 915-18.

[71]E. E. Agerbo, M. M. Nordentoft and P. B. Mortensen, "Familial, Psychiatric, and Socioeconomic Risk Factors for Suicide in Young People: Nested Case-Control Study," *British Medical Journal* 325, no. 7355 (2002): 74-77.

[72]Goldsmith, *Reducing Suicide,* p. 2.

[73]Joiner, *Why People Die,* p. 174.

[74]Jamison, *Night Falls Fast,* p. 197.

[75]Conner et al., "Reactive Aggression," p. 413; M. Krakowski, "Violence and Se-rotonin: Influence of Impulse Control, Affect Regulation, and Social Func-tioning," *The Journal of Neuropsychiatry and Clinical Neurosciences* 15, no. 3 (2003): 294-305; Williams, *Cry of Pain,* p. 125; Joiner, *Why People Die,* pp. 179-84.

[76]Kushner, *American Suicide,* p. 120.

[77]CDC, "Suicide Contagion and the Reporting of Suicide: Recommendations from a National Workshop," *MMWR: Recommendations and Reports* 43, no. RR-6 (1994): 9-18.

[78]T. E. Joiner et al., "Childhood Physical and Sexual Abuse and Lifetime Number of Suicide Attempts: A Persistent and Theoretically Important Relationship," *Behaviour Research and Therapy* 45, no. 3 (2007): 539-47; Office of the Surgeon General and Office of Population Affairs, *The Surgeon General's Call to Action to Promote Sexual Health and Responsible Sexual Behavior* (Rockville, MD: Office of the Surgeon General, 2001).

[79]The National Violent Death Reporting System—which tracks violent deaths, including suicide, in 16 states—reports that in 2009 31.97 percent of suicides were related to intimate partner problems. CDC, wisqars.cdc.gov:8080/nvdrs/ nvdrsDisplay.jsp.

[80]K. Devries et al., "Violence Against Women Is Strongly Associated with Suicide Attempts: Evidence from the WHO Multi-Country Study on Women's Health and Domestic Violence Against Women," *Social Science and Medicine* 73, no. 1 (2011): 79-86; C. M. Rennison, *Intimate Partner Violence, 1993–2001* (Washington, DC: U.S. Department of Justice, Bureau of Justice Statistics, 2003). A. J. Sedlak et al., *Fourth National Incidence Study of Child Abuse and Neglect (NIS–4): Report to Congress, Executive Summary* (Washington, DC: U.S. Department of Health and Human Services, Administration for Children and Families, 2010).

[81]R. L. Marquet et al., "The Epidemiology of Suicide and Attempted Suicide in Dutch General Practice 1983–2003," *BMC Family Practice* 6, no. 45 (2005). Durkheim noted the preservation effects of marriage and the risks of sin-gleness in the nineteenth century. Durkheim, *Suicide: A Study,* p. 173; P. Corcoran, "Suicide and Marital Status in Northern Ireland," *Social Psychiatry and Psychiatric Epidemiology* 45, no. 8 (2010): 795-800; M. Stroebe, W. Stroebe and G. Abakoumkin, "The Broken Heart: Suicidal Ideation in Bereavement," *American Journal of Psychiatry* 162, no. 11 (2005): 2178-80; Agerbo, Nordentoft and Mortensen, "Familial, Psychiatric, and Socioeconomic," pp. 74-77.

[82]M. M. Miller et al., "The Association Between Changes in Household Firearm Ownership and Rates of Suicide in the United States, 1981–2002," *Injury Prevention* 12, no. 3 (2006): 178-82; M. S. Kaplan et al., "Factors Associated with Suicide by Firearm Among U.S. Older Adult Men," *Psychology of Men and Masculinity* 13, no. 1 (2012): 65-74.

[83]N. Kreitman, V. Carstairs and J. C. Duffy, "Association of Age and Social Class with Suicide Among Men in Great Britain," *Journal of Epidemiology and Community Health* 45, no. 3 (1991): 195-202.

[84]F. Luo et al., "Impact of Business Cycles on US Suicide Rates, 1928–2007," *American Journal of Public Health* 101 (2011): 1139-46; Kessler et al., "Trends in Suicide," pp. 2487-95.

[85]M. A. Ilgen et al., "Pain and Suicidal Thoughts, Plans and Attempts in the United States," *General Hospital Psychiatry* 30 (2008): 521-27.

[86]R. Eynan et al., "The Association Between Homelessness and Suicidal Ideation and Behaviors: Results of a Cross-Sectional Survey," *Suicide and Life-Threatening Behavior* 32, no. 4 (2002): 418-27.

[87]M. Kaplan et al., "Suicide Among Male Veterans: A Prospective Population-Based Study," *Journal of Epidemiology and Community Health* 61, no. 7 (2007): 619-24.

[88]Kushner, *American Suicide*, p. 88.

[89]R. R. Garofalo et al., "Sexual Orientation and Risk of Suicide Attempts Among a Representative Sample of Youth," *Archives of Pediatrics and Adolescent Medicine* 153 (1999): 487-93; S. C. Gilman et al., "Risk of Psychiatric Disorders Among Individuals Reporting Same-Sex Sexual Partners in the National Comorbidity Survey," *American Journal of Public Health* 91, no. 6 (2001): 933-39; M. King et al., "A Systematic Review of Mental Disorder, Suicide, and Deliberate Self Harm in Lesbian, Gay and Bisexual People," *BMC Psychiatry* 8 (2008): 70; G. Remafedi et al., "The Relationship Between Suicide Risk and Sexual Orientation: Results of a Population-Based Study," *American Journal Of Public Health* 88, no. 1 (1998): 57-60.

[90]E. Miller, C. McCullough and J. Johnson, "The Association of Family Risk Factors with Suicidality Among Adolescent Primary Care Patients," *Journal of Family Violence* 27, no. 6 (2012): 523-29.

[91]Miller, Rathus and Linehan, *Dialectical Behavior Therapy*, p. 20.

[92]A. Beautrais, "Child and Young Adolescent Suicide in New Zealand," *Australian and New Zealand Journal Of Psychiatry* 35, no. 5 (2001): 647-53. Mościcki, "Epidimiology of Suicide," p. 49.

[93]M. S. Gould et al., "Psychosocial Risk Factors of Child and Adolescent Completed Suicide," *Archives of General Psychiatry* 53, no. 12 (1996): 1155-62.

[94]W. Styron, *Darkness Visible: A Memoir of Madness* (New York: Random House, 1990), p. 39.

[95]Durkheim, *Suicide: A Study,* pp. 277-78.

[96]I. W. Borowsky, M. Ireland and M. D. Resnick, "Adolescent Suicide Attempts: Risks and Protectors," *Pediatrics* 107, no. 3 (2001): 485-93.

[97]McKeon, *Suicidal Behavior,* p. 33.

[98]L. A. Brenner et al., "Suicidality and Veterans with a History of Traumatic Brain Injury: Precipitating Events, Protective Factors, and Prevention Strategies," *Rehabilitation Psychology* 54, no. 4 (2009): 390-97.

[99]N. A. Skopp et al., "Childhood Adversity and Suicidal Ideation in a Clinical Military Sample: Military Unit Cohesion and Intimate Relationships as Protective Factors," *Journal of Social and Clinical Psychology* 30, no. 4 (2011): 361-77.

[100]S. Stack, "The Effect of the Decline in Institutionalized Religion on Suicide, 1954-1978," *Journal for the Scientific Study of Religion* 22, no. 3 (1983): 239-52.

[101]D. B. Larson and S. S. Larson, "Spirituality's Potential Relevance to Physical and Emotional Health: A Brief Review of Quantitative Research," *Journal of Psychology and Theology* 31, no. 1 (2003): 37-51.

[102]S. Hamdan et al., "Protective Factors and Suicidality in Members of Arab Kindred," *Crisis: The Journal of Crisis Intervention and Suicide Prevention* 33, no. 2 (2012): 80-86.

[103]Y. Lee, "Validation of Reasons for Living and Their Relationship with Suicidal Ideation in Korean College Students," *Death Studies* 36, no. 8 (2012): 712-22; M. Oquendo et al., "Protective Factors Against Suicidal Behavior in Latinos," *Journal of Nervous and Mental Disease* 193, no. 7 (2005): 438-43. To access a copy of the reasons for living scale, go to depts.washington.edu/brtc/files/ RFL72.pdf.

[104]M. M. Linehan et al., "Reasons for Staying Alive When You Are Thinking of Killing Yourself: The Reasons for Living Inventory," *Journal of Consulting and Clinical Psychology* 51, no. 2 (1983): 276-86.

[105]M. A. Marty, D. L. Segal and F. L. Coolidge, "Relationships Among Dispositional Coping Strategies, Suicidal Ideation, and Protective Factors Against Suicide in Older Adults," *Aging and Mental Health* 14, no. 8 (2010): 1015-23.

[106]P. Qin and P. Mortensen, "The Impact of Parental Status on the Risk of Completed Suicide," *Archives of General Psychiatry* 60, no. 8 (2003): 797-802.

[107]E. Miller, C. McCullough and J. Johnson, "The Association of Family Risk Factors with Suicidality Among Adolescent Primary Care Patients," *Journal of Family Violence* 27, no. 6 (2012): 523-29; S. D. Walsh, A. Edelstein and D. Vota, "Suicidal Ideation and Alcohol Use Among Ethiopian Adolescents in Israel: The Relationship with Ethnic Identity and Parental Support," *European Psychologist* 17, no. 2 (2012): 131-42; D. Li et al., "Gratitude and Suicidal Ideation and Suicide Attempts Among Chinese Adolescents: Direct, Mediated, and

Moderated Effects," *Journal of Adolescence* 35, no. 1 (2012): 55-66; M. S. Gould and R. A. Kramer, "Youth Suicide Prevention," *Suicide and Life Threatening Behaviors* 31, no. s1 (2001): 6-31.

[108]Kushner discusses the problem that statistics are based on the supposition that one individual suicide behaves just like every other suicide, which is certainly not the case. Kushner, *American Suicide*, p. 72. P. G. Quinnett, *Counseling Suicidal People: A Therapy of Hope*, 3rd ed. (Spokane, WA: QPR Institute, 2009), p. 40.

[109]McKeon, *Suicidal Behavior*, p. 24.

[110]Source unknown.

[111]Jamison, *Night Falls Fast*, p. 25.

CHAPTER 2: SHATTERING MYTHS ABOUT SUICIDE

[1]K. Greene-McCreight, *Darkness Is My Only Companion: A Christian Response to Mental Illness* (Grand Rapids: Brazos, 2006), p. 28. Used by permission. J. T. Stout, *Bipolar Disorder: Rebuilding Your Life* (Costa Mesa, CA: Shepherd, 2002).

[2]F. Schaeffer, *Crazy for God* (Cambridge, MA: Da Capo, 2007), p. 138.

[3]L. A. Brenner et al., "Suicidality and Veterans with a History of Traumatic Brain Injury: Precipitating Events, Protective Factors, and Prevention Strategies," *Rehabilitation Psychology* 54, no. 4 (2009): 390-97; K. Dervic et al., "Moral or Religious Objections to Suicide May Protect Against Suicidal Behavior in Bipolar Disorder," *Journal Of Clinical Psychiatry* 72, no. 10 (2011): 1390-96; K. Dervic et al., "Religious Affiliation and Suicide Attempt," *American Journal of Psychiatry* 161, no. 12 (2004): 2303-8.

[4]M. E. McCullough and B. B. Willoughby, "Religion, Self-Regulation, and Self-Control: Associations, Explanations, and Implications," *Psychological Bulletin* 135, no. 1 (2009): 69-93.

[5]Ibid.

[6]C. H. Spurgeon, "Joy and Peace in Believing," sermon 692, Metropolitan Tabernacle Pulpit, May 20, 1866, www.spurgeongems.org/vols10-12/chs692.pdf.

[7]R. Bainton, *Here I Stand: A Life of Martin Luther* (New York: Abingdon, 1950).

[8]J. R. Watt, *Choosing Death: Suicide and Calvinism in Early Modern Geneva* (Kirksville, MO: Truman State University Press, 2001), p. 10.

[9]In a letter from Carnell to Harold John Ockenga dated June 25, 1961, Carnell wrote, "I was suffering from severe depression. . . . I was in the hospital ten days, during which time I received five shock treatments. The depression abated a good deal, and I was released. Since then I have been an outpatient with the Wells Medical Group of Arcadia, having received my 6th and 7th shock treatments. Right now I am feeling quite good. I hope it keeps up." R. Nelson, *The Making and Unmaking of an Evangelical Mind: The Case of*

Edward John Carnell (Cambridge, MA: Cambridge University Press, 1987), p. 113. Carnell also wrote, "Insomnia has plagued me from adolescence until now." E. J. Carnell, *Christian Commitment* (New York: Macmillan, 1957), p. 10. "He would never be free of barbituric dependence." Nelson, *Making and Unmaking,* p. 113.

[10]P. A. Seaman, "A Moth in the Heart," in *Children of Jonah,* ed. J. T. Clemons (Sterling, VA: Capital, 2001), p. 39; D. Connelly, *After Life: What the Bible Really Says* (Downers Grove, IL: InterVarsity Press, 1994), p. 51.

[11]Kushner describes Mather as having "nightmares in which Satan attempted to take advantage of his depressive state," where he considered suicide but resisted the temptation. H. I. Kushner, *American Suicide: A Psychocultural Exploration* (New Brunswick, NJ: Rutgers University Press, 1989), p. 26.

[12]J. Donne, *Biathanatos,* ed. William A. Clebsch (Chico, CA: Scholars, 1983), p. 3.

[13]Carnell, *Christian Commitment,* p. 11.

[14]The cororner's verdict was: "Death was caused by pulmonary congestion and edema due to barbiturate intoxication, suffered at an undetermined time, on the estimated date of April 14, 1967, at the Claremont Hotel, Oakland, California. . . . I find death undetermined whether accidental or suicidal." Nelson, *Making and Unmaking,* pp. 117, 120.

[15]L. V. Baldwin, *There Is a Balm in Gilead: The Cultural Roots of Martin Luther King, Jr.* (Minneapolis: Fortress, 1991), pp. 109-10.

[16]K. Mason, *When the Pieces Don't Fit: Making Sense of Life's Puzzles* (Grand Rapids: Discovery House, 2008).

[17]M. McMinn, *Sin and Grace in Christian Counseling* (Downers Grove, IL: IVP Academic, 2008), p. 154.

[18]H. R. Fedden, *Suicide: A Social and Historical Study* (London: Peter Davies, 1938), p. 309.

[19]Kushner, *American Suicide,* p. 21.

[20]A. Y. Hsu, *Grieving a Suicide: A Loved One's Search for Comfort, Answers and Hope* (Downers Grove, IL: InterVarsity Press, 2002), p. 89.

[21]L. Carr and G. Carr, *Fierce Goodbye: Living in the Shadow of Suicide* (Scottdale, PA: Herald, 2004), p. 107.

[22]Nelson, *Making and Unmaking,* p. 116.

[23]T. Wright, *The Life of William Cowper* (London: T. Fisher Unwin, 1892), pp. 60-61, 105, 208.

[24]McCullough and Willoughby, "Religion, Self-Regulation," pp. 69-93.

[25]D. B. Larson and S. S. Larson, "Spirituality's Potential Relevance to Physical and Emotional Health: A Brief Review of Quantitative Research," *Journal of Psychology and Theology* 31, no. 1 (2003): 37-51.

[26]K. I. Pargament et al., "Religious Coping Methods as Predictors of Psychological, Physical and Spiritual Outcomes Among Medically Ill Elderly Patients: A Two-year Longitudinal Study," *Journal of Health Psychology* 9, no. 6 (2004): 713-30.

[27]J. B. Green, *Body, Soul, and Human Life: The Nature of Humanity in the Bible* (Grand Rapids: Baker Academic, 2008), pp. 29-31.

[28]Beck and Demarest write, "Although body and spirit are separate entities ontologically, in this life they are intricately united." J. R. Beck and B. Demarest, *The Human Person in Theology and Psychology: A Biblical Anthropology for the Twenty-First Century* (Grand Rapids: Kregel, 2005), p. 141.

[29]Ibid., p. 153; G. W. Moon, "A Transformational Approach," in S. P. Greggo and T. A. Sisemore, *Counseling and Christianity: Five Approaches* (Downers Grove, IL: IVP Academic, 2012), p. 136; Green, *Body, Soul,* p. 179.

[30]C. Plantinga Jr., *Not the Way It's Supposed to Be* (Grand Rapids: Eerdmans, 1995), p. 140.

[31]D. Willard, *The Spirit of the Disciplines: Understanding How God Changes Lives* (San Francisco: HarperSanFrancisco, 1988), p. 70.

[32]J. T. Maltsberger, T. Jobe and D. G. Stauffacher, "Supporting the Family of a Suicidal Person: Those Who Live in Fear," in D. C. Clark, *Clergy Response to Suicidal Persons and Their Family Members* (Chicago: Exploration, 1993), p. 79.

[33]M. G. Hubbard, *More Than an Aspirin: A Christian Perspective on Pain and Suffering* (Grand Rapids: Discovery House, 2009), p. 91.

[34]Greene-McCreight, *Darkness Is My Only Companion,* p. 59.

[35]A. B. Spencer and W. D. Spencer, *Joy Through the Night: Biblical Resources for Suffering People* (Downers Grove, IL: InterVarsity Press, 1994), p. 127.

[36]Greene-McCreight, *Darkness Is My Only Companion,* p. 130.

[37]E. Robins, *The Final Months: A Study of the Lives of 134 Persons Who Committed Suicide* (New York: Oxford University Press, 1994), p. 206.

[38]I. Bolton with C. Mitchell, *My Son . . . My Son . . . : A Guide to Healing After Death, Loss or Suicide* (Roswell, GA: Bolton Press Atlanta, 2005), p. 31.

[39]Robins, *The Final Months,* pp. 200-201.

[40]K. R. Jamison, *Night Falls Fast: Understanding Suicide* (New York: Vintage, 1999), p. 82.

[41]T. Joiner, *Myths About Suicide* (Cambridge, MA: Harvard University Press, 2010), p. 171.

[42]E. S. Shneidman, *The Suicidal Mind* (New York: Oxford University Press, 1996), p. 56.

[43]D. B. Biebel and S. L. Foster, *Finding Your Way After the Suicide of Someone You Love* (Grand Rapids: Zondervan, 2005), p. 27.

[44]Ibid., p. 14.

[45]Hsu, *Grieving a Suicide*, p. 29.

[46]Ibid., p. 17.

[47]Ibid., p. 89.

[48]E. R. Ellis and G. N. Allen, *Traitor Within: Our Suicide Problem* (Garden City, NY: Doubleday, 1961), p. 176.

[49]Joiner, *Myths About Suicide*, p. 44.

[50]Kushner, *American Suicide*, p. 2.

[51]Joiner, *Myths About Suicide*, p. 86.

[52]T. Joiner Jr., *Why People Die by Suicide* (Cambridge, MA: Harvard University Press, 2007), p. 35.

[53]E. Stengel, *Suicide and Attempted Suicide* (Harmondsworth, UK: Penguin, 1964), p. 99; M. Williams, *Cry of Pain: Understanding Suicide and Self-Harm* (London: Penguin, 1997), p. 150.

[54]S. R. Blauner, *How I Stayed Alive When My Brain Was Trying to Kill Me: One Person's Guide to Suicide Prevention* (New York: William Morrow, 2002), p. 219.

[55]M. Z. Brown, K. Comtois and M. M. Linehan, "Reasons for Suicide Attempts and Nonsuicidal Self-Injury in Women with Borderline Personality Disorder," *Journal of Abnormal Psychology* 111, no. 1 (2002): 198-202.

[56]B. M. Barraclough et al., "A Hundred Cases of Suicide: Clinical Aspects," *British Journal of Psychiatry* 125 (1974): 355-73.

[57]W. Styron, *Darkness Visible: A Memoir of Madness* (New York: Random House, 1990), p. 33.

[58]Ibid., p. 83.

[59]Ibid., p. 62

[60]Robins, *The Final Months*, p. 410.

[61]Ibid., p. 94.

[62]J. B. Luoma, C. E. Martin and J. L. Pearson, "Contact with Mental Health and Primary Care Providers Before Suicide: A Review of the Evidence," *The American Journal of Psychiatry* 159, no. 6 (2002): 909-16; P. Wang, P. Berglund and R. Kessler, "Patterns and Correlates of Contacting Clergy for Mental Disorders in the United States," *Health Services Research* 38, no. 2 (2003): 647-73.

[63]Robins, *The Final Months*, p. 248.

[64]Ibid., p. 399.

[65]Ibid., p. 355.

[66]Ibid.

[67]M. Gould et al., "Evaluating Iatrogenic Risk of Youth Suicide Screening Programs: A Randomized Controlled Trial," *The Journal of the American Medical Association* 293, no. 13 (2005): 1635-43.

[68]Robins, *The Final Months*, p. 377.

[69]Shneidman, *The Suicidal Mind*, p. 74.

[70]Ibid., p. 46.

[71]ABC News, "Man Survives Suicide Jump from Golden Gate Bridge," April 28, 2006, www.abcnews.go.com/GMA/story?id=1900628.

[72]Shneidman, *The Suicidal Mind*, p. 133.

[73]R. McKeon, *Suicidal Behaivor*, in the series Advances in Psychotherapy: Evidence-Based Practice (Cambridge, MA: Hogrefe and Huber, 2009), p. 15.

[74]Jamison, *Night Falls Fast*, pp. 206-7; J. Sun et al., "Seasonality of Suicide in Shandong China, 1991–2009: Associations with Gender, Age, Area and Methods of Suicide," *Journal of Affective Disorders* 135, no. 1-3 (2011): 258-66.

[75]T. Joiner et al., *The Interpersonal Theory of Suicide: Guidance for Working with Suicidal Clients* (Washington, DC: American Psychological Association, 2009), p. 14. For specific statistics, see Joiner, *Why People Die*, pp. 128-29.

[76]Jamison, *Night Falls Fast*, pp. 94-95.

[77]G. Maldonado and J. F. Kraus, "Variation in Suicide Occurrence by Time of Day, Day of the Week, Month, and Lunar Phase," *Suicide and Life-Threatening Behavior* 21, no. 2 (1991): 174-87.

[78]Robins, *The Final Months*, p. 284.

CHAPTER 3: SUICIDE AND CHRISTIAN THEOLOGY

[1]S. R. Blauner, *How I Stayed Alive When My Brain Was Trying to Kill Me: One Person's Guide to Suicide Prevention* (New York: William Morrow, 2002).

[2]E. R. Ellis and G. N. Allen, *Traitor Within: Our Suicide Problem* (Garden City, NY: Doubleday, 1961), p. 176.

[3]E. S. Shneidman, *The Suicidal Mind* (New York: Oxford University Press, 1996).

[4]E. Robins, *The Final Months: A Study of the Lives of 134 Persons Who Committed Suicide* (New York: Oxford University Press, 1994), p. 229.

[5]J. W. von Goethe, *The Sorrows of Young Werther* (New York: Vintage Classic, 1971).

[6]Shneidman, *The Suicidal Mind*, p. 45.

[7]K. Mason et al., "Clergy Referral of Suicidal Individuals: A Qualitative Study," *Journal of Pastoral Care and Counseling* 65, no. 3 (2011).

[8]J. T. Clemons, *What Does the Bible Say About Suicide?* (Minneapolis: Fortress, 1990), p. 97.

[9]For example, Smedes writes, "When I was a child, I heard compassionate people comfort the loved ones of a suicide victim with the assurance that anyone who commits suicide is insane at that moment. So, being mad, a suicide victim would not be held accountable by God, despite the sin. But they were wrong of course." L. B. Smedes, "Good Question: Is Suicide Unforgiveable?" *Christianity Today*, July 10, 2000, www.christianitytoday.com/ct/2000/july10/30.61.html.

[10]M. Luther, *Works of Luther*, ed. and trans. Jaroslav Pelikan (Philadelphia: Fortress, 1967), 54:29.

[11]Biebel and Foster argue that the sixth commandment was not a "general prohibition against killing anyone, since the Israelites, with God's blessing, killed plenty of their enemies after they received the commandments. Nor does it seem to apply to suicide." D. B. Biebel and S. L. Foster, *Finding Your Way After the Suicide of Someone You Love* (Grand Rapids: Zondervan, 2005), p. 123.

[12]H. R. Fedden, *Suicide: A Social and Historical Study* (London: Peter Davies, 1938), pp. 10, 31; A. J. Droge and J. D. Tabor, *A Noble Death: Suicide and Martyrdom Among Christians and Jews in Antiquity* (San Francisco: HarperCollins, 1992).

[13]Droge and Tabor, *A Noble Death*.

[14]Ibid., p. 129.

[15]Ibid., p. 131.

[16]Ibid., p. 188.

[17]St. Ambrose of Milan, *Letter* 37, Christian Classics Ethereal Library, Calvin College, www.ccel.org/ccel/pearse/morefathers/files/ambrose_letters_04_letters31_40.htm.

[18]J. Donne, *Biathanatos*, ed. William A. Clebsch (Chico, CA: Scholars Press, 1983), pp. 24-25.

[19]Fedden, *Suicide*, p. 120.

[20]Donne, *Biathanatos*, p. 37.

[21]Ibid., pp. 42, 46-47, 60-61, 81, 96.

[22]A. Alvarez, *The Savage God: A Study of Suicide* (New York: Random House, 1972), p. 165.

[23]F. Winslow, *The Anatomy of Suicide* (Boston: Milford House, 1972), p. 38.

[24]D. Bonhoeffer, *Ethics*, vol. 6, ed. I. Tödt et al., trans. R. Krauss, C. C. West and D. W. Stott (Minneapolis: Fortress), p. 200.

[25]A. Y. Hsu, *Grieving a Suicide: A Loved One's Search for Comfort, Answers and Hope* (Downers Grove, IL: InterVarsity Press, 2002), p. 100.

[26]Winslow comments, "If I am commanded not to shed the blood of another man because he is made in the *image of God*, I am not justified in shedding my own blood, as I stand in the same relation to the Deity as my fellow-men." Winslow, *Anatomy of Suicide*, p. 37.

[27]Augustine, *City of God* 1.20; see also 1.17, 1.18, 1.22, 1.24, 1.25, 1.26, 1.27. In addition, see Augustine's tract *Against Gaudentius*.

[28]Droge and Tabor, *A Noble Death*, p. 175.

[29]J. Bels, "La mort volontaire dans l'oeuvre de saint Augustin," *Revue de l'histoire des religions* 187, 164 (1975). Droge and Tabor specify, "Augustine was not the first to draw this distinction, as we have seen, but it was he who reinforced it

and established it in a way that has endured to the present day." Droge and Tabor, *A Noble Death,* p. 179.

[30]Joiner notes that many Muslim clergy distinguish between self-martyrdom and suicide. T. Joiner, *Why People Die by Suicide* (Cambridge, MA: Harvard University Press, 2005), p. 142.

[31]T. Aquinas, *Summa Theologiae* 42.124 (New York: McGraw-Hill, 1966), p. 43.

[32]Bonhoeffer, *Ethics,* p. 200.

[33]G. K. Chesterton, *Orthodoxy* (New York: John Lane, 1908), p. 134. He also writes, "Obviously. A martyr is a man who cares so much for something outside him, that he forgets his own personal life. A suicide is a man who cares so little for anything outside him, that he wants to see the last of everything. One wants something to begin: the other wants everything to end. . . . The suicide is ignoble because he has not this link with being: he is a mere destroyer; spiritually, he destroys the universe." *Orthodoxy,* p. 133.

[34]Clemons mentions early councils at Guadix (305), Carthage (348) and Braga (363). Clemons, *What Does the Bible Say,* p. 79. Fedden adds the Council of Auxerre (A.D. 578), the Antisidor Council (A.D. 590), the Council of Hereford (A.D. 673), the Council of Troyes (A.D. 878), the A.D. 967 decree of King Edgar and the Synod of Nîmes (1284). Fedden, *Suicide,* pp. 134, 135, 144. Alvarez adds the Council of Toledo (A.D. 693). Alvarez, *The Savage God,* p. 71. Durkheim mentions the Council of Arles. E. Durkheim, *Suicide: A Study in Sociology,* trans. John A. Spaulding and George Simpson (New York: Free Press, 1951), p. 327. Stengel adds the Council of Nîmes, 1184. E. Stengel, *Suicide and Attempted Suicide* (Harmondsworth, UK: Penguin, 1964), p. 60. Watt also mentions the Synod of Nîmes in 1284. J. R. Watt, *Choosing Death: Suicide and Calvinism in Early Modern Geneva* (Kirksville, MO: Truman State University Press, 2001), p. 86.

[35]Stengel, *Suicide and Attempted,* p. 59. Fedden, *Suicide: A Social,* p. 115.

[36]Fedden, *Suicide,* p. 133.

[37]T. López Bardón, "Councils of Braga," in *The Catholic Encyclopedia* (New York: Robert Appleton, 1907). Droge and Tabor, *A Noble Death,* p. 5.

[38]Aquinas, *Summa Theologiae* 2.2.64.5.

[39]Calvin discussed suicide in two sermons, on Saul and his armor bearer and Ahithophel. Watt, *Choosing Death,* pp. 67-68.

[40]Chesterton, *Orthodoxy,* pp. 131-32. This is a similar perspective to that of Wittgenstein, who wrote, "If suicide is allowed then everything is allowed." L. Wittgenstein, *Notebooks 1914–1916,* trans. G. E. M. Anscombe (New York: Harper, 1961).

[41]"*Le suicide doit être une vocation.*" (Suicide must be a vocation.) J. Rigaut, "*Je serai sérieux comme le plaisir,*" *Revue Littérature* 17 (December 1920), www .larevuedesressources.org/je-serai-serieux-comme-le-plaisir,1900.html.

[42]Bonhoeffer, *Ethics*, p. 198.

[43]D. Bonhoeffer, *Letters and Papers from Prison*, ed. C. Gremmels et al., trans. I. Best et al. (Minneapolis: Fortress, 2010), 8:64.

[44]For a discussion see J. A. Gallagher, "A Catholic Perspective on Suicide," in *Clergy Response to Suicidal Persons and Their Family Members*, ed. D. C. Clark (Chicago: Exploration 1993), p. 22.

[45]Clemons writes, "Roman Catholic canon law was changed in 1983 to permit known suicides to receive in some cases, full funeral rites." Clemons, *What Does the Bible Say*, p. 9. See paragraph 2281 of the *Catechism of the Catholic Church*, www.vatican.va/archive/ENG0015/_INDEX.HTM.

[46]See paragraph 2283 of the *Catechism of the Catholic Church*, www.vatican.va/archive/ENG0015/_INDEX.HTM.

[47]The Carrs write, "The evidence, then, is that there is neither valid biblical nor 'natural' grounds for the church's condemnation of suicide as an unforgivable sin. It is an act that we do not want to condone or encourage, yet there is no evidence that it brings eternal damnation to its successful practitioners. . . . God's grace is sufficient." I. Carr and G. Carr, *Fierce Goodbye: Living in the Shadow of Suicide* (Scottdale, PA: Herald, 2004), p. 103.

[48]Smedes, "Good Question," www.christianitytoday.com/ct/2000/july10/30.61.html.

[49]Donne, *Biathanatos*, p. 10.

[50]Carr and Carr, *Fierce Goodbye*, p. 45.

[51]Hsu, *Grieving a Suicide*.

[52]Bonhoeffer, *Ethics*, p. 199.

[53]Smedes, "Good Question," www.christianitytoday.com/ct/2000/July10/30.61.html.

[54]Burton writes, "Thus of [the suicide's] goods and bodies we can dispose; but what shall become of their souls, God alone can tell; His mercy may come *inter pontem et fontem, inter gladium et jugulum*, [betwixt the bridge and the brook, the knife and the throat]. *Quod cuiquam contigit, cuivis potest* [what happens to someone may happen to anyone]. Who knows how he may be tempted? It is his case, it may be thine: *Quae sua sors hodie est, cras fore vestra potest.* We ought not to be so rash and rigorous in our censures as some are; charity will judge and hope the best; God be merciful unto us all!" R. Burton, *The Anatomy of Melancholy*, vol. 1 (London: Dent, 1964), p. 439.

[55]K. Greene-McCreight, *Darkness Is My Only Companion: A Christian Response to Mental Illness* (Grand Rapids: Brazos, 2006), p. 97.

[56]D. Wilkerson, *Suicide* (Lindale, TX: David Wilkerson Publications, 1978), p. 29.

[57]"The Bible says our body is the temple of the Holy Ghost. To destroy that temple is to blaspheme. It is an unpardonable sin." Ibid., p. 40.

[58]S. Harper, "A Wesleyan Arminian View," in *4 Views on Eternal Security*, ed. J. Matthew Pinson (Grand Rapids: Zondervan, 2002), p. 239.

[59]Ibid., p. 243.

[60]For an in-depth discussion of "the equality of sins dissolves all concrete sins in an ocean of undifferentiated sinfulness," see M. Volf, *Exclusion and Embrace: A Theological Exploration of Identity, Otherness, and Reconciliation* (Nashville: Abingdon, 1996), p. 82. See also Chesterton, *Orthodoxy*, p. 133.

[61]As Williams has noted, "What would Hume, as an empiricist, have made of the evidence which has now emerged about the aftermath of suicide? In many instances suicide appears to have such a devastating effect on the survivors that, if it were only the balance of suffering one were examining, one could conclude that the suicide was not ethically justifiable." M. Williams, *Cry of Pain: Understanding Suicide and Self-Harm* (London: Penguin, 1997), p. 104.

[62]C. Plantinga Jr., *Not the Way It's Supposed to Be* (Grand Rapids: Eerdmans, 1995), p. 21.

[63]Ibid., p. 22.

[64]Some do not. For example, Fedden believes that suicide is amoral: "There is something very niggard, very middle-class, very non-conformist, in judging a life by its exodus." Fedden, *Suicide*, p. 13. Gesundheit believes Judaism considers suicide a sin. B. Gesundheit, "Suicide—A Halakhic and Moral Analysis of Masekhet Semahot, Chapter 2, Laws 1-6," *Tradition* 35, no. 3 (2001): 31-51. In Islam, God punishes suicide. See the Qur'an 4:29.

[65]Durkheim, *Suicide: A Study*, p. 327.

[66]Mason et al., "Clergy Referral."

[67]Szasz dissents. See T. Szasz, "The Case Against Suicide Prevention," *American Psychologist* 41, no. 7 (1986): 806-12.

[68]T. Joiner et al., *The Interpersonal Theory of Suicide: Guidance for Working with Suicidal Clients* (Washington, DC: American Psychological Association, 2009), p. 168.

[69]Plantinga, *Not the Way It's Supposed to Be*, p. 20. He goes on to say social and cultural forces sometimes "push, draw, stress, and limit human beings in countless ways," pp. 64-65.

[70]Smedes, "Good Question," www.christianitytoday.com/ct/2000/july10/30.61 .html.

[71]Mason et al., "Clergy Referral."

[72]"Suicide," Assemblies of God, ag.org/top/beliefs/contempissues_17_suicide.cfm.

[73]*Catechism of the Catholic Church* 3.2.2.5, www.vatican.va/archive/ccc_css/ archive/catechism/p3s2c2a5.htm. "In 1983, the Roman Catholic Church removed suicide from the list of mortal sins." Suicide Prevention Resource Center, *The Role of Faith Communities in Preventing Suicide: A Report of an Interfaith Suicide Prevention Dialogue* (Newton, MA: Education Development Center, 2009), p. 27.

[74]www.elca.org/en/Faith/Faith-and-Society/Social-Messages/Suicide-Prevention.

[75]General Convention, *Journal of the General Convention of the . . . Episcopal Church, Denver, 2000* (New York: General Convention, 2001), p. 173.

[76]Stanley S. Harakas, "The Stand of the Orthodox Church on Controversial Issues," Greek Orthodox Archdiocese of America, www.goarch.org/ourfaith/controversialissues.

[77]"Consensus Statement on Suicide and Suicide Prevention," Suicide Prevention Resource Center, March 12–13, 2008, www.sprc.org/sites/sprc.org/files/library/Consensus_Statement.pdf.

[78]"The Nature and Value of Human Life," Presbyterian Church USA, www.pcusa.org/resource/nature-and-value-human-life.

[79]Clemons, *What Does the Bible Say.*

[80]"Prevention of Lesbian, Gay, Bisexual, and Transgender Youth Suicide," July 6, 1999, United Church of Christ General Synod, www.ucc.org/assets/pdfs/1999-PREVENTION-OF-LESBIAN-GAY-BISEXUAL-AND-TRANSGENDER-SUICIDE.pdf.

[81]*The Book of Discipline of the United Methodist Church* (Nashville: United Methodist Publishing House, 2004), www.archives.umc.org/interior.asp?mid=1735. Also, see Suicide Prevention Resource Center, Appendix E, *The Role of Faith Communities*, p. 29.

[82]William H. Nicholson, "How to Help Someone Who Wants to Commit Suicide," Anchorage Moravian Church, November 11, 2004, www.alaskamoravian.org/artman/publish/article_19.shtml.

CHAPTER 4: THEORIES OF SUICIDE

[1]K. Lewin, *Field Theory in Social Science: Selected Theoretical Papers*, ed. D. Cartwright (New York: Harper and Row, 1951), p. 169.

[2]As cited by R. Burton, *The Anatomy of Melancholy* (London: Dent, 1964), 1:177.

[3]See Chrysostom's seventeenth epistle to Olympia, as cited in Burton, *Anatomy of Melancholy*, p. 259.

[4]Aquinas, *Summa Theologiae* 35. Melancholy, of course, existed before then. For example, Egyptian monks experienced melancholy or acedia, and Dante's fifth circle confined the melancholy, which provides supportive evidence that melancholy existed before the Renaissance. H. R. Fedden, *Suicide: A Social and Historical Study* (London: Peter Davies, 1938), p. 169.

[5]F. Winslow, *The Anatomy of Suicide* (Boston: Milford House, 1972), p. 126.

[6]Burton, *Anatomy of Melancholy*, pp. 169-70.

[7]Ibid., pp. 210-11, 219, 301, 331, 333, 336, 339, 346, 372.

[8]J. R. Watt, *Choosing Death: Suicide and Calvinism in Early Modern Geneva*

(Kirksville, MO: Truman State University Press, 2001), p. 11. Watt also notes that Anglican physicians "Alexander Crichton and William Pargeter, who both wrote in the 1790s, accused the Methodists of contributing to suicide by nurturing the terror of hell, leading people to melancholy and despair" (p. 118).

[9]Burton, *Anatomy of Melancholy*, pp. 429-30.

[10]Ibid., p. 431.

[11]H. I. Kushner, *American Suicide: A Psychocultural Exploration* (New Brunswick, NJ: Rutgers University Press, 1989), pp. 19, 28.

[12]Winslow, *Anatomy of Suicide*, p. 229.

[13]Ibid., p. 241.

[14]Ibid., pp. 45, 136.

[15]Ibid., p. 338.

[16]E. Durkheim, *Suicide: A Study in Sociology*, trans. John A. Spaulding and George Simpson (New York: Free Press, 1951), p. 67.

[17]Ibid., p. 313.

[18]Ibid., pp. 324, 312. Durkheim also believed that this suicidal tendency increased from youth to older adulthood. He noted that the suicidal tendency was ten times greater in older adulthood than in youth.

[19]Ibid., p. 388. Durkheim notes that older social forms of organization such as the family unit or clan had disappeared over time and were not being replaced.

[20]Ibid., p. 185. Watt specifies, "A thorough examination of the data demonstrates that there was a dramatic increase in suicide in the eighteenth century, particularly after 1750, an increase that cannot be dismissed as the result of lost records or lax investigations for one era and complete registers and strict inquests for another." Watt, *Choosing Death*, p. 13.

[21]Durkheim, *Suicide: A Study*, p. 85.

[22]Ibid., pp. 213, 158, 221. Durkheim argues that societal integration is important because only a society is able to communicate to individual members their worth and the value of their lives; an individual's smaller horizon limits him or her from an accurate appraisal (p. 213). Durkheim also believed that the suicide rate was higher among Protestants than among Catholics because Catholicism dominated and controlled the lives of its adherents (p. 158). Durkheim writes that societies that practice altruistic suicide are highly integrated with individuals "almost completely absorbed in the group" (p. 221).

[23]Ibid., pp. 246, 258. Durkheim believed crises cause suicides because they are "disturbances of the collective order" (p. 246), resulting in society's insufficient presence in individuals "leaving people without a check-rein" (p. 258).

[24]Kushner, *American Suicide*, p. 61.

[25]S. Freud, "Mourning and Melancholia," in *Standard Edition of the Complete*

Psychological Works of Sigmund Freud, ed. and trans. James Strachey et al. (London: Hogarth, 1957), 14:239-58.

[26]"The aim of all life is death." S. Freud, *Beyond the Pleasure Principle*, trans. and ed. James Strachey (New York: W. W. Norton, 1961), p. 46.

[27]Freud, "Mourning and Melancholia," p. 248.

[28]Ibid., pp. 252, 246.

[29]I. Bolton with C. Mitchell, *My Son . . . My Son . . . : A Guide to Healing After Death, Loss or Suicide* (Roswell, GA: Bolton Press Atlanta, 2005), p. 9.

[30]A. Wenzel, G. K. Brown and A. T. Beck, *Cognitive Therapy for Suicidal Patients: Scientific and Clinical Applications* (Washington, DC: American Psychological Association, 2009), p. 4.

[31]E. S. Shneidman, *The Suicidal Mind* (New York: Oxford University Press, 1996), p. 4.

[32]Ibid., p. 25.

[33]Ibid., p. 13.

[34]R. McKeon, *Suicidal Behavior*, in the series Advances in Psychotherapy: Evidence-Based Practice (Cambridge, MA: Hogrefe and Huber, 2009), p. 28. Shneidman, *The Suicidal Mind*, p. 131.

[35]Shneidman, *The Suicidal Mind*, p. 151.

[36]M. Williams, *Cry of Pain: Understanding Suicide and Self-Harm* (London: Penguin, 1997), pp. xii, 152.

[37]Ibid., p. 153.

[38]Ibid., pp. 162, 92, 171.

[39]Ibid., p. 173.

[40]Ibid., p. 215.

[41]R. R. van der Sande et al., "Psychosocial Intervention Following Suicide Attempt: A Systematic Review of Treatment Interventions," *Acta Psychiatrica Scandinavica* 96, no. 1 (1997): 43-50. Wenzel and colleagues note that their theory is compatible with Joiner's and with Rudd's. Wenzel, Brown and Beck, *Cognitive Therapy*, pp. 58-59. They go on, "We agree with Joiner that cognitions about failures in life, such as failed belongingness or burdensomeness, are necessary for suicidal crises to develop" (p. 76). Joiner and colleagues write, "The [interpersonal] theory is amenable to, and easily integrated into, a range of cognitive-interpersonal approaches." T. Joiner et al., *The Interpersonal Theory of Suicide: Guidance for Working with Suicidal Clients* (Washington, DC: American Psychological Association, 2009), p. 193. As far as Linehan's theory, Joiner writes, "The current framework and Linehan's model are thus quite compatible; she has identified processes that can be viewed as relatively distal in the causal chain leading up to suicidal behavior; the processes, in turn, may lay the groundwork for the relatively more proximal factors emphasized here" (p. 42).

[42]A. L. Miller, J. H. Rathus and M. M. Linehan, *Dialectical Behavior Therapy with Suicidal Adolescents* (New York: Guilford, 2007), p. 28. Dialectical behavior therapy targets first life-interfering behaviors, then therapy-interfering behaviors, and last behaviors that interfere with quality of life.

[43]Wenzel, Brown and Beck, *Cognitive Therapy*.

[44]A. T. Beck, G. Brown and R. A. Steer, "Prediction of Eventual Suicide in Psychiatric Inpatients by Clinical Ratings of Hopelessness," *Journal of Consulting and Clinical Psychology* 57, no. 2 (1989): 309-10; A. T. Beck et al., "Relationship Between Hopelessness and Ultimate Suicide: A Replication with Psychiatric Outpatients," *The American Journal of Psychiatry* 147, no. 2 (1990): 190-95; G. K. Brown et al., "Risk Factors for Suicide in Psychiatric Outpatients: A 20-Year Prospective Study," *Journal of Consulting and Clinical Psychology* 68, no. 3 (2000): 371-77; D. McMillan et al., "Can We Predict Suicide and Non-Fatal Self-Harm with the Beck Hopelessness Scale? A Meta-Analysis," *Psychological Medicine* 37, no. 6 (2007): 769-78. M. Spokas et al., "Suicide Risk Factors and Mediators Between Childhood Sexual Abuse and Suicide Ideation Among Male and Female Suicide Attempters," *Journal of Traumatic Stress* 22, no. 5 (2009): 467-70.

[45]Wenzel, Brown and Beck, *Cognitive Therapy*, p. 119; L. R. Pollock and J. M. G. Williams, "Problem-Solving in Suicide Attempters," *Psychological Medicine* 34, no 1 (2004): 163-67.

[46]Wenzel, Brown and Beck, *Cognitive Therapy*, p. 65.

[47]Ibid., p. 128.

[48]Ibid., p. 191.

[49]Ibid., p. 192.

[50]Ibid.

[51]Ibid., p. 193.

[52]Ibid., pp. 10, 94, 132.

[53]M. M. Linehan, *Cognitive-Behavioral Treatment of Borderline Personality Disorder* (New York: Guilford, 1993); McKeon, *Suicidal Behavior*, p. 40.

[54]Y. Lee, "Validation of Reasons for Living and Their Relationship with Suicidal Ideation in Korean College Students," *Death Studies* 36, no. 8 (2012): 712-22; M. Oquendo et al., "Protective Factors Against Suicidal Behavior in Latinos," *Journal of Nervous and Mental Disease* 193, no. 7 (2005): 438-43.

[55]McKeon, *Suicidal Behavior*, p. 45.

[56]Miller, Rathus and Linehan, *Dialectical Behavior Therapy*, p. 38.

[57]Ibid., p. 35.

[58]M. M. Linehan et al., "Two-Year Randomized Controlled Trial and Follow-Up of Dialectical Behavior Therapy vs. Therapy by Experts for Suicidal Behaviors and Borderline Personality Disorder," *Archives of General Psychiatry* 63, no. 7

(2006): 757-66. The important aspect of this study is that dialectical behavior therapy was not compared to treatment as usual but to community treatment by experts and was found to outperform community treatment by experts on suicidal behavior treatment targets.

[59]J. H. Rathus and A. L. Miller, "Dialectical Behavior Therapy Adapted for Suicidal Adolescents," *Suicide and Life-Threatening Behavior* 32, no. 2 (2002): 146-57.

[60]T. Joiner, *Why People Die by Suicide* (Cambridge, MA: Harvard University Press, 2005), pp. 96-97, 47.

[61]T. Joiner et al., *The Interpersonal Theory*, pp. 42, 136.

[62]Ibid., p. 101.

[63]Ibid., p. 6.

[64]D. W. Cox et al., "Suicide in the United States Air Force: Risk Factors Communicated Before and at Death," *Journal of Affective Disorders* 133 (2011): 398-405; T. E. Joiner et al., "Main Predictions of the Interpersonal-Psychological Theory of Suicidal Behavior: Empirical Tests in Two Samples of Young Adults," *Journal of Abnormal Psychology* 118, no. 3 (2009): 634-46; K. A. Van Orden et al., "Suicidal Desire and the Capability for Suicide: Tests of the Interpersonal-Psychological Theory of Suicidal Behavior Among Adults," *Journal of Consulting and Clinical Psychology* 76, no. 1 (2008): 72-83.

[65]Joiner et al., *The Interpersonal Theory*, p. 111.

[66]Genes account for 70 percent of fearlessness. T. Joiner, "Lonely at the Top: Why Men Are the Lonely Sex," presentation given for the Massachusetts Coalition for Suicide Prevention, Northeast Region, September 20, 2012, Bedford, MA.

[67]Joiner, *Why People Die*, p. 118.

[68]J. G. Saxe, "The Blind Men and the Elephant," in *The Poems of John Godfrey Saxe: Complete in One Volume* (Boston: Ticknor and Fields, 1868), p. 259.

[69]P. Wang, P. Berglund and R. Kessler, "Patterns and Correlates of Contacting Clergy for Mental Disorders in the United States," *Health Services Research* 38, no. 2 (2003): 647-73.

[70]C. G. Ellison et al., "The Clergy as a Source of Mental Health Assistance: What Americans Believe," *Review of Religious Research* 48, no. 2 (2006): 190-211, 197.

[71]K. Mason et al., "Clergy Referral of Suicidal Individuals: A Qualitative Study," *Journal of Pastoral Care and Counseling* 65, no. 3 (2011).

[72]D. Lester, "Religiosity and Personal Violence: A Regional Analysis of Suicide and Homicide Rates," *Journal of Social Psychology* 127, no. 6 (1987): 685-86; J. Neeleman, "Regional Suicide Rates in the Netherlands: Does Religion Still Play a Role?" *International Journal of Epidemiology* 27, no. 3 (1998): 466-72; S. Stack, "The Effect of Religious Commitment: A Cross National Analysis," *Journal of Health and Social Behavior* 24 (1983): 362-74; S. Stack, "The Effect of the Decline in Institutionalized Religion on Suicide, 1954–1978," *Journal for*

the Scientific Study of Religion 22, no. 3 (1983): 239-52; F. Van Tubergen et al., "Denomination, Religious Context, and Suicide: Neo-Durkheimian Multilevel Explanations Tested with Individual and Contextual Data," *American Journal of Sociology* 111, no. 3 (2005): 797-823.

[73]M. J. Alexander et al., "Coping with Thoughts of Suicide: Techniques Used by Consumers of Mental Health Services," *Psychiatric Services* 60, no. 9 (2009): 1214-21.

[74]A. Holmes, *All Truth Is God's Truth* (Grand Rapids: Eerdmans, 1977), p. 8; J. D. Carter and B. Narramore, *The Integration of Psychology and Theology: An Introduction* (Grand Rapids: Zondervan), p. 73.

[75]K. Mason et al., "Clergy referral."

[76]Nearly half the psalms are lament—for example, Psalm 89.

[77]K. Mason et al., "Clergy referral."

[78]F. Watts, K. Dutton and L. Gulliford, "Human Spiritual Qualities: Integrating Psychology and Religion," *Mental Health, Religion and Culture* 9, no. 3 (2006): 277-89.

CHAPTER 5: HELPING SOMEONE IN A SUICIDE CRISIS

[1]D. G. Stauffacher and D. C. Clark, "Recognizing Suicidal Risk," in D. C. Clark, *Clergy Response to Suicidal Persons and Their Family Members* (Chicago: Exploration, 1993), pp. 35-36.

[2]H. Hendin et al., "Recognizing and Responding to a Suicide Crisis," *Suicide and Life-Threatening Behavior* 31, no. 2 (2001): 115-28.

[3]A. Wenzel, G. K. Brown and A. T. Beck, *Cognitive Therapy for Suicidal Patients: Scientific and Clinical Applications* (Washington, DC: American Psychological Association, 2009), p. 142.

[4]Ibid.

[5]Possible depression (early morning awakening, loss of interest in golf and friendships), loss of his good name, loss of the affair, social withdrawal.

[6]T. Joiner, *Myths About Suicide* (Cambridge, MA: Harvard University Press, 2010), p. 65.

[7]L. Barnes, R. M. Ikeda and M. Kresnow, "Help-Seeking Behavior Prior to Nearly Lethal Suicide Attempts," *Suicide and Life-Threatening Behavior* 32, suppl. (2001): 68-75.

[8]P. Wang, P. Berglund and R. Kessler, "Patterns and Correlates of Contacting Clergy for Mental Disorders in the United States," *Health Services Research* 38, no. 2 (2003): 647-73.

[9]P. A. Seaman, "A Moth in the Heart," in *Children of Jonah*, ed. J. T. Clemons (Sterling, VA: Capital Books, 2001), p. 42.

[10]M. S. Gould et al., "Evaluating Iatrogenic Risk of Youth Suicide Screening Programs: A Randomized Controlled Trial," *Journal of the American Medical Association* 293, no. 13 (2005): 1635-43.

[11]T. Joiner et al., *The Interpersonal Theory of Suicide: Guidance for Working with Suicidal Clients* (Washington, DC: American Psychological Association, 2009), p. 178.

[12]J. Peterson, J. Skeem and S. Manchak, "If You Want to Know, Consider Asking: How Likely Is It That Patients Will Hurt Themselves in the Future?" *Psychological Assessment* 23, no. 3 (2011): 626-34.

[13]L. L. Morrison and D. L. Downey, "Racial Differences in Self-Disclosure of Suicidal Ideation and Reasons for Living: Implications for Training," *Cultural Diversity and Ethnic Minority Psychology* 6, no. 4 (2000): 374-86.

[14]K. A. Busch, J. Fawcett and D. G. Jacobs, "Clinical Correlates of Inpatient Suicide," *Journal of Clinical Psychiatry*, 64, no. 1 (2003): 14-19.

[15]R. McKeon, *Suicidal Behavior*, in the series Advances in Psychotherapy: Evidence-Based Practice (Cambridge, MA: Hogrefe and Huber, 2009), p. 77. Wenzel, Brown and Beck, *Cognitive Therapy*, p. 140; A. L. Miller, J. H. Rathus and M. M. Linehan, *Dialectical Behavior Therapy with Suicidal Adolescents* (New York: Guilford, 2007), p. 67.

[16]McKeon, *Suicidal Behavior*, p. 21.

[17]S. Goldsmith et al., *Reducing Suicide: A National Imperative* (Washington, DC: National Academies Press, 2002), p. 5; A. T. Beck, G. Brown and R. A. Steer, "Prediction of Eventual Suicide in Psychiatric Inpatients by Clinical Ratings of Hopelessness," *Journal of Consulting and Clinical Psychology* 57, no. 2 (1989): 309-10; M. Williams, *Cry of Pain: Understanding Suicide and Self-Harm* (London: Penguin, 1997), p. 185.

[18]L. C. Range and E. Knott, "Twenty Suicide Assessment Instruments: Evaluation and Recommendations," *Death Studies* 21, no. 1 (1997): 25-58; D. Shaffer et al., "The Columbia Suicide Screen: Validity and Reliability of a Screen for Youth Suicide and Depression," *Journal of the American Academy of Child and Adolescent Psychiatry* 43 (2004): 71-79; United States Preventive Services Task Force, *Screening for Depression: Recommendations and Rationale*, 3rd ed. (Washington, DC: Office of Disease Prevention and Health Promotion, 2002).

[19]T. Joiner, *Why People Die by Suicide* (Cambridge, MA: Harvard University Press, 2005), p. 207; T. Joiner et al., *The Interpersonal Theory of Suicide: Guidance for Working with Suicidal Clients* (Washington, DC: American Psychological Association, 2009), p. 72; Wenzel, Brown and Beck, *Cognitive Therapy*, p. 140.

[20]P. M. Lewinsohn, P. Rohde and J. R. Seeley, "Adolescent Suicidal Ideation and Attempts: Prevalence, Risk Factors, and Clinical Implications," *Clinical Psychology: Science And Practice* 3, no. 1 (1996): 25-46.

[21]Wenzel, Brown and Beck, *Cognitive Therapy*, pp. 9, 139.

[22]Joiner et al., *The Interpersonal Theory*, p. 60.

[23]McKeon, *Suicidal Behavior*, p. 6.

[24]See the Acquired Capability for Suicide Scale, Joiner et al., *The Interpersonal Theory*, p. 61.

[25]E. K. Mościcki, "Epidemiology of Suicide," in *The Harvard Medical School Guide to Suicide Assessment and Intervention*, ed. Douglas G. Jacobs (San Francisco: Jossey-Bass, 1999), p. 43.

[26]McKeon, *Suicidal Behavior*, p. 34.

[27]Joiner et al., *The Interpersonal Theory*, p. 86.

[28]In *Nally v. Grace Community Church*, where a young man visited multiple times with multiple pastors and later killed himself, the Supreme Court of California decided that pastors are not held to the same standards of care as mental health professionals. *Nally v. Grace Community Church*, 47 Cal.3d 278 (1988), law.justia.com/cases/california/cal3d/47/278.html.

[29]For Joiner and colleagues' list, see Joiner et al., *The Interpersonal Theory*, p. 75.

[30]Mościcki, "Epidemiology of Suicide," p. 45; Goldsmith et al., *Reducing Suicide*, p. 5.

[31]K. Mason et al., "Clergy Referral of Suicidal Individuals: A Qualitative Study," *Journal of Pastoral Care and Counseling* 65, no. 3 (2011).

[32]M. A. Hubble, B. L. Duncan and S. D. Miller, *The Heart and Soul of Change: What Works in Therapy* (Washington, DC: American Psychological Association, 2000).

[33]T. Jobe, J. H. Shackelford and D. G. Stauffacher, "How to Get Professional Help for a Suicidal Person and Remain Involved," in Clark, *Clergy Response*, p. 67.

[34]Stauffacher and Clark, "Recognizing Suicidal Risk," p. 37.

[35]Wenzel, Brown and Beck, *Cognitive Therapy*, pp. 144-45.

[36]Joiner et al., *The Interpersonal Theory*, p. 95.

[37]S. R. Blauner, *How I Stayed Alive When My Brain Was Trying to Kill Me: One Person's Guide to Suicide Prevention* (New York: William Morrow, 2002), p. 149.

[38]M. S. Berk et al., "A Cognitive Therapy Intervention for Suicide Attempters: An Overview of the Treatment and Case Examples," *Cognitive and Behavioral Practice* 11 (2004): 265-77; Wenzel, Brown and Beck, *Cognitive Therapy*, p. 277.

[39]Rev. Chad Varah, an Anglican priest, started the Samaritans.

[40]M. S. Gould et al., "An Evaluation of Crisis Hotline Outcomes, Part 2: Suicidal Callers," *Suicide and Life-Threatening Behavior* 37, no. 3 (2007): 338-52.

[41]M. Rudd, M. Mandrusiak and T. E. Joiner Jr., "The Case Against No-Suicide Contracts: The Commitment to Treatment Statement as a Practice Alternative," *Journal of Clinical Psychology* 62, no. 2 (2006): 243-51; Wenzel, Brown and Beck, *Cognitive Therapy*, p. 145.

[42]"Suicide Prevention Alert," Office of the Ombudsman for Mental Health and Mental Retardation, State of Minnesota, 2002, mn.gov/omhdd/images/suicide-prevention-alert.pdf.

[43]B. L. Drew, "Self-Harm Behavior and No-Suicide Contracting in Psychiatric Inpatient Settings," *Archives of Psychiatric Nursing* 15, no. 3 (2001): 99-106.

[44]Joiner, *Why People Die,* p. 213.

[45]T. L. Farrow, A. F. Simpson and H. B. Warren, "The Effects of the Use of 'No-Suicide Contracts' in Community Crisis Situations: The Experience of Clinicians and Consumers," *Brief Treatment and Crisis Intervention* 2, no. 3 (2002): 241-46.

[46]For Joiner and colleagues' list see Joiner et al., *The Interpersonal Theory,* p. 75.

[47]McKeon, *Suicidal Behavior,* p. 35.

[48]Stauffacher and Clark, "Recognizing Suicidal Risk," p. 38.

[49]Jobe, Shackelford and Stauffacher, "How to Get Professional Help," p. 69.

[50]McKeon, *Suicidal Behavior,* p. 55.

[51]A. Beautrais, "The Contribution to Suicide Prevention of Restricting Access to Methods and Sites," *Crisis: The Journal of Crisis Intervention and Suicide Prevention* 28, no. 1 (2007): 1-3; Williams, *Cry of Pain,* p. 187.

[52]K. Hawton, "Restriction of Access to Methods of Suicide as a Means of Suicide Prevention," in *Prevention and Treatment of Suicidal Behavior: From Science to Practice,* ed. K. Hawton (New York: Oxford University Press, 2005), p. 281.

[53]R. H. Seiden, "Where Are They Now? A Follow-Up Study of Suicide Attempters from the Golden Gate Bridge," *Suicide and Life-Threatening Behavior* 8 (1978): 203-16.

[54]M. M. Miller et al., "The Association Between Changes in Household Firearm Ownership and Rates of Suicide in the United States, 1981–2002," *Injury Prevention* 12, no. 3 (2006): 178-82.

[55]For Joiner and colleagues' list see Joiner et al., *The Interpersonal Theory,* p. 75.

[56]E. Stengel, *Suicide and Attempted Suicide* (Harmondsworth, UK: Penguin, 1964), p. 71.

[57]M. K. Nock et al., "Cross-National Prevalence and Risk Factors for Suicidal Ideation, Plans and Attempts," *British Journal of Psychiatry* 192, no. 2 (2008): 98-105.

[58]G. Borges et al., "A Risk Index for 12-Month Suicide Attempts in the National Comorbidity Survey Replication (NCS-R)," *Psychological Medicine: A Journal of Research in Psychiatry and the Allied Sciences* 36, vol. 12 (2006): 1747-57; H. M. Hoberman and B. D. Garfinkel, "Completed Suicide in Children and Adolescents," *American Academy of Child and Adolescent Psychiatry Journal* 27, no. 6 (1988): 689-95; K. R. Jamison, *Night Falls Fast: Understanding Suicide* (New York: Vintage, 1999), p. 189; O. Simon et al., "Characteristics of Impulsive Suicide Attempts and Attempters," *Suicide and Life-Threatening Behavior* 32, 1 suppl. (2001): 49-59.

[59]G. Larkin, R. Smith and A. Beautrais, "Trends in US Emergency Department

Visits for Suicide Attempts, 1992–2001," *Crisis* 29, vol. 2 (2008): 73-80; E. Salinsky and C. Loftis, "Shrinking Inpatient Psychiatric Capacity: Cause for Celebration or Concern?" *Issue Brief National Health Policy Forum* 1, no. 823 (2007): 1-21.

[60]L. J. Baraff, N. Janowicz and J. R. Asarnow, "Survey of California Emergency Departments About Practices for Management of Suicidal Patients and Resources Available for Their Care," *Annals of Emergency Medicine* 48, vol. 4 (2006): 452-58.

[61]Jobe, Shackelford and Stauffacher, "How to Get Professional Help," pp. 59-71; Clark, *Clergy Response*, p. 68.

[62]O. Bennewith et al., "General Practice Based Intervention to Prevent Repeat Episodes of Deliberate Self-Harm," *British Medical Journal* 324, vol. 7348 (2002); McKeon, *Suicidal Behavior*, p. 1. Miller, Rathus and Linehan, *Dialectical Behavior Therapy*, p. 202; J. Waterhouse and S. Platt, "General Hospital Admission in the Management of Parasuicide: A Randomised Controlled Trial," *British Journal of Psychiatry* 156 (1990): 236-42.

[63]Joint Commission on the Accreditation of Health Care Organizations. *Sentinel Event Data, Event Type by Year, 1995-Fourth Quarter.* Retrieved November 2, 2011 from www.jointcommission.org/sentinel_event_data_general. W. Styron, *Darkness Visible: A Memoir of Madness* (New York: Random House, 1990), p. 70.

[64]Joiner et al., *The Interpersonal Theory*, p. 149.

[65]L. J. Baraff, N. Janowicz and J. R. Asarnow, "Survey of California Emergency Departments About Practices for Management of Suicidal Patients and Resources Available for Their Care," *Annals of Emergency Medicine* 48, no. 4 (2006): 452-58.

[66]Douglas G. Jacobs et al., "Practice Guideline for the Assessment and Treatment of Patients with Suicidal Behavior," *Psychiatry Online,* November 2003, psychiatryonline.org/content.aspx?bookid=28&sectionid=1673332.

[67]K. Greene-McCreight, *Darkness Is My Only Companion: A Christian Response to Mental Illness* (Grand Rapids: Brazos, 2006), p. 32.

[68]A. G. Weaver and H. G. Koenig, "Elderly Suicide, Mental Health Professionals and the Clergy: A Need for Clinical Collaboration," *Death Studies* 20, no. 5 (1996): 495.

[69]Jobe, Shackelford and Stauffacher, "How to Get Professional Help," p. 69.

[70]Greene-McCreight, *Darkness Is My Only Companion*, p. 35.

[71]Joiner, *Why People Die*, pp. 96-97.

[72]McKeon, *Suicidal Behavior*, p. 53.

[73]Joiner, *Myths About Suicide*, p. 123.

[74]Joiner, *Why People Die*, p. 226.

[75]L. M. Chatters et al., "Church-Based Social Support and Suicidality Among

African Americans and Black Caribbeans," *Archives of Suicide Research* 15, no. 4 (2011): 337-53.

[76]T. D. Doty and S. Spencer-Thomas, *The Role of Faith Communities in Suicide Prevention: A Guidebook for Faith Leaders* (Westminster, CO: Carson J. Spencer Foundation, 2009), p. 12.

[77]J. A. Motto, "Suicide Prevention for High-Risk Persons Who Refuse Treatment," *Suicide: A Quarterly Journal of Life-Threatening Behavior* 6, no. 4 (1976): 223-30.

[78]G. L. Carter et al., "Postcards from the EDge: 24-Month Outcomes of a Randomised Controlled Trial for Hospital-Treated Self-Poisoning," *British Journal of Psychiatry* 191, no. 6 (2007): 548-53.

[79]G. Vaiva et al., "Effect of Telephone Contact on Further Suicide Attempts in Patients Discharged from an Emergency Department: Randomised Controlled Study," *BMJ: Clinical Research Edition* 332, no. 7552 (2006): 1241-45.

[80]Mason, "Clergy Referral."

[81]Blauner, *How I Stayed Alive*, p. 224.

[82]E. J. Langer and J. Rodin, "The Effects of Choice and Enhanced Personal Responsibility for the Aged: A Field Experiment in an Institutional Setting," *Journal of Personality and Social Psychology* 34 (1976): 191-98.

[83]L. A. Brenner et al., "Suicidality and Veterans with a History of Traumatic Brain Injury: Precipitating Events, Protective Factors, and Prevention Strategies," *Rehabilitation Psychology* 54, no. 4 (2009): 390-97.

[84]Joiner, *Why People Die*, p. 47.

[85]K. J. Kaplan and M. B. Schwartz, *A Psychology of Hope: A Biblical Response to Tragedy and Suicide* (Grand Rapids: Eerdmans, 2008).

[86]McKeon, *Suicidal Behavior*, p. 63.

[87]A. Y. Hsu, *Grieving a Suicide: A Loved One's Search for Comfort, Answers and Hope* (Downers Grove, IL: InterVarsity Press, 2002), p. 134.

[88]D. Hollinger, "A Theology of Death," in *Suicide: A Christian Response: Crucial Considerations for Choosing Life*, ed. Timothy J. Demy and Gary P. Stewart (Grand Rapids: Kregel, 1998), p. 261.

[89]Greene-McCreight, *Darkness Is My Only Companion*, p. 88.

[90]Mason, "Clergy Referral."

[91]Greene-McCreight, *Darkness Is My Only Companion*, p. 13.

[92]M. G. Hubbard, *More Than an Aspirin: A Christian Perspective on Pain and Suffering* (Grand Rapids: Discovery House, 2009), p. 278.

[93]Jamison, *Night Falls Fast*, p. 105.

[94]Taken from J. R. Beck and B. Demarest, *The Human Person in Theology and Psychology: A Biblical Anthropology for the Twenty-First Century* (Grand Rapids: Kregel, 2005), pp. 187-88, 189.

[95]L. L. Townsend, *Suicide: Pastoral Responses* (Nashville: Abingdon, 2006), p. 44.

CHAPTER 6: HELPING A SURVIVOR OF ATTEMPTED SUICIDE

[1]A. Alvarez, *The Savage God: A Study of Suicide* (New York: Random House, 1972).

[2]L. Townsend, *Suicide: Pastoral Responses* (Nashville: Abingdon, 2006), p. 72.

[3]M. Williams, *Cry of Pain: Understanding Suicide and Self-Harm* (London: Penguin, 1997).

[4]K. Mason et al., "Clergy Referral of Suicidal Individuals: A Qualitative Study," *Journal of Pastoral Care and Counseling* 65, no. 3 (2011).

[5]Ibid.

[6]E. S. Shneidman, *The Suicidal Mind* (New York: Oxford University Press, 1996), p. 131.

[7]S. R. Blauner, *How I Stayed Alive When My Brain Was Trying to Kill Me: One Person's Guide to Suicide Prevention* (New York: William Morrow, 2002), p. 144.

[8]This may be why some people refer to a "*failed* attempt" and a "*successful* suicide*," unfortunate language because suicide is never a success.

[9]Cowper is author of the hymn "God Moves in a Mysterious Way." T. Wright, *The Life of William Cowper* (London: T. Fisher Unwin, 1892).

[10]F. Winslow, *The Anatomy of Suicide* (Boston: Milford House, 1972), p. 145.

[11]Wright, *The Life of William Cowper*, pp. 108-9.

[12]J. T. Clemons, *What Does the Bible Say About Suicide?* (Minneapolis: Fortress, 1990), p. 23.

[13]U.S. Department of Health and Human Services, *Mental Health: A Report of the Surgeon General* (Rockville, MD: U.S. Department of Health and Human Services, Substance Abuse and Mental Health Services Administration, Center for Mental Health Services, National Institutes of Health, National Institute of Mental Health, 1999).

[14]S. S. Canetto, "Women and Suicidal Behavior: A Cultural Analysis," *American Journal or Orthopsychiatry* 78, no. 2 (2008): 259-66. See also E. R. Dahlen and S. Canetto, "The Role of Gender and Suicide Precipitant in Attitudes Toward Nonfatal Suicidal Behavior," *Death Studies* 26, no. 2 (2002): 99-116.

[15]T. Joiner, *Myths About Suicide* (Cambridge, MA: Harvard University Press, 2010), p. 44.

[16]Silverman et al., "Rebuilding the Tower of Babel: A Revised Nomenclature for the Study of Suicide and Suicidal Behaviors, Part II: Suicide-Related Ideations, Communications and Behaviors," *Suicide and Life-Threatening Behavior* 37, no. 3 (2007): 264-77.

[17]E. Stengel, *Suicide and Attempted Suicide* (Harmondsworth, UK: Penguin, 1964).

[18]Williams, *Cry of Pain*.

[19]Shneidman, *The Suicidal Mind*.

[20]R. McKeon, *Suicidal Behavior*, in the series Advances in Psychotherapy: Evidence-Based Practice (Cambridge, MA: Hogrefe and Huber, 2009).

[21]S. J. Gibb, A. L. Beautrais and D. M. Fergusson, "Mortality and Further Suicidal Behaviour After an Index Suicide Attempt: A 10-Year Study," *Australian and New Zealand Journal of Psychiatry* 39, nos. 1-2 (2005): 95-100. C. Haw et al., "Repetition of Deliberate Self-Harm: A Study of the Characteristics and Subsequent Deaths in Patients Presenting to a General Hospital According to Extent of Repetition," *Suicide and Life-Threatening Behavior* 37, no. 4 (2007): 379-96.

[22]Joiner, T. 2005. *Why People Die by Suicide* (Cambridge, MA: Harvard University Press, 2007); A. L. Beautrais, "Further Suicidal Behavior Among Medically Serious Suicide Attempters," *Suicide and Life-Threatening Behavior* 34, no. 1 (2004): 1-11.

[23]E. Harris and B. Barraclough, "Suicide as an Outcome for Mental Disorders: A Meta-Analysis," *British Journal of Psychiatry* 170, no. 3 (1997): 205-28; J. Cooper et al., "Suicide After Deliberate Self-Harm: A 4-Year Cohort Study," *The American Journal of Psychiatry* 162, no. 2 (2005): 297-303.

[24]K. Hawton, *Prevention and Treatment of Suicidal Behavior* (New York: Oxford University Press, 2005), p. 6.

[25]M. S. Gould et al., "Youth Suicide Risk and Preventive Interventions: A Review of the Past 10 Years," *Journal of the American Academy of Child and Adolescent Psychiatry* 42, no. 4 (2003): 386.

[26]E. K. Mościcki, "Epidemiology of Suicide," in *The Harvard Medical School Guide to Suicide Assessment and Intervention* (San Francisco: Jossey Bass, 1999), pp. 40-51; Joiner, *Why People Die*.

[27]S. Goldsmith et al., *Reducing Suicide: A National Imperative* (Washington, DC: National Academies Press, 2002).

[28]K. Hawton and L. Harriss, "How Often Does Deliberate Self-Harm Occur Relative to Each Suicide? A Study of Variations by Gender and Age," *Suicide and Life-Threatening Behavior* 38, no. 6 (2008): 650-60.

[29]Stengel, *Suicide and Attempted*, p. 83.

[30]Ibid.

[31]Gibb, Beautrais and Fergusson, "Mortality and Further Suicidal Behaviour," pp. 95-100.

[32]D. Wilkerson, *Suicide* (Lindale, TX: David Wilkerson Publications, 1978), p. 76.

[33]A. Wenzel, G. K. Brown and A. T. Beck, *Cognitive Therapy for Suicidal Patients: Scientific and Clinical Applications* (Washington, DC: American Psychological Association, 2009).

[34]Ibid., p. 6.

[35]See also Beck's Suicide Intent Scale with Four Factors: Expectancies and At-

titudes, Premeditation, Precautions Against Intervention, and Oral Communication. Wenzel, Brown and Beck, *Cognitive Therapy*, p. 24.

[36]Williams, *Cry of Pain*, pp. 81-82.

[37]Mental health professionals don't drive a person to the hospital because of the potential liability if the person jumped out of the vehicle.

[38]G. Pittman, "Many Self-Harm Patients Don't Get Psych Evaluation," Reuters, September 7, 2011; L. J. Baraff, N. Janowicz and J. R. Asarnow, "Survey of California Emergency Departments About Practices for Management of Suicidal Patients and Resources Available for Their Care," *Annals of Emergency Medicine* 48, no. 4 (2006): 452-58.

[39]Baraff, Janowicz and Asarnow, "Survey of California Emergency Departments," pp. 452-58.

[40]Stengel, *Suicide and Attempted*.

[41]T. Joiner et al., *The Interpersonal Theory of Suicide: Guidance for Working with Suicidal Clients* (Washington, DC: American Psychological Association, 2009), p. 88; K. R. Jamison, *Night Falls Fast: Understanding Suicide* (New York: Vintage, 1999), p. 149.

[42]L. Appleby et al., "Suicide Within 12 Months of Contact with Mental Health Services: National Clinical Survey," *BMJ: Clinical Research Edition* 318, no. 7193 (1999): 1235-39.

[43]Jamison, *Night Falls Fast*, pp. 114-15; K. A. Busch, J. Fawcett and D. G. Jacobs, "Clinical Correlates of Inpatient Suicide," *Journal of Clinical Psychiatry* 64, no. 1 (2003): 14-19; H. G. Morgan and P. Priest, "Suicide and Other Unexpected Deaths Among Psychiatric In-Patients: The Bristol Confidential Inquiry," *British Journal of Psychiatry* 158 (1991): 368-74.

[44]*Nally v. Grace Community Church*, 47 Cal.3d 278 (1988), law.justia.com/cases/california/cal3d/47/278.html.

[45]Williams, *Cry of Pain*.

[46]Mościcki, "Epidemiology of Suicide," pp. 40-51.

[47]M. Alexander et al., "Coping with Thoughts of Suicide: Techniques Used by Consumers of Mental Health Services," *Psychiatric Services* 60, no. 9 (2009): 1214-21. See also A. G. Weaver and H. G. Koenig, "Elderly Suicide, Mental Health Professionals and the Clergy: A Need for Clinical Collaboration," *Death Studies* 20, no. 5 (1996): 495.

[48]K. Mason et al., "Clergy Referral of Suicidal Individuals: A Qualitative Study," *Journal of Pastoral Care and Counseling* 65, no. 3 (2011).

[49]K. Greene-McCreight, *Darkness Is My Only Companion: A Christian Response to Mental Illness* (Grand Rapids: Brazos, 2006), p. 137.

[50]Jamison, *Night Falls Fast*, pp. 258-59.

[51]McKeon, *Suicidal Behavior*.

[52]Ibid.

[53]Appleby et al., "Suicide Within 12 Months," pp. 1235-39. See also Cooper et al., "Suicide After Deliberate Self-Harm," pp. 297-303.

[54]Gibb, Beautrais and Fergusson, "Mortality and Further Suicidal Behaviour," pp. 95-100.

[55]Jamison, *Night Falls Fast*, p. 153.

[56]T. C. Welu, "A Follow-Up Program for Suicide Attempters: Evaluation of Effectiveness," *Suicide and Life-Threatening Behavior* 7, no. 1 (1977): 17-30.

[57]McKeon, *Suicidal Behavior*, p. 77.

[58]G. G. O'Brien et al., "Deliberate Self-Harm and Predictors of Out-Patient Attendance," *British Journal of Psychiatry* 150 (1987): 246-47.

[59]R. Kessler et al., "Trends in Suicide Ideation, Plans, Gestures, and Attempts in the United States, 1990–1992 to 2001–2003," *The Journal of the American Medical Association* 293, no. 20 (2005): 2493.

[60]A. L. Berman, D. A. Jobes and M. M. Silverman, *Adolescent Suicide: Assessment and Intervention*, 2nd ed. (Washington, DC: American Psychological Association, 2006).

[61]J. A. Cramer and R. Rosenbeck, "Compliance with Medication Regimens for Mental and Physical Disorders," *Psychiatric Services* 49 (1988): 196-201.

[62]J. A. Urquhart, "A Call for a New Discipline," *Pharmacology Technology* 11 (1987): 16-17.

[63]S. D. Cochran, "Preventing Medical Noncompliance in the Outpatient Treatment of Bipolar Affective Disorders," *Journal of Consulting and Clinical Psychology* 52 (1984): 873-78.

[64]Health Insurance Portability and Accountability Act of 1996, www.hhs.gov/ocr/privacy.

[65]Jamison, *Night Falls Fast*.

[66]Joiner, *Why People Die*, p. 165.

[67]K. J. Kaplan and M. B. Schwartz, *A Psychology of Hope: A Biblical Response to Tragedy and Suicide* (Grand Rapids: Eerdmans, 2008); K. Dervic et al., "Religious Affiliation and Suicide Attempt," *The American Journal Of Psychiatry* 161, no. 12 (2004): 2303-8.

[68]Shneidman, *The Suicidal Mind*.

[69]K. Hawton, "Psychosocial Treatments Following Attempted Suicide: Evidence to Inform Clinical Practice," in *Prevention and Treatment of Suicidal Behavior: From Science to Practice* (New York: Oxford University Press, 2005), p. 198.

[70]Williams, *Cry of Pain*.

CHAPTER 7: HELPING THE HELPERS

[1]K. R. Jamison, *Night Falls Fast: Understanding Suicide* (New York: Vintage, 1999), p. 259.

[2]W. Styron, *Darkness Visible: A Memoir of Madness* (New York: Random House, 1990), p. 77.

[3]L. Pessoa, "On the Relationship Between Emotion and Cognition," *Nature Reviews Neuroscience* 9 (2008): 148-58.

[4]E. Kennedy-Moore and J. C. Watson, *Expressing Emotion: Myths, Realities, and Therapeutic Strategies* (New York: Guilford Press, 1999), p. 7.

[5]A. L. Miller, J. H. Rathus and M. M. Linehan, *Dialectical Behavior Therapy with Suicidal Adolescents* (New York: Guilford, 2007), p. 188.

[6]Unpublished interviews with five pastors about their experiences following a suicide in their faith community. The student assistant who worked with me was Heather Thornburg.

[7]L. L. Townsend, *Suicide: Pastoral Responses* (Nashville: Abingdon, 2006), p. 93.

[8]Unpublished data from interviews with fifteen pastors. The student assistant who worked with me was Elizabeth Bousa.

[9]S. R. Blauner, *How I Stayed Alive When My Brain Was Trying to Kill Me: One Person's Guide to Suicide Prevention* (New York: William Morrow, 2002), p. 211.

[10]Ibid., p. 209.

[11]J. Asarnow, M. S. Berk and L. J. Baraff, "Family Intervention for Suicide Prevention: A Specialized Emergency Department Intervention for Suicidal Youths," *Professional Psychology: Research and Practice* 40, no. 2 (2009): 118-25.

[12]A. Spirito et al., "An Intervention Trial to Improve Adherence to Community Treatment by Adolescents After a Suicide Attempt," *Journal of the American Academy of Child and Adolescent Psychiatry* 41, no. 4 (2002): 435-42.

[13]R. McKeon, *Suicidal Behavior*, in the series Advances in Psychotherapy: Evidence-Based Practice (Cambridge, MA: Hogrefe and Huber. 2009).

[14]"AAS Recommendations for Inpatient and Residential Patients Known to Be at Elevated Risk for Suicide," American Association of Suicidology, 2008 www.sui cidology.org/c/document_library/get_file?folderId=231&name=DLFE-106.pdf.

[15]For a list of warning signs see the American Association of Suicidology, www .suicidology.org/ncpys/warning-signs-risk-factors.

[16]M. S. Berk et al., "A Cognitive Therapy Intervention for Suicide Attempters: An Overview of the Treatment and Case Examples," *Cognitive and Behavioral Practice* 11 (2004): 265-77.

[17]Asarnow, Berk and Baraff, "Family Intervention," pp. 118-25.

[18]Miller, Rathus and Linehan, *Dialectical Behavior Therapy*, p. 111.

[19]E. Bernstein, "After a Suicide: Privacy on Trial," *Wall Street Journal*, March 24, 2007; M. Carmichael, "MIT Reexamines Campus Efforts after 2 Suicides," *Boston Globe*, November 9, 2011; *Jain v. Iowa* 617 N.W.2d 293 (Iowa 2000); *White v. University of Wyoming* 954 P.2d 983; P. Lake and N. Tribbensee, "The

Emerging Crisis of College Student Suicide: Law and Policy Responses to Serious Forms of Self-Inflicted Injury," *Stetson Law Review* 32 (2005): 134.

[20]Jamison, *Night Falls Fast,* p. 262.

[21]K. R. Jamison and K. Hawton, "The Burden of Suicide and Clinical Suggestions
for Prevention," in *Prevention and Treatment of Suicidal Behavior: From
Science to Practice,* ed. K. Hawton (New York: Oxford University Press, 2005),
p. 189.

[22]Ibid., p. 261.

[23]H. Hendin et al., "Problems in Psychotherapy with Suicidal Patients," *American
Journal of Psychiatry* 163, no. 1 (2006): 67-72.

[24]Miller, Rathus and Linehan, *Dialectical Behavior Therapy,* p. 205.

[25]Ibid., p. 189. The National Violent Death Reporting System—which tracks
violent deaths, including suicide, in 16 states—reports that in 2009 31.97
percent of suicides were related to intimate partner problems. CDC, wisqars
.cdc.gov:8080/nvdrs/nvdrsDisplay.jsp.

[26]Miller, Rathus and Linehan, *Dialectical Behavior Therapy,* p. 238.

[27]R. Joiner, *Why People Die by Suicide* (Cambridge, MA: Harvard University
Press, 2005), p. 96.

[28]Asarnow, Berk and Baraff, "Family Intervention," pp. 118-25.

[29]Miller, Rathus and Linehan, *Dialectical Behavior Therapy,* p. 194.

[30]Ibid., p. 43.

[31]Blauner, *How I Stayed Alive,* p. 261.

[32]H. J. Markman, S. M. Stanley and S. L. Blumberg, *Fighting for Your Marriage:
Positive Steps for Preventing Divorce and Preserving a Lasting Love* (San Francisco: Jossey-Bass, 2001).

[33]See www.prepinc.com.

[34]Miller, Rathus and Linehan, *Dialectical Behavior Therapy,* p. 191.

[35]Ibid., p. 106.

[36]Ibid.

[37]Ibid., p. 107.

[38]D. Baumrind, "The Influence of Parenting Style on Adolescent Competence
and Substance Use," *Journal of Early Adolescence* 11, no. 1 (1991): 56-95.

[39]Miller, Rathus and Linehan, *Dialectical Behavior Therapy,* p. 112.

[40]Ibid., p. 200.

[41]Ibid., p. 58.

[42]Ibid.

[43]Ibid., p. 200.

[44]Ibid., p. 113.

[45]Unpublished data from interviews with fifteen pastors. The student assistant
who worked with me was Elizabeth Bousa.

[46]S. D. Govig, *In the Shadow of Our Steeples: Pastoral Presence for Families Coping with Mental Illness* (Binghamton, NY: Haworth Pastoral, 1999).

[47]L. G. Calhoun and R. G. Tedeschi, "Posttraumatic Growth: The Positive Lessons of Loss," in *Meaning Reconstruction and the Experience of Loss,* ed. R. A. Niemeyer (Washington DC: American Psychological Association, 2001), p. 168.

[48]A. J. Weaver et al., "Mental Health Issues Among Clergy and Other Religious Professionals: A Review of Research," *Journal of Pastoral Care and Counseling* 56, no. 4 (2002): 393-403.

[49]R. J. Wicks, *The Resilient Clinician* (New York: Oxford University Press, 2007), Kindle edition, chap. 2.

[50]C. A. Chessick et al., "Current Suicide Ideation and Prior Suicide Attempts of Bipolar Patients as Influences on Caregiver Burden," *Suicide and Life-Threatening Behavior* 37, no. 4 (2007): 482-91.

[51]Wicks, *Resilient Clinician,* chap. 1.

[52]A. D. Hart, "Burnout: Prevention and Cure," images.acswebnetworks .com/1/48/Burnout.pdf.

[53]K. Mason et al., "Clergy Referral of Suicidal Individuals: A Qualitative Study," *Journal of Pastoral Care and Counseling* 65, no. 3 (2011).

[54]Unpublished data from interviews with fifteen pastors. The student assistant who worked with me was Elizabeth Bousa.

[55]K. S. Pope and M. J. T. Vasquez, *Ethics in Psychotherapy and Counseling: A Practical Guide*, 3rd ed. (San Francisco: John Wiley and Sons, 2007), p. 61.

[56]J. T. Maltsberger, T. Jobe and D. G. Stauffacher, "Supporting the Family of a Suicidal Person: Those Who Live in Fear," in D. C. Clark, *Clergy Response to Suicidal Persons and Their Family Members* (Chicago: Exploration, 1993), p. 80.

[57]R. Anderson, *The Soul of Ministry: Forming Leaders for God's People* (Louisville, KY: Westminster John Knox, 1997), p. 81.

[58]Unpublished data from interviews with fifteen pastors. The student assistant who worked with me was Elizabeth Bousa.

[59]Ibid.

[60]Unpublished interviews with five pastors about their experiences following a suicide in their faith community. The student assistant who worked with me was Heather Thornburg.

[61]Unpublished data from interviews with fifteen pastors. The student assistant who worked with me was Elizabeth Bousa.

[62]Ibid.

[63]Mason, "Clergy Referral."

[64]J. L. Farrell and D. A. Goebert, "Collaboration Between Psychiatrists and Clergy in Treating Serious Mental Illness," *Psychiatric Services* 59, no. 4 (2008).

[65]Calhoun and Tedeschi, "Posttraumatic Growth," p. 161.

[66]Ibid., p. 158.

[67]R. G. Tedeschi and R. J. McNally, "Can We Facilitate Posttraumatic Growth in Combat Veterans?" *American Psychologist* 66, no. 1 (2011): 19-24.

CHAPTER 8: HELPING SUICIDE SURVIVORS

[1]B. Rubel, *But I Didn't Say Goodbye: For Parents and Professionals Helping Child Suicide Survivors* (Kendall Park, NJ: Griefwork Center, 2000), pp. xiv.

[2]Ibid., p. xx.

[3]D. E. Ness and C. R. Pfeffer, "Sequelae of Bereavement Resulting from Suicide," *The American Journal of Psychiatry* 147, no. 3 (1990): 279-85.

[4]D. B. Biebel and S. L. Foster, *Finding Your Way After the Suicide of Someone You Love* (Grand Rapids: Zondervan, 2005), p. 133.

[5]W. Leane and R. Shute, "Youth Suicide: The Knowledge and Attitudes of Australian Teachers and Clergy," *Suicide and Life-Threatening Behaviors* 28, no. 2 (1998): 165-73.

[6]C. S. Lewis, *A Grief Observed* (London: Faber and Faber, 1961), p. 7.

[7]K. R. Jamison, *Night Falls Fast: Understanding Suicide* (New York: Vintage, 1999), p. 295.

[8]C. Fine, *No Time to Say Goodbye: Surviving the Suicide of a Loved One* (New York: Doubleday, 1997), p. 191.

[9]Ibid., p. 200.

[10]Ibid., p. 68.

[11]Jamison, *Night Falls Fast*, p. 297.

[12]Fine, *No Time*, p. 152.

[13]Biebel and Foster, *Finding Your Way*, p. 112.

[14]T. Joiner, *Myths About Suicide* (Cambridge, MA: Harvard University Press, 2010), p. 119.

[15]Fine, *No Time*, p. 27.

[16]I. Bolton with C. Mitchell, *My Son . . . My Son . . . : A Guide to Healing After Death, Loss or Suicide* (Roswell, GA: Bolton Press Atlanta), p. 14.

[17]Ibid., p. 28.

[18]E. Goffman, *Stigma: Notes on the Management of Social Identity* (New York: Simon and Schuster, 1963), p. 3.

[19]L. Range and L. Calhoun, "Responses Following Suicide and Other Types of Death: The Perspective of the Bereaved," *Omega: Journal of Death and Dying* 21, no. 4 (1990): 311-20.

[20]Jamison, *Night Falls Fast*, p. 299.

[21]M. I. Solomon, "The Bereaved and the Stigma of Suicide," *Omega: Journal of Death and Dying* 13, no. 4 (1982-83): 377-87.

[22]Fine, *No Time*, p. 137.

[23]Bolton with Mitchell, *My Son,* p. 105.

[24]Ibid., p. 42.

[25]S. Freud, *Letters of Sigmund Freud,* ed. Ernst L. Freud, trans. Tania and James Stern (Mineola, NY: Courier Dover, 1992), p. 65.

[26]Bolton with Mitchell, *My Son,* p. 49.

[27]Fine, *No Time,* p. 85.

[28]Jamison, *Night Falls Fast,* p. 294.

[29]Biebel and Foster, *Finding Your Way,* p. 39.

[30]Ibid., p. 11.

[31]Fine, *No Time,* p. 95.

[32]Bolton with Mitchell, *My Son,* p. 54.

[33]Biebel and Foster, *Finding Your Way,* p. 84.

[34]Fine, *No Time,* p. 155.

[35]A. Y. Hsu, *Grieving a Suicide: A Loved One's Search for Comfort, Answers and Hope* (Downers Grove, IL: InterVarsity Press, 2002), p. 33.

[36]D. A. Brent et al., "The Impact of Adolescent Suicide on Siblings and Parents: A Longitudinal Follow-up," *Suicidal and Life-Threatening Behavior* 26 (1996): 253-59.

[37]P. Qin and P. Mortensen, "The Impact of Parental Status on the Risk of Completed Suicide," *Archives of General Psychiatry* 60, no. 8 (2003): 797-802.

[38]Bolton with Mitchell, *My Son,* p. 15.

[39]Ibid., p. 107.

[40]Biebel and Foster, *Finding Your Way,* p. 68.

[41]L. Carr and G. Carr, *Fierce Goodbye: Living in the Shadow of Suicide* (Scottdale, PA: Herald, 2004), p. 109.

[42]Biebel and Foster, *Finding Your Way,* pp. 10-11.

[43]Fine, *No Time,* p. 120.

[44]Biebel and Foster, *Finding Your Way,* p. 29.

[45]E. S. Shneidman, *The Suicidal Mind* (New York: Oxford University Press, 1996), pp. 14-15.

[46]Fine, *No Time,* p. 73.

[47]Biebel and Foster, *Finding Your Way,* p. 100.

[48]Fine, *No Time,* p. 70.

[49]Carr and Carr, *Fierce Goodbye,* p. 127.

[50]N. B. Webb, "The Child and Death," in *Helping Bereaved Children: A Handbook for Practitioners,* ed. N. B. Webb (New York: Guilford, 1993), p. 4.

[51]Joiner, *Myths About Suicide,* p. 227.

[52]Webb, "The Child," p. 4.

[53]Biebel and Foster, *Finding Your Way,* pp. 102-3.

[54]R. A. Niemeyer, *Meaning Reconstruction and the Experience of Loss* (Washington, DC: American Psychological Association, 2001).

[55]Lewis, *A Grief Observed*, p. 46. He goes on, "I thought I could describe a *state*; make a map of sorrow. Sorrow, however, turns out to be not a state but a process" (p. 47).

[56]E. Jennings, "Words About Grief," *The Collected Poems*, ed. Emma Mason (Manchester, UK: Carcanet, 2012), p. 485. Used with permission.

[57]T. W. Barrett and T. B. Scott, "Suicide Bereavement and Recovery Patterns Compared with Nonsuicide Bereavement Patterns," *Suicide and Life-Threatening Behavior* 20, no. 1 (1990): 1-15.

[58]Bolton with Mitchell, *My Son*, p. 69.

[59]Hsu, *Grieving a Suicide*, p. 22.

[60]Fine, *No Time*, p. 89.

[61]Bolton with Mitchell, *My Son*, p. 103.

[62]Ibid., p. 107.

[63]T. Work, "Advent's Answer to the Problem of Evil," *International Journal of Systematic Theology* 2, no. 1 (2000): p. 103.

[64]Hsu, *Grieving a Suicide*, p. 143.

[65]Lewis, *A Grief Observed*, pp. 24-25.

[66]H. J. M. Nouwen, *The Inner Voice of Love: A Journey Through Anguish to Freedom* (New York: Image Books Doubleday, 1996), p. 103.

[67]N. Wolterstorff, *Lament for a Son* (Grand Rapids: Eerdmans, 1987), p. 25.

[68]Bolton with Mitchell, *My Son*, p. 111.

[69]Biebel and Foster, *Finding Your Way*, p. 21.

[70]Fine, *No Time*, p. 44.

[71]Hsu, *Grieving a Suicide*, p. 144.

[72]Wolterstorff, *Lament for a Son*, p. 34.

[73]Bolton with Mitchell, *My Son*, p. 111.

[74]Hubbard, *More Than an Aspirin*, p. 91. See also Heb 11:35-37.

[75]Wolterstorff, *Lament for a Son*, p. 34.

[76]T. Joiner Jr., *Why People Die by Suicide* (Cambridge, MA: Harvard University Press, 2007), p. 5.

[77]Bolton with Mitchell, *My Son*, p. 66.

[78]Hubbard, *More Than an Aspirin*, p. 261

[79]Biebel and Foster, *Finding Your Way*, p. 109.

[80]Bolton with Mitchell, *My Son*, p. 111.

[81]Biebel and Foster, *Finding Your Way*, p. 29.

[82]Bolton with Mitchell, *My Son*, p. 107.

[83]Wolterstorff, *Lament for a Son*, p. 76.

[84]Bolton with Mitchell, *My Son*, p. 111.

[85]Carr and Carr, *Fierce Goodbye*, p. 31.

[86]Hubbard, *More Than an Aspirin*, p. 278. For example, see Psalm 102.

[87]A. Weems, *Psalms of Lament* (Louisville, KY: Westminster John Knox, 1995).

[88]*Surviving a Suicide Loss: A Financial Guide* (New York: American Foundation for Suicide Prevention, 2005).

[89]Bolton with Mitchell, *My Son*, p. 111.

[90]Ibid.

[91]L. Vandecreek and K. Mottram, "The Religious Life During Suicide Bereavement: A Description," *Death Studies* 33, no. 8 (2009): 741-61.

[92]Ibid., p. 26. See also Biebel and Foster, *Finding Your Way*, p. 50.

[93]Carr and Carr, *Fierce Goodbye*, p. 38.

CHAPTER 9: HELPING THE FAITH COMMUNITY

[1]Bishop Thomas Shaw, personal communication, Nov. 20, 2011.

[2]Michael Cooper, "Bishop David E. Johnson, 61, Dies From Gunshot," *New York Times*, January 17, 1995, www.nytimes.com/1995/01/17/obituaries/bishop -david-e-johnson-61-dies-from-gunshot.html.

[3]Mother Beth Maynard, personal communication, July 27, 2011.

[4]T. Joiner, *Why People Die by Suicide* (Cambridge, MA: Harvard University Press, 2005), pp. 224-25.

[5]Unpublished data from interviews with fifteen pastors. The student assistant who worked with me was Elizabeth Bousa.

[6]E. Goffman, *Stigma: Notes on the Management of Social Identity* (New York: Simon and Schuster, 1963), p. 6; W. W. Rankin et al., "The Stigma of Being HIV-Positive in Africa," *PLoS Med* 2, no. 8 (2005).

[7]I. Roldán, "AIDS Stigma in the Puerto Rican Community: An Expression of Other Stigma Phenomenon in Puerto Rican Culture," *Interamerican Journal of Psychology* 41, no. 1 (2007).

[8]M. Requarth, *After a Parent's Suicide: Helping Children Heal* (Sebastopol, CA: Healing Hearts, 2006), p. 96.

[9]Unless otherwise noted, this and all other clergy quotes in this chapter come from unpublished interviews with five pastors about their experiences after a suicide in their faith community. The student assistant who worked with me was Heather Thornburg.

[10]A. Y. Hsu, *Grieving a Suicide: A Loved One's Search for Comfort, Answers and Hope* (Downers Grove, IL: InterVarsity Press, 2002), p. 66.

[11]"CDC Recommendations for a Community Plan for the Prevention and Containment of Suicide Clusters," *MMWR* 37, no. S-6 (1988): 1-12.

[12]L. Wissow et al., "Cluster and Regional Influences on Suicide in a Southwestern American Indian Tribe," *Social Science and Medicine* 53 (2001): 1115-24.

[13]H. R. Fedden, *Suicide: A Social and Historical Study* (London: Peter Davies, 1938), p. 299.

[14]E. Durkheim, *Suicide: A Study in Sociology* trans. John A. Spaulding and George Simpson (New York: Free Press, 1951), p. 97.

[15]Fedden, *Suicide*, p. 298.

[16]M. Gould, P. Jamieson and D. Romer, "Media Contagion and Suicide Among the Young," *American Behavioral Scientist* 46, no. 9 (2003): 1269; L. Coleman, *The Copycat Effect* (New York: Simon and Schuster, 2004); J. W. von Goethe, *The Sorrows of Young Werther* (New York: Vintage Classic, 1971).

[17]K. R. Jamison, *Night Falls Fast: Understanding Suicide* (New York: Vintage, 1999), p. 278.

[18]A. Alvarez, *The Savage God: A Study of Suicide* (New York: Random House, 1972), p. 210.

[19]S. J. Surtees, "Suicide and Accidental Death at Beachy Head," *British Medical Journal* 284 (1982): 321-24.

[20]T. Joiner, *Myths About Suicide* (Cambridge, MA: Harvard University Press, 2010), p. 143.

[21]E. K. Mościcki, "Epidemiology of Suicide," in *The Harvard Medical School Guide to Suicide Assessment and Intervention*, ed. Douglas G. Jacobs (San Francisco: Jossey-Bass, 1999), p. 49.

[22]M. Williams, *Cry of Pain: Understanding Suicide and Self-harm* (London: Penguin, 1997), pp. 131-32.

[23]Ibid., p. 136.

[24]A. Schmidtke and H. Häfner, "The Werther Effect After Television Films: New Evidence for an Old Hypothesis," *Psychological Medicine* 18, no. 3 (1988): 665-76.

[25]A. Beautrais, "The Contribution to Suicide Prevention of Restricting Access to Methods and Sites," *Crisis: The Journal of Crisis Intervention and Suicide Prevention* 28, no. 1 (2007): 1-3.

[26]M. Gould and D. Shaffer, "The Impact of Suicide in Television Movies: Evidence of Imitation," *New England Journal of Medicine* 315, no. 11 (1986): 690-94.

[27]Jamison, *Night Falls Fast*, pp. 279-80.

[28]Williams, *Cry of Pain*, pp. 131-32.

[29]Suicide Prevention Resource Center, *After a Suicide: Recommendations for Religious Services and Other Public Memorial Observances* (Newton, MA: Education Development Center, 2004); *Reporting on Suicide: Recommendations for the Media* (Centers for Disease Control and Prevention, et al.), www .sprc.org/sites/sprc.org/files/library/sreporting.pdf.

[30]Jamison, *Night Falls Fast*, p. 144.

[31]Gould, Jamieson and Romer, "Media Contagion," p. 1269.

[32]L. J. Nicoletti, "Morbid Topographies: Placing Suicide in Victorian London," in *A Mighty Mass of Brick and Smoke: Victorian and Edwardian Representations of London* (New York: Rodopi, 2007), pp. 13-14.

[33]F. Winslow, *The Anatomy of Suicide* (Boston: Milford House, 1972), p. 96.

[34]Gould, Jamieson and Romer, "Media Contagion," p. 1269.

[35]M. Requarth, *After a Parent's Suicide: Helping Children Heal* (Sebastopol, CA: Healing Hearts, 2006), p. 120.

[36]Jamison, *Night Falls Fast,* p. 279.

[37]Mościcki, "Epidemiology of Suicide," p. 49.

[38]D. M. Cutler, E. L. Glaeser and K. E. Norberg, "Explaining the Rise in Youth Suicide," in *Risky Behavior Among Youths: An Economic Analysis*, ed. J. Gruber (Chicago: University of Chicago Press, 2001), pp. 219-69.

[39]D. B. Goldston et al., "Cultural Considerations in Adolescent Suicide Prevention and Psychosocial Treatment," *American Psychologist* 63, no. 1 (2008): 14-31; T. Joiner, *Why People Die*, pp. 30, 168.

[40]Durkheim, *Suicide: A Study*, p. 96.

[41]D. M. Velting and M. S. Gould, "Suicide Contagion," in *Review of Suicidology*, ed. R. W. Maris, M. M. Silverman and S. Canetto (New York: Guilford, 1997), pp. 96-137.

[42]Suicide Prevention Resource Center, *After a Suicide*, p. 10.

[43]Ibid.

[44]Ibid.

[45]Requarth, *After a Parent's Suicide*, p. 122.

[46]T. D. Doty and S. Spencer-Thomas, *The Role of Faith Communities in Suicide Prevention: A Guidebook for Faith Leaders* (Westminster, CO: Carson J. Spencer Foundation, 2009), p. 29.

[47]Ibid., p. 39.

[48]D. B. Biebel and S. L. Foster, *Finding Your Way After the Suicide of Someone You Love* (Grand Rapids: Zondervan, 2005), p. 169.

[49]From *The Journey: A Meditation with Words and Music,* Festival Service Book 7, The Royal School of Church Music, Croydon, as cited in L. Carr and G. Carr, *Fierce Goodbye: Living in the Shadow of Suicide* (Scottdale, PA: Herald, 2004) p. 104. Used by permission of Coventry Cathedral.

[50]Suicide Prevention Resource Center, *Choosing and Implementing a Suicide Prevention Gatekeeper Training Program* (training course), slide 6.

[51]Doty and Spencer-Thomas, *Role of Faith Communities,* p. 14.

[52]Joiner, *Myths About Suicide*, p. 65.

[53]R. H. Aseltine Jr. and R. DeMartino, "An Outcome Evaluation of the SOS Suicide Prevention Program," *American Journal of Public Health* 94, no. 3 (2004): 446-51.

[54]M. S. Gould et al., "Youth Suicide Risk and Preventive Interventions: A Review of the Past 10 Years," *Journal of the American Academy of Child and Adolescent Psychiatry* 42, no. 4 (2003): 386.

[55]T. Joiner et al., *The Interpersonal Theory of Suicide: Guidance for Working with Suicidal Clients* (Washington, DC: American Psychological Association, 2009), p. 177.

[56]P. A. Wyman et al., "Randomized Trial of a Gatekeeper Program for Suicide Prevention: 1-Year Impact on Secondary School Staff," *Journal of Consulting and Clinical Psychology* 76, no. 1 (2008): 104-15.

[57]T. Jobe, J. H. Shackelford and D. G. Stauffacher, "How to Get Professional Help for a Suicidal Person and Remain Involved," in D. C. Clark, *Clergy Response to Suicidal Persons and Their Family Members* (Chicago: Exploration, 1993), p. 66.

[58]Doty and Spencer-Thomas, *Role of Faith Communities,* p. 12.

[59]U.S. Department of Health and Human Services (HHS) Office of the Surgeon General and National Action Alliance for Suicide Prevention, *2012 National Strategy for Suicide Prevention: Goals and Objectives for Action* (Washington, DC: HHS, 2012).

[60]Ibid., p. 40.

CONCLUSION

[1]C. G. Ellison et al., "The Clergy as a Source of Mental Health Assistance: What Americans Believe," *Review of Religious Research* 48, no. 2 (2006): 190-211.

[2]S. Harris, *Your Breakthrough Is Guaranteed: Seven Simple Steps That Will Help Insure Your Success in Every Area of Life* (CreateSpace Independent Publishing Platform [an Amazon company], 2010).

[3]K. Mason, *When the Pieces Don't Fit: Making Sense of Life's Puzzles* (Grand Rapids: Discovery House, 2008).

[4]L. A. Brenner et al., "Suicidality and Veterans with a History of Traumatic Brain Injury: Precipitating Events, Protective Factors, and Prevention Strategies," *Rehabilitation Psychology* 54, no. 4 (2009): 390-97.

[5]E. Miller, C. McCullough and J. Johnson, "The Association of Family Risk Factors with Suicidality Among Adolescent Primary Care Patients," *Journal of Family Violence* 27, no. 6 (2012): 523-29.

[6]N. A. Skopp et al., "Childhood Adversity and Suicidal Ideation in a Clinical Military Sample: Military Unit Cohesion and Intimate Relationships as Protective Factors," *Journal of Social and Clinical Psychology* 30, no. 4 (2011): 361-77.

[7]S. Stack, "The Effect of the Decline in Institutionalized Religion on Suicide, 1954–1978," *Journal for the Scientific Study of Religion* 22, no. 3 (1983): 239-52.

[8]M. E. McCullough and B. B. Willoughby, "Religion, Self-Regulation, and Self-Control: Associations, Explanations, and Implications," *Psychological Bulletin* 135, no. 1 (2009): 69-93.

[9]Ibid.

[10]D. B. Larson and S. S. Larson, "Spirituality's Potential Relevance to Physical and Emotional Health: A Brief Review of Quantitative Research," *Journal of Psychology and Theology* 31, no. 1 (2003): 37-51.

[11]L. Dossey, *Healing Words: The Power of Prayer and the Practice of Medicine* (San Francisco: HarperSanFrancisco, 1993), pp. 252-53.

[12]M. Alexander et al., "Coping with Thoughts of Suicide: Techniques Used by Consumers of Mental Health Services," *Psychiatric Services* 60, no. 9 (2009): 1214-21.

[13]M. A. Marty, D. L. Segal and F. L. Coolidge, "Relationships Among Dispositional Coping Strategies, Suicidal Ideation, and Protective Factors Against Suicide in Older Adults," *Aging and Mental Health* 14, no. 8 (2010): 1015-23.

[14]Y. Lee, "Validation of Reasons for Living and Their Relationship with Suicidal Ideation in Korean College Students," *Death Studies* 36, no. 8 (2012): 712-22; M. Oquendo et al., "Protective Factors Against Suicidal Behavior in Latinos," *Journal of Nervous and Mental Disease* 193, no. 7 (2005): 438-43.

[15]T. Joiner, *Why People Die by Suicide* (Cambridge, MA: Harvard University Press, 2005), p. 96.

[16]D. Li et al., "Gratitude and Suicidal Ideation and Suicide Attempts Among Chinese Adolescents: Direct, Mediated, and Moderated Effects," *Journal of Adolescence* 35, no. 1 (2012): 55-66.

[17]W. Leane and R. Shute, "Youth Suicide: The Knowledge and Attitudes of Australian Teachers and Clergy," *Suicide and Life-Threatening Behavior* 28, no. 2 (1998): 165-73.

[18]K. I. Pargament, N. A. Murray-Swank and N. Tarakeshwar, "Editorial: An Empirically-Based Rationale for a Spiritually-Integrated Psychotherapy," *Mental Health, Religion and Culture* 8, no. 3 (2005): 155-65.

[19]Ellison et al., "The Clergy as a Source," p. 197.

[20]A. A. Hohmann and D. B. Larson, "Psychiatric Factors Predicting Use of Clergy," in *Psychotherapy and Religious Values*, ed. E. L. Worthington (Grand Rapids: Baker, 1993); P. Wang, P. Berglund and R. Kessler, "Patterns and Correlates of Contacting Clergy for Mental Disorders in the United States," *Health Services Research* 38, no. 2 (2003): 647-73.

IVP PRAXIS

EQUIPPING LEADERS FOR MINISTRY

God has called us to ministry. But it's not enough to have a vision for ministry if you don't have the practical skills for it. Nor is it enough to do the work of ministry if what you do is headed in the wrong direction. We need both vision *and* expertise for effective ministry. We need *praxis*.

Praxis puts theory into practice. It brings cutting-edge ministry expertise from visionary practitioners. You'll find sound biblical and theological foundations for ministry in the real world, with concrete examples for effective action and pastoral ministry. Praxis books are more than the "how to" – they're also the "why to." And because *being* is every bit as important as *doing*, Praxis attends to the inner life of the leader as well as the outer work of ministry. Feed your soul, and feed your ministry.

If you are called to ministry, you know you can't do it on your own. Let Praxis provide the companions you need to equip God's people for life in the kingdom.

www.ivpress.com/praxis